Gerald M. Weinberg

Quality
Software
Management

Volume
3
Congruent
Action

Dorset House Publishing
353 West 12th Street
New York, New York 10014

Library of Congress Cataloging in Publication Data
(Revised for vol. 3)

Weinberg, Gerald M.
    Quality software management.

    Includes bibliographical references and indexes.
    Contents: v. 1. Systems thinking -- v. 2. First-
order measurement -- v. 3. Congruent action.
    1. Computer software--Development--Management.
2. Computer software--Quality control. I. Title.
QA76.76.D47W45 1991   005.1'068   91-18061
ISBN 0-932633-28-5

Cover Design: Dennis Stillwell

Distributed in the English language in Singapore, the Philippines, and Southeast
Asia by Toppan Co., Ltd., Singapore and in the English language in Japan by
Toppan Co., Ltd., Tokyo, Japan.

Printed in the United States of America

Library of Congress Catalog Number: 91-18061
ISBN: 0-932633-28-5   12 11 10 9 8 7 6 5 4 3

*I think it only appropriate
to dedicate Volume 3 to III
and the other Campers*

Acknowledgments

I want to acknowledge the important contributions of the following people to the improvement of this book through reviews, discussions, demonstrations, experiments, and examples:

Wayne Bailey	Payson Hall	David Robinson
Jim Batterson	Naomi Karten	Dan Starr
Jinny Batterson	Norm Kerth	Eileen Strider
Lee Copeland	Mark Manduke	Wayne Strider
Michael Dedolph	David McClintock	Dani Weinberg
Peter de Jager	Lynne Nix	Janice Wormington
Phil Fuhrer	Judy Noe	Gus Zimmerman
Dawn Guido	Bill Pardee	

I also thank the Change Artists and others in my client organizations, as well as numerous participants in the Problem Solving Leadership seminars, the Organizational Change Shop, the Quality Software Management seminars, the CompuServe Software Engineering Management Forum, the Washington DPMA study group, and other educational experiences. Among them: Tom Bragg, Rich Cohen, Arthur George, Ed Hand, Andy Hardy, Steve Heller, Sue Petersen, Brian Richter, Ben Sano, and Mark Weisz.

In this book, I credit each person who made a contribution, except that I have disguised all people and clients from whom I've obtained confidential information. I hope that someday they will experience working in an environment in which they needn't be afraid to tell their stories.

Contents

Preface

> *We discovered that the key reason for our lack of competitiveness was poor management—by worldwide, not U.S., standards. We were being wiped out by the Japanese because thoy were better managers. It wasn't robotics, or culture, or morning calisthenics and the company songs—It was profossional managers who understood their business and paid attention to detail.*[1]
> — Vaughn Beals

In the four decades I've spent in the software business, I've learned that there are three fundamental abilities you need to do a quality job of managing software engineering:

1. the ability to understand complex situations so you can plan a project and then observe and act so as to keep the project going according to plan, or modify the plan

2. the ability to observe what's happening and to understand the significance of your observations in terms of effective adaptive actions

3. the ability to act appropriately in difficult interpersonal situations, even though you may be confused, or angry, or so afraid you want to run away and hide

All three abilities are essential for quality software management, but I didn't want to write a large, imposing book. Therefore, like any quality manager of software, I decomposed the project into three smaller projects, each addressing one of these three fundamental abilities. *Volume 1, Systems Thinking* deals with the first ability—the ability to understand complex situations. *Volume 2, First-Order Measurement* deals with the ability to observe what's happening and to understand the significance of your observations. This third volume, *Congruent Action,* will deal with the ability to act appropriately even in the presence of strong feelings.

Now for an apology: Like most software managers, my initial estimate for this total work was optimistic. As a result, I cannot finish what I have to say in this volume, and I will require a fourth. In the fourth and final volume, I will treat the question of organizational change: how you can use all the tools I give you in *Volumes 1, 2,* and *3* to manage a large organization and to transform your own organization into a congruent one. By congruent, I mean that an organization not only understands the concepts of good software engineering, but also practices them.

How can organizations achieve this level? They must have managers who are able to

- take in information about actual and desired performance
- process that information congruently
- act in an appropriate manner

In short, organizations need managers whose personal effectiveness will tie together all of the components of effective software engineering management. Some of that personal effectiveness comes from training and experience from past projects, and some of it comes from the ability to take in what's happening in current projects. Even more of it comes from past experience of a more general kind: experience as a human being functioning in the world.

Some managers shouldn't have been chosen as managers in the first place, and they likely didn't even want to be chosen. Unfortunately, their organizations don't appreciate that choosing managers for other than managerial potential is a mistake. Some managers are well-chosen, but few appreciate that management is as much dependent on technique as any other profession and that even the most able managers must be trained.

Managers themselves must take responsibility for upgrading the quality of management, for changing their own attitudes and thinking patterns before they try to impose changes on everyone else. What are you doing to get congruent management in your own organization? What are you doing to become a more congruent manager yourself? This volume is devoted to helping all of you get a fresh start so that you can decide if you really want to be a manager and, if so, to develop your full potential to lead the way to a true profession of software engineering.

Part I
Managing Yourself

*When I am, as it were, completely by myself, entirely alone, and of good cheer
... it is on such occasions that my ideas flow best and most abundantly. Whence
and how they come I know not, nor can I force them. ... Nor do I hear in my
imagination the parts in sequence, but I hear them, as it were, all at once. What
a delight that is I cannot tell.*

— Wolfgang Amadeus Mozart

In his classic article on software engineering, Fred Brooks exposes our tendency to
seek a "silver bullet"—some new technical breakthrough that would magically set
software engineering to rights. Then he delivers the message of his title: "There is
no silver bullet."[1]

Unfortunately, Brooks's audience doesn't seem to want to hear his message. I
have seen very little evidence of software engineering managers giving up their
search for the silver bullet. I do hear Brooks quoted by managers opposing someone else's technical idea. "Apparently, you think you've got a silver bullet," they
say, mockingly. "Don't you know that Fred Brooks says there is no silver bullet?"
Then, having humiliated their opponent, they continue with the sale of their own
silver bullets.

Even though none of these silver bullets have hit their target, some software
organizations are producing high-quality work. After observing many of these
high-quality organizations, I'd like to amend Brooks's aphorism to read

There is no silver bullet, but sometimes there is a Lone Ranger.

In every high-quality software organization that I have visited, I have discovered at
least one Lone Ranger and several Tontos acting as backup. In Part I, I want to
show what differentiates the Lone Rangers and their Tontos from the other characters—those who never manage to do much of anything memorable unless they are
the villains.

1
Why Congruence Is Essential to Managing

You're writing a gospel
A chapter a day,
By things that you do
By things that you say.
People read what you write
Whether faithless or true,
Say, what is the gospel
According to you?
— Children's poem

To produce high-quality software, we need high-quality, effective software engineering managers. This book is about how to become such a manager.

Until now, such managers have been rare in software engineering. During my long career as a software developer, I never had such a manager, so I believed that they didn't exist. More than that, I believed they were unnecessary—and I was right. Such high-quality managers were unnecessary to produce mediocre software. In my years as a consultant, however, I've met many high-quality managers, and I've learned they are necessary if you want to go beyond mediocrity.

Perhaps your experience is much like mine. Perhaps you haven't met many high-quality software engineering managers or you don't believe that high-quality software requires high-quality managers. In either case, you'll have to take my word for their necessity.

Even if you believe in the necessity of effective managers, you may not agree with my explanation of what it takes to be effective. You may believe, for instance,

3

that an effective manager simply needs to understand the concepts of software engineering, not practice them. This erroneous belief is the cause of a great deal of trouble, and is extremely difficult for intelligent people to overcome. At least it was for me. For many years, I enjoyed the superiority of thinking that if I knew what to do, it didn't much matter if I actually did it. That opinion made it easy for me to be a nonparticipating critic.

I've met many others like me in the software business, so I need to first convince you of the error of your ways. This first chapter introduces the idea of congruence and tackles the question, Why must actions be congruent with thoughts?

1.1 Knowing versus Doing

The two previous volumes in this series discuss that in order to manage an engineering system by feedback control[1] (Figure 1-1), a manager in the role of a controller needs to perform four activities:

- plan what should happen
- observe what significant things are really happening
- compare the observed with the planned
- take actions needed to bring the actual closer to the planned

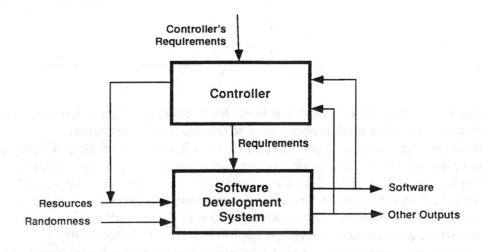

Figure 1-1.   The feedback model of a software development system requires the transfer of information about the system's performance plus requirements for the controller to compare with that information. This is the model that distinguishes the more desirable Steering (Pattern 3) organization from the less desirable Oblivious (Pattern 0), Variable (Pattern 1), and Routine (Pattern 2) organizations.

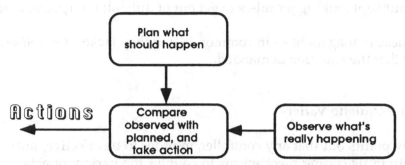

Figure 1-2.   In Steering (Pattern 3) organizations, the manager's job is to control a process that produces a desired product or service. The manager plans what should happen, then observes what actually happens. The manager designs an action based on the difference between the planned and the actual results, and the actions are then fed back into the process being controlled.

Volume 1 of this series focuses on planning, and *Volume 2* concentrates on observing and comparing. This volume as well as the next focuses on *action* (see Figure 1-2).

The focus on action may seem strange to those of you who believe that once the planning is done, the right actions must follow. I used to believe this myself. I have experienced many ineffective managers, and I attributed their ineffectiveness to their lack of brains: They simply didn't know what to do. Much later, I learned that this wasn't always their problem. I have witnessed hundreds of instances when managers knew quite well what to do but were somehow incapable of doing it. Let me give a few examples:

- A manager knew that there was not the slightest hope of completing a project on time, but was unable to admit it to her manager in order to open a discussion of alternative plans or approaches.
- Another manager knew that adding developers to his late project would only make it later, but he was unable to risk the appearance of doing nothing.
- A manager knew that screaming at people would only make things worse, but was unable to stop screaming at them.
- A manager knew that an employee smelled so bad the other employees weren't able to work with him, but was unable to speak to the employee about it.
- A manager knew that a certain person was right for an assignment, but assigned another person because he disliked the best candidate.
- A manager knew that a project shouldn't proceed without a clear understanding of the problem being solved, but he was unable to resist the eagerness of the developers to get started writing code.

- A manager knew that she shouldn't make promises she couldn't keep, but kept making promises to get out of difficult interpersonal situations.

What all these managers have in common is that they lacked the self-esteem to act in the way that the situation demanded.

1.2 Law of Requisite Variety

W.R. Ashby points out that any controller, in order to be effective, must have sufficient variety in its coping mechanisms to counter the variety of actions that could be exhibited by the system being controlled.[2] Ashby's Law of Requisite Variety says that the action taken by the controller must be *congruent* with the situation, in that there is at least one controller action to deal with each possible system action. The managers who couldn't do what they knew they should do lacked the requisite variety of actions to perform their jobs effectively.

For purposes of control, it doesn't matter *why* these managers were unable to exhibit the requisite variety of action. The reason may be that the managers (acting as controller) lack a plan or lack the observations needed to compare the plan to what's really happening (as *Volumes 1* and *2* discuss extensively). Or the reason may be that the managers know what to do but are incapable of actually doing it, especially during periods of stress.

When people are not tapping their full variety of potential actions, they are coping *incongruently*. According to the Law of Requisite Variety, managers acting incongruently are likely to be incapable of controlling the system they are trying to control. This book is about increasing the congruence of your actions, especially when you are under stress, and thus improving your ability to manage for the quality you desire.

1.3 The Importance of Congruent Management

The significance of congruent management extends beyond individual projects to the process of raising the general cultural level of the entire organization. As Bill Curtis, former director of the Process Program at the Software Engineering Institute (SEI), observes

> If an organization is trying to build a general management infrastructure at the same time it is trying to improve its software process, then it will take longer to achieve the next level.[3]

Even further, Watts Humphrey and Curtis, SEI's first two directors of the Process Program, note

A defined engineering process cannot overcome the instability created by the absence of sound management practices. Occasionally, unusually capable and forceful managers can withstand such pressures.[4]

Now, it seems to me that these observations could lead in one of two directions.

1. Try to introduce defined engineering practices into an organization in order to overcome instability even if the organization has incapable and weak managers.

2. Try to seek out and cultivate unusually capable and forceful managers within the organization.

The SEI is pursuing path 1, which is appropriate for an organization whose clients are organizations. This volume will pursue path 2, which is appropriate because that's my audience: Individuals who want to become "unusually capable and forceful managers."

1.4 The Number One Random Process Element

It's extremely important that the SEI and other institutions pursue path 1, even though it's not my chosen path. For one thing, this path is the one we in computing have always pursued and the one we know better: figuring out ways to achieve quality by eliminating people from the equation. Secondly, it has had some phenomenal successes.

I recently read about William Shanks, who in the 19th century took twenty years to compute pi to 707 digits, but made a mistake in the 528th decimal place. I also read about D.H. Lehmer, who in the 1930s proved that the 257th Mersenne number was prime, taking two hours a day for a year to do it.

These two cases can serve as examples of how tools have helped increased quality and productivity. Today, to compute pi to 707 decimal places, I can invoke a program called Mathematica on my desktop with the instruction

```
N[Pi,707]
```

Ten seconds later, I have my 707 places, all correct this time. To determine if 2^{257-1} is prime, I write

```
PrimeQ[2^257-1]
```

Ten seconds later, my Macintosh™ asserts that this is true.

Because of software technology, I have achieved truly spectacular increases in performance, cost, and quality. But these two problems share an important characteristic: They involve essentially no management!

If they did involve management, the spectacular gains made possible by tools would evaporate. What would happen in your organization if a customer submitted a request to compute pi to 707 decimal places? Is this a ten-second job?

I had a number of my students conduct this pi-to-707-decimal-places test in their organizations, secretly asking a customer to submit the request. Here were some of the results:

- After one week, the request form was returned by a clerk with the comment "Incorrectly completed."
- The request form was never returned, never acted on, and never heard of again three months later. (This was the most frequent "response.")
- The customer received a call from a secretary to schedule a meeting with an analyst. The analyst had no available time for more than a month.
- The request form was returned in two days with pi to ten decimal places penciled in.
- The request form was returned in ten days marked "You're not serious!"
- Several replies were in terms of programming estimates, which ranged from three weeks to four months.
- Two customers were referred to other customers—one who was using Mathematica and one using Maple (which are similar mathematical applications). These other customers graciously solved the problem in a few minutes.
- One customer got a printout of pi to 707 decimal places, actually 1,000 decimal places.
- One customer was asked on the phone whether he wanted a printout or a file on disk. He asked for the file, and was given it by hand less than an hour later.

To me, this silly little survey simply confirms what I have observed directly in dozens of organizations. The variation in service produced by these organizations didn't come from the differences in technology, because all had access to the same technology. The variation came from the differences in management. In software work today,

Management is the number one random process element.

You don't have to take my word for it because you can use your own experience. Recall the best and the worst software engineering managers you have known. How much did their organizations or projects differ on performance? on cost? on quality?

Now, ask any quality specialist how to go about improving quality, and nine times out of ten you will hear

1.   Identify your number one random process element.

2.   Take steps to reduce the randomness in that element.

The problem, of course, is not that simple because those very managers are the people in charge of changing the process. In other words,

The number one random process element stands in the way of improving all the other random process elements.

For some strange reason, many people attempting to change organizations continue to make the same mistake. They assume that the same people who got us into this mess will somehow be the best people to lead us out of it. All the management tools in the world will not help if the managers are incongruent:

- if they are too self-centered to see and hear what's really happening
- if they are too muddled to understand what should happen
- if they are too fearful to carry out carefully planned actions

When managers are incongruent and not emotionally centered, all of our fancy cybernetic models are full of sound and fury, but signify nothing. A controller that cannot control itself is worse than no controller at all:

If you cannot manage yourself, you have no business managing others.

The personal effectiveness of people is what integrates all the other components of software engineering management. You'll never get a Steering (Pattern 3) organization with Routine (Pattern 2) managers. Instead, you start by getting the effective managers, then they'll lead the others.

1.5 The Road Ahead

These observations furnish the overall vision of this volume. The challenge we all face is to remove every obstacle that managers encounter in using full and appropriate variety in their actions. To accomplish this goal, we must first address the largest source of management incongruence: the way managers are chosen in the first place. That's the subject of Chapter 2. Next, in Chapter 3, I address the strongest variety-reducing factor: low self-esteem that causes managers to act incongruently rather than in a way they know they should.

Even when incongruent coping behaviors are recognized and avoided, managers still face many obstacles to requisite variety. A manager's unconscious preferences toward employees' age, gender, and numerous other characteristics affect the manager's actions. We must expose the most common of these preferences: personality, temperament, culture, gender, age, physical capacity, and mode of perception, then learn what a manager can do to make them conscious.

Consciousness, however, is not sufficient to change actions. We must also examine how people become addicted to their destructive behaviors, and how much more than logic or morality is needed to overcome addictions.

Finally, we must examine the managers' relationships to the most effective variety-producing tool at their disposal: other people. We need to examine how managers can improve their interactions with individual workers, colleagues, and bosses. More than that, we need to explore the special relationships that exist between managers and teams.

That's a big menu, but merely being aware of all these issues won't help at all without lots of practice. The sooner we get on with the reading, the sooner we'll be able to go into action.

1.6 Helpful Hints and Suggestions

1. One of the surest indicators of incongruent managers is their belief that they have power and that the power is one-sided. When a project fails, the employees, the customers, the vendors, or the fates are to blame; when it succeeds, it's due to brilliant management.

2. The powerful concepts of congruence and requisite variety will appear throughout this book in a number of forms. The key underlying concept will always be matching two things, usually thoughts or feelings on the one hand and words or behaviors on the other.

3. As you proceed through this book, you'll read about many techniques of how to act congruently. As you read, remember that underlying all of these techniques is an awareness and an acceptance that you always have choices about how to respond. Whenever you find yourself saying, either to yourself or others, "I had no choice," you know that you were acting incongruently and not using your full potential as a controller.

1.7 Summary

✓   This book is about how you can become the kind of high-quality, effective software engineering manager needed to produce high-quality software. First and foremost among the requirements for you to develop into such a manager is the ability to act in congruence with your beliefs.

✓   If we borrow from the field of cybernetics, managers can be seen as controllers of feedback systems. To manage an engineering system by feedback control, a manager as the controller needs to

- plan what should happen
- observe what significant things are really happening
- compare the observed with the planned
- take actions needed to bring the actual closer to the planned

✓ Effective managers must know what to do, but they must also be able to act in accordance with that knowledge.

✓ Ashby's Law of Requisite Variety says that the action taken by the controller must be congruent with the situation. When people are not tapping their full variety of potential actions, they are coping incongruently.

✓ For control purposes, it doesn't matter why managers are unable to exhibit the requisite variety of action. Managers acting incongruently may not be capable of controlling the system they are trying to control, and thus of producing high-quality software, regardless of the reasons for their incongruence.

✓ Technology is obviously important to the consistent delivery of high-quality software and software services, but in today's software organizations, management is the number one random process element. In addition, management stands in the way of improving all the other random process elements.

✓ The personal effectiveness of people is what integrates all the other components of software engineering management. You'll never get a Steering (Pattern 3) organization with Routine (Pattern 2) managers. Instead, you start by getting the effective managers, then they will lead the others.

✓ In this volume, I'll address the major obstacles that managers face in using full and appropriate variety in their actions.

1.8 Practice

1. In reviewing an early draft of this book, my colleague Jim Batterson suggested the following: Another common meaning of congruence is doing what you say you will do. It's really frustrating to work for a manager whom you cannot count on to do what he or she says. Discuss how this definition of congruence is related to the one based on requisite variety.

2. Still another common meaning of congruence is that you appear on the outside the same way you feel inside. Discuss how this definition of congruence is related to the one based on requisite variety.

3.   Discuss how all three definitions of congruence are related to the geometric concept of congruence, as when two triangles are congruent.

4.   Give some examples of when you observed a manager who knew what to do, but was unable to do it. Give some examples when you were that manager.

5.   Another reviewer, Norm Kerth, contributed this suggestion: Review your past management training, textbooks, and articles. Which ones urge congruence and which urge incongruence? Which honor the human component and which ones ignore it, or try to suppress it?

6.   Again, as suggested by Norm Kerth: With congruence as a guiding theme, examine the biographies of leaders you admire. In particular, ask yourself, How did these leaders respond when they were told that they didn't have choices? How did they influence the choices available to others?

2

Choosing
Management

*Distrust any enterprise
that requires new clothes.*
— Henry David Thoreau

Why are congruent managers so hard to find in software engineering? Perhaps this difficulty has something to do with the way organizations choose and develop their managers, or the way managers themselves choose the job. If the right people aren't selected for the job, no wonder they're incongruent.

This chapter explores the topic of choosing management. The title is intentionally ambiguous, because it refers to both

- how the organization chooses its management
- how the individual chooses a career in management

If you don't understand the difference between these two choices, perhaps it never occurred to you that if you were chosen (or not chosen) as a manager by the organization, you had the final choice. Pretending that you don't have a choice is a sure sign of incongruence and hardly the best way to start your management career.

2.1 Where the Payoff Is

I have derived Figure 2-1 from a figure in Barry Boehm's classic study of software engineering economics. The figure is also reproduced on the bookcover, which seems to acknowledge that it reflects the central findings of his entire book.[1] In the book, Boehm isolates a number of "cost drivers," of which the four in the figure are indicated to be the most important. By studying these drivers—tools, people, systems, and management—we can determine which areas ought to be given management priority.

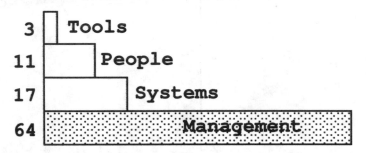

Figure 2-1.   Boehm describes the management category as having the most influence on software costs, but he doesn't give an estimate. I derived the estimate in this chart from six management actions that Boehm says are often each "responsible for doubling software development costs."

Top managers could use Figure 2-1 as a high-level guide showing where best to concentrate their organizational improvement efforts. Suppose the elements of the chart had not been labeled, so that all you could see was a list of four impact ratios—3, 11, 17, and 64. If you were managing a software engineering organization, where would you spend most of your time seeking improvement? Obviously, the factor of 64 would be the first place to look for improvement, and that place is *management*.

The question seems absurd, except for the fact that most managers answer the question in reverse order of the chart if they are given only the categories—tools, people, systems, and management. Perhaps the reason certain drivers are bigger than others is that management spends so little time paying attention to them.

This reverse emphasis is certainly true of the Software Engineering Institute's research. By counting and classifying the content of all published abstracts[2] in a summary of their first five years of sponsored research, I produced the graph shown in Figure 2-2.

2.2 The One-Dimensional Selection Model of Management

In my experience consulting with a number of software engineering organizations, I've found that the distribution of effort in these organizations closely parallels that

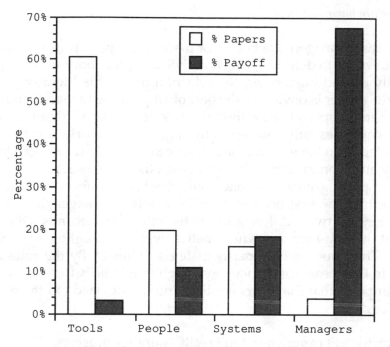

Figure 2-2.   A graph of the breakdown of the SEI's sponsored research among four areas in the first five years of its existence. The plot shows the percentage of payoff in various areas according to my interpretation of Boehm's data, versus the percentage of papers published by the SEI in the same areas in the period 1086 to 1991.

of the SEI's sponsored research. For example, when I showed Figure 2-2 to a manager at the XYZ Company, he argued that their efforts to improve management were much more significant than the four percent shown by the SEI. Here's what he told me: "Perhaps we don't spend as much money as you would like on management tools or training, but we spend an enormous amount of time rating and ranking our employees, and these rankings are used to determine which ones we should promote into management."

Upon hearing this remark, the scales fell from my eyes. In the XYZ Company, there may be plenty of effort devoted to improving management, but this effort is based on a faulty model of human beings. At the same time, I realized that many of my clients use this same faulty model, which I call the One-Dimensional Selection Model. This model is based on three faulty assumptions, namely:

- Managers are born, not made.
- People can be ranked on a one-dimensional scale.
- The scale for programming is the same as the scale for management.

Let's examine why each of these assumptions is a myth.

2.2.1 Managers are born, not made

If you believe that managers are born, not made, then your principal interest and effort will be devoted to detecting which individuals were born to wear the crown. In some family-owned businesses, the selection process is literally genetic. The eldest son of the owner is obviously the best of all possible managers, but a daughter will do if there happens to be a shortage of sons. Perhaps I shouldn't mock this model: Many countries and businesses throughout the world use this model to choose their rulers, and have been doing so for centuries. As far as I can tell, they're not necessarily any worse off than those that use other methods.

The rule of primogeniture has one undisputed advantage: its lack of ambiguity. You believe that the first-born son will be a better manager than the second-born, even if they are twins differing in age by only a few seconds. Of course, you also know that the first-born son will be better than any daughter, no matter when she was born. The rules are only partly male chauvinistic: By the rules of succession common in European aristocracy, any daughter will be better than a nephew.

The assumption that managers are born, not made, leads to three significant action prejudices:

- Maturity and experience don't really count for much.
- The only really important thing is to choose the right people to manage.
- Management training is largely a waste of time.

In terms of software cultural patterns, these are similar to the assumptions that Variable (Pattern 1) managers make about programmers.[3] In the anthropological view, biases amount to a "mana" model: Certain people have big magic (mana) and certain people don't.

Is such a model correct? I don't think so; the American Management Association doesn't think so; the Harvard Business School doesn't think so. But many of my clients think so. Some of them say they don't think so, but their actions belie their words.

2.2.2 People can be ranked on a one-dimensional scale

If you are too much of a republican to believe in the efficacy of primogeniture, you will need another selection rule for choosing your managers, but it would be nice to have one that is similarly unambiguous. Many organizations use rating systems to produce, for each employee, a single number. This number shows how "good" that employee is, so by putting all the numbers together, they can achieve a linear ranking of all employees, from best to worst. If, for instance, there are 80,000 employees, the best employee will be ranked number 1, and the worst will be ranked number 80,000.

In other organizations, there is no individual employee rating, but there are rankings within each work unit that are combined eventually to produce a ranking for the entire organization. Is this ranking system valid? I personally would never knowingly participate in such a ranking because it violates some of my deepest principles. That doesn't mean I'm right in believing such systems are nonsensical, but only that I don't believe in certain things. I leave that question to the wisdom and experience of my readers, many of whom have participated in these ranking exercises.

2.2.3 *The scale for programming is the same as the scale for management*

Even if the first two assumptions were valid, we would still have to face the issue of whether the best people for one type of job will be the best for another. Would the best King of England also make the best computer programmer? Or, more germane to our topic, *Will the best programmers make the best managers?*

In more than three decades in the information systems business, I can recall hardly a week passing without someone asking me this question. I believe there is very little connection between what it takes to make a decent programmer and what it takes to make a decent manager. Some attributes do support both jobs, others are important to one and not the other, while still others are important to one and devastating to the other. My strongest suspicion is that it all balances out, so that programmers picked at random would be just as good at managing as programmers picked according to any ranking system. And the random method would be a lot cheaper.

2.3 Effects of Applying the Model

As a result of these three assumptions, all of which I believe are faulty, the strongest technical people are typically promoted to management. Usually, the first promotion is to the job of technical team leader. Success in the job of technical team leader does correlate with success as a programmer, as I have discussed at length in *Becoming a Technical Leader.*[4] But a technical team leader is not a manager in the usual sense of that word, although titles can certainly confuse the issue.

2.3.1 *Loss of the true sense of the management task*

In a Variable (Pattern 1) organization, there may be many layers of management because each manager's span of control is small. The typical "manager" is a technical leader whose team consists of two or three or four people, and whose job is precisely to be the best technical worker on the team. This structure is the most effective way that a Variable organization has of dealing with the differences among programmers and tasks. Variability is not reduced by developing a consistent process, but by this leader's taking away the parts of the technical work that prove difficult for some other team member.

For this technique to work, each person must be managed over the shoulder, especially at the bottom level. The team leader then knows quickly when something is not going according to plan and steps in to take the task away and do it personally.

When working well, this approach means that the best technical person tackles the toughest technical jobs, even though it's not known in advance which jobs those will be. If the team leader does this job properly, the less skilled people get a chance to learn how to handle tough assignments, and the overall technical capability of the organization grows. But if it's handled poorly, the team leader becomes overloaded and the team members don't really learn a thing—except to feel that they're incompetent.

2.3.2 Loss of technical capability

The promotion to technical team leader based on technical competence thus makes a good deal of sense, especially if the promotion is coupled with some attention to coaching or mentoring skills. When the practice is extended to true management ranks—that is, above the team leader level—the rationale is lost. The first and most obvious effect is shown in Figure 2-3. Even if the best programmers make the best managers, the practice of moving the best programmers into management obviously reduces the average as well as the best technical capabilities of the organization.

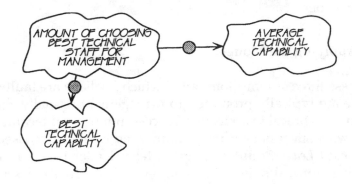

Figure 2-3.   Even if the best programmers make the best managers, promoting them into management reduces the average, as well as the best, technical capabilities of the organization.

2.3.3 Loss of people and loss of satisfaction

That's only the first-order effect, however. As Figure 2-4 shows, when technical capability diminishes, the technical staff can become less satisfied, and retaining the best remaining programmers may become difficult. Also, staff development tends to depend on the examples set by the best technical staff members. If these people are continuously removed, staff development slows, which also has a negative effect on job satisfaction and retention.

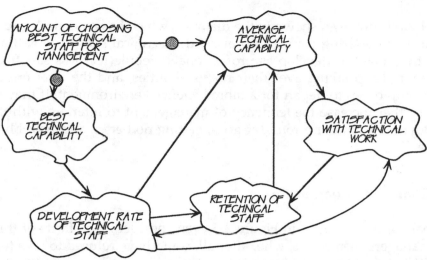

Figure 2-4.   When technical capability diminishes, satisfaction of the technical staff goes down, as does the organization's ability to retain good programmers. Also, staff development tends to decrease when the best technical staff is continually removed, and this also affects job satisfaction and retention.

2.3.4 Interference effects

An additional set of effects is shown in Figure 2-5. Effective team leaders who move into management tend to have difficulty keeping their hands off the technical work. After all, this kind of work is what made their reputations. When they aren't feeling very successful as managers, their tendency to interfere increases, perhaps under pressure from *their own* managers. And, of course, if the average technical capability of the organization keeps decreasing, managers will be less successful and therefore under even more pressure to interfere—thus creating another strong positive feedback loop.

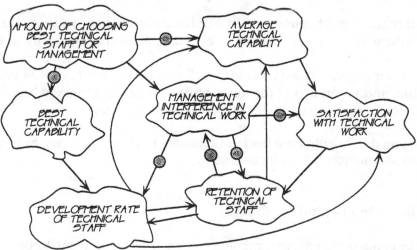

Figure 2-5.   The full dynamic of using technical capability as the criterion for selecting managers.

This loop is not even shown in the diagram, which has enough destructive loops as it stands. Interfering managers prevent the technical staff from getting the experience they need to develop as professionals. People feel less satisfied when their managers keep taking over their responsibilities, and the interference may even cause employees to depart for a more beneficial environment. If they do leave, this may further increase the tendency of management to interfere with the remaining employees. Round and round it goes, getting no better, and possibly getting a lot worse.

2.4 Choice and Congruence

No part of the dynamic in Figure 2-5 even considers the effects of this practice on the managers themselves, who, after all, could have refused to take the managerial jobs. What could be more incongruent than taking a job you don't want and are not qualified for? Yet most of the hundreds of software engineering managers I have interviewed on the subject have admitted that they didn't want to leave their technical work for a management position. Here are some typical comments from those managers:

✓ "I was at the top of my game, so why would I want to enter a new game where I would be at the bottom?"

✓ "I didn't want to manage anybody, but if I wanted to advance my career, there was no place else to go, except out."

✓ "Quite frankly, I did it mostly for the money. I was pretty much at the ceiling for technical work, and now I'm making almost twice as much. And I'm still sorry most of the time that I couldn't ask my family to live on less."

Not all managers, of course, are this unhappy with their decision. But if my admittedly informal survey is reasonably accurate, a good many of them are, at least at first.

If your organization promotes you into management because you are a technical whiz, and if you accept the job in spite of what you think is best, you start your quest for congruent action with one very big strike against you:

If you don't really want the job of manager in the first place, everything you do as manager will be incongruent.

2.5 The Vision Behind the Choice

To be a congruent, effective manager, then, you must want to be a manager. But that's not most important. Many studies of managerial success show that the most effective managers are not primarily seeking to advance their careers, but to advance their vision of what can be accomplished by the organization. Many software engineers, frustrated with what they could accomplish in their technical positions, move into management. Perhaps this is not a bad starting place, though it takes much more than frustration to make an effective manager.

I extensively explore the role of vision in my book *Becoming a Technical Leader*,[5] so I don't intend to repeat myself here. I do want to announce some limitations on what this volume can do for you. My work has been devoted to helping people who hold visions that I personally consider worthwhile. I have studiously avoided helping people who I felt were

- participating in illegal or unethical activities
- seeking to further their own interests at the expense of others (I have no objection to people furthering their own interests. I do that all the time myself.)
- seeking to inflict their personal psychological issues on others (We all have our own needs, but we don't all seek management power so we can make others satisfy them.)

If you want to learn how to use your management position to gain sexual favors from your employees or get promoted to a job you don't deserve, this current book won't help you. At least, I certainly *hope* it won't help you. My experience with this type of manager says that their employees *always* see through their unworthy visions, no matter what they say.

On the other hand, I do have some idea of where such unworthy visions come from, and I'd like to believe that self-understanding might help turn some of these people around. But I'm no preacher, so I don't expect to save any souls. If your vision already involves helping yourself by somehow helping others, I want this book to teach you how to help others by helping yourself.

2.6 Helpful Hints and Suggestions

1. There is an additional assumption underlying the practice of selecting managers from among the best of the technical staff. Why should managers come from the technical staff at all? Recently, for instance, I've noticed that a number of my clients are finding outstanding project managers among the ranks of housewives with grown children. In a successful software company, one of these women explained her success with the remark, "Raising three teenagers is precisely the background you need to manage the computer scientists they hire around here." Reading this, my colleague Norm Kerth suggests that managers might find more food for thought in watching reruns of *The Cosby Show* than in studying the management philosophy of Attila the Hun.

2.   Even if taking the best technical performers into management were always the correct choice, the policy does not come without difficulties. As Linda Hill notes,

> Isolated by this star status, the new managers had limited first-hand opportunities to observe their managers handling the interpersonal difficulties that can arise in working with less proficient subordinates. And because they had been successful, they had encountered relatively few difficulties or conflicts with superiors or peers.[6]

In short, the policy of choosing the best individual performers tends to bring into management those who have the least experience handling interpersonal difficulties up, down, or across the ladder.

Another problem is that the best technical performers are more likely to look back fondly at their technical success and regret making the change to management. The best technical people strongly identify with other technical professionals and, as a result, experience the greatest loss and the greatest stress in losing their technical status. Some of them can become quite critical of the people who work for them who are not strong technically, regardless of other skills they bring to the table.

3.   My reviewer Peter de Jager, upon reading this chapter, suggests another reason why technical experts may be moved into management without regard to the effect on productivity:

> A disturbing non-event took place at this year's PC Expo in New York. A panel was brought together to discuss the issues of personal computer productivity. Our goal was to define some simple, but effective, strategies to deliver significant productivity increases. ... Out of more than 82,000 attendees, only one person attended the panel.
>
> Perhaps the low level of productivity has nothing to do with technology. ... Perhaps it has something to do with the fact that 81,999 technology managers were not interested in a productivity discussion. ... Perhaps they are not interested in business. Perhaps they are only interested in technology. ... Perhaps ...[7]

And perhaps this state of affairs is self-perpetuating, in that these same managers are the ones who pick their successors.

4.   A fellow consultant as well as my most challenging critic, Jinny Batterson, introduced me to the book *Love and Profits* by James A. Autry, whose vision of management is very similar to mine. For one thing, he reminds us that the charter to manage really comes from below:

> Management is, in fact, a sacred trust in which the well-being of other people is put in your care during most of their waking hours. It is a trust

placed upon you first by those who put you in the job, but more important than that, it is a trust placed upon you after you get the job by those whom you are to manage.[8]

5.   Another fellow consultant Naomi Karten believes that managers are made, not born, but warns, "The fact that the American Management Association and Harvard Business School agree wouldn't persuade me if I didn't. They have a profit motive for believing that managers can be made." I have a similar motive, so be warned.

6.   Payson Hall, a consultant and astute student of project management, offers another way that managers often get set up for failure: "The new project manager is made a managing leader who also has the technical responsibility. This combination is quite difficult, since when things aren't going well on the project, what is usually needed is NOT another person at the oars, but a good captain to organize the crew in the storm. Yet, as you said, the former techies tend to dive for the safety of their expertise under stress, the result being a loss of perspective."

2.7 Summary

✓   Congruent managers are hard to find in software engineering, partly because of the way the organizations choose and develop their managers.

✓   Boehm says, "Poor management can increase software costs more rapidly than any other factor." A cost driver of 64 would be a conservative estimate for management, because of the many ways poor management can increase costs—or even create total project failure.

✓   Managers often seem to allocate improvement effort in reverse order of cost-driver impact, putting least effort into the most important driver, management itself.

✓   The One-Dimensional Selection Model for managers is based on three faulty assumptions, namely:

   •   Managers are born, not made.
   •   People can be ranked on a one-dimensional scale.
   •   The scale for programming is the same as the scale for management.

As a result of this model, we tend to move the strongest technical people to management, a practice that weakens both management and the technical staff.

✓   Team leaders can be effective at improving software quality, but the job of team leader is not the same as the job of manager. Nor will the best team leaders necessarily make the best managers.

✓   Technical people who don't want to be managers but are promoted anyway are starting their management careers in an incongruent position, one that will be difficult to improve over time.

✓   People who go into management to pursue an unworthy vision will be unworthy managers. I hope this book won't help them.

2.8 Practice

1.   Try this experiment: Refer to a computer trade publication such as *Datamation* or *Computerworld*. Calculate the amount of advertising space given to tools and compare it with the space given to management. The results may suggest why many software engineering managers have been driven by the vendors' claims about the wonders of tools.

2.   You can perform a similar experiment by studying the titles of computer books. In fact, if you study the titles of my books, you'll find that most of them are about software tools. In my old age, I've realized the error of my ways. That's why I'm leaving most of the tool business to my younger colleagues and concentrating on improving the effectiveness of the other three factors: people, systems (specifically, their complexity), and management.

3.   Diagram some of the effects on managers of the practice of moving the best technical workers into management. Also diagram some of the effects on the remaining technical staff.

4.   If the best programmers don't necessarily become the best managers, what other criteria should be used to select managers?

5.   Where would be good places to look outside of the technical staff for people with aptitude and experience for software engineering management?

6.   I hesitate to offer advice on how to select managers to somebody whose situation I don't know. My colleague Phil Fuhrer suggests, however, that some more insightful ways of choosing managers, even if not ideal, would be a useful addition to this chapter. So in response to Phil's request, here are some ideas, all of which I have seen used appropriately in practice at one time or another:

- Use peer nomination.
- Select the most experienced at managing in other areas of life.
- Choose the most mature.
- Select those who want it the most.
- Select those who have the best reason for wanting it.
- Select those who aspire to a career in management.
- Put a number of candidates through extensive management training, then choose according to how well they apply their training.
- Use a consulting firm specializing in management selection.
- Draw lots.
- Pick the person with the most formal education in management.
- Choose the one who has demonstrated the best leadership qualities.
- Go outside the technical organization and pick a proven manager.
- Grow them using a master/apprentice model.
- Use an intelligent combination of the above methods.

Discuss the pros and cons of each of the above methods. What other methods can you suggest?

7. As suggested by my colleague Norm Kerth: How can you create an environment in which those individuals who are interested in managing can naturally experiment with different styles of management? How can you create an environment in which they will be encouraged to grow into effective managers?

3
Styles of Coping

There is no value-judgment more important to man—no factor more decisive to his psychological development and motivation—than the estimate he passes on himself.

This estimate is ordinarily experienced by him not in the form of a conscious verbalized judgment, but in the form of a feeling that can be hard to isolate and identify because he experiences it constantly; it is part of every other feeling, it is involved in his every emotional response.[1]
— N. Branden

If we believe in the importance of management, have some competence for management, and have chosen a career in management for all the right reasons, why do we fail to act in accordance with what we know is good management practice? One reason is that we are not always utterly logical creatures, but have feelings as well as thoughts. When these inner feelings are strong enough, they translate into characteristic styles of coping. These styles, in turn, translate into effective or ineffective management actions.

An example of effective, congruent interaction might be nothing more than a low-stress communication in which everybody went away undiminished, and out of which came some useful work. In fact, it's hard to write dramatically about congruence, because congruent interactions aren't very dramatic; we all just act sensibly, are considerate of one another, get our work done, and enjoy what we're doing.

Since everybody in an organization is responsible for controlling something, and since incongruent coping behavior reduces the variety needed for effective control, it's possible to measure an organization's health through the people's characteristic coping styles.

3.1 Coping Congruently: The Self, Other, and Context

When we act congruently, we are, consciously or unconsciously, taking into account three general areas: the self, other (or empathic), and context (Figure 3-1).

✓ **Self**: We must consider our own needs and capabilities. For instance, managers who try to attend every technical meeting may overload all their available time, and thus be unable to do the managerial job, or even to make any real technical contribution.

✓ **Other**: We must consider the needs and capabilities of other people. For instance, if a programmer is perfectly capable of writing readable code but refuses to do so, then testing and maintaining that code will be a great burden, if not an impossibility.

✓ **Context**: We must consider the reality of the context in which we are operating. For instance, if a manager insists on sticking with an old design that can no longer handle the task, the project may be doomed no matter how hard everyone works. Or if a manager in a start-up company spends money as if the company had a billion-dollar cash balance, the organization may be out of business before its software product is ready for market.

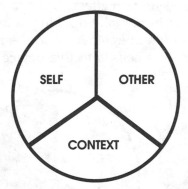

Figure 3-1.   In order to cope effectively with the world, we must consider three essential components—the self, other, and context—and balance their requirements all at the same time. To do this is to behave congruently.

Under ordinary circumstances, such congruent coping is the rule, but if circumstances were always ordinary, we wouldn't need managers. Under stress, people tend to lose their balance, and one or more of these three essential components may be lost to the others, leading to a characteristic incongruent coping style.[2] Even when stress is not too great, if feelings of self-esteem are low, they are manifest much more dramatically in characteristic incongruent coping styles as described by the family therapist and my mentor Virginia Satir. She identified five styles: blaming, placating, superreasonable, loving or hating, and irrelevant. Let's look at each of these in turn, then see how each can be a signal of a poorly managed software situation.

3.2 Blaming

When people fail to take other people into account, they fall into a blaming posture. Here are some typical blaming actions you may see in software organizations (underlined words are stressed in this style of speaking):

✓ *Manager, as programmer arrives late for a meeting:* "You're <u>always</u> late. You <u>never</u> show <u>any</u> consideration for <u>other</u> people."

✓ *Programmer, when asked by manager to volunteer to talk to a job applicant:* "Why don't <u>you</u> do it <u>yourself</u>? <u>I'm</u> not going to do <u>your</u> job for you. If you were better <u>organized</u>, you wouldn't need to ask <u>me</u> such things."

✓ *Manager, when marketing manager asks about the possibility of revising the requirements:* "You <u>never</u> get the requirements right the first time. If I told you <u>once</u>, I've told you a <u>thousand</u> times: Do the job <u>right</u> the <u>first</u> time, then you won't bother <u>me</u> with revisions."

When blaming, a person is saying, in effect, "*I am everything; you are nothing.*" Of course, this stance comes not from really thinking "I am everything," but just the opposite. Directing the attention at another person—and blaming is often accompanied by a pointed finger—is a self-protective device to distract others from the inadequacy that the blamer feels.

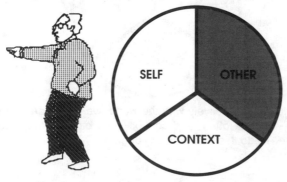

Figure 3-2.   When people are blaming, they exclude other people from consideration. Their pointed finger and aggressive posture is an attempt (usually unconscious) to hide their feelings of inadequacy.

Like all incongruent coping, blaming arises from feelings of low self-esteem. When I blame, I attempt to build myself up by tearing down others because I don't have the confidence that I can amount to much any other way. Blaming usually fools people who are unsophisticated, or whose own self-esteem is at a low ebb. The knowledgeable observer, however, sees the amount of blaming as a sure measure of how inadequate the blamer feels. Moreover, if blaming is the preferred management style, it becomes a measure of how far an organizational environment has degenerated.

3.3 Placating

One of the reasons that blamers so often fool people is that many of their victims are habitual placaters. When people forget to take themselves into account, they fall into a placating posture. From this humble position, placaters readily believe the blamer who tells them, *"You are nothing."* Here are some typical ways placaters would try to cope with the same three situations:

✓   *Manager, as programmer arrives late for a meeting:* "I'm sorry we have so many meetings. I'll try not to have so many in the future."

✓   *Programmer, when asked by manager to volunteer to talk to a job applicant:* "I don't know how I'll find the time, but I'll manage somehow, even though I'll probably miss most of my schedules. But I don't understand why you'd choose me to do it. There are lots of people here who are better programmers, and better at interviewing."

✓   *Manager, when marketing manager asks about the possibility of revising the requirements:* "I'm awfully sorry, I should have anticipated that requirement. We'll find some way to do it, but the schedule may have to slip. No? That's not okay? I guess it's very important to you. I'm sorry I brought it up. Of course we'll find some way to get it done on time. I can work Sunday. My kids won't mind too much. Their mother can take them to drug rehabilitation class in her wheelchair."

Placating, of course, also comes from low self-esteem, and at least has the advantage of being a bit more honest than blaming. I feel lousy about myself, and I translate this into *"I am nothing; you are everything."*

Placating may easily go undetected because placaters are so accommodating. When I placate, I may not hear my own whining, see my slumping posture, or notice that I'm holding my breath, but other people will detect it if they know what to observe. If they fail to observe what I'm doing, they may not notice the placating until I fail to deliver on my many promises. Or they may fall for my manipulation and, out of pity, let me off the hook.

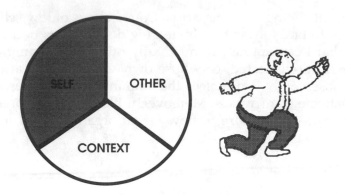

Figure 3-3.   When people placate, they exclude themselves from consideration. Paradoxically, their submissive posture is intended (usually unconsciously) to make other people sorry for them, and so give them what they want.

A very common pattern in dysfunctional organizations is a blaming boss with placating subordinates (Figure 3-4). Such a boss never understands that the blaming hurts in at least two ways:

- The placating employee is likely to agree to anything, no matter how unreasonable.
- The placating employee is likely to resent the boss and, consciously or unconsciously, work less effectively in delivering on the promise.

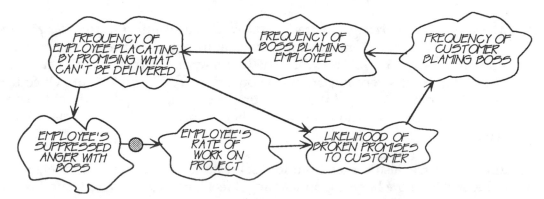

Figure 3-4.   A very common pattern is a blaming boss locked in a never-ending cycle with a placating employee. In this specific case, the blaming leads the placating employee to promise what probably cannot be delivered, and the chance of delivery is made worse because the employee harbors hidden anger at the boss, which is translated into a work slowdown or a series of "innocent" mistakes. The boss, in turn, is following another common pattern: placating in response to the customer's blaming, then blaming the employee.

To add to this dynamic, blaming bosses often broadcast their blame when others are watching, and if any of the spectators are inclined to placate, they may also get involved in a similar dynamic. Public blaming is like skunk spray—it sticks to everyone within range.

Another reaction of the placater to the blamer is shown in Figure 3-4. The customer blames the boss for nondelivery, and the boss, unable to respond to the customer but disinclined to keep anger bottled up, turns around and blames the employee. This shows that blaming and placating are not "wired" into people. Each of us knows how to do each of the incongruent coping styles, though we each have favorites that we exhibit when our self-esteem is low enough. If the favorite doesn't work, we'll switch to one of the others, continuing this incongruent dance as long as it works (if you can call this working).

We can see the malleability of coping postures in Figure 3-5, which shows the dynamic of the sudden switch of roles between blaming and placating. Most married couples are able to make this switch dozens of times a day, and bosses and their employees can be as adept as an old married couple. An experienced observer can pinpoint the state of a software organization by picking up on the quantity of blaming and placating among members of the organization.

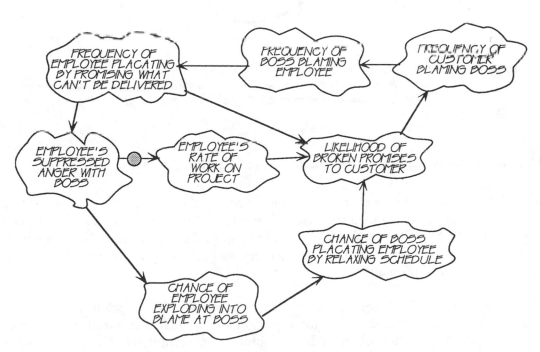

Figure 3-5.   A common variation of the blaming/placating dynamic is the sudden switch in roles when the placater has swallowed enough abuse, and suddenly throws it all back at the boss. The boss then becomes a placater and relaxes some requirement, which leads to the customer's blaming the boss again, starting another cycle.

3.4 Superreasonable

Superreasonable behavior is a little more difficult to notice or use as a measurement of organizational health. That's because superreasonable people try to hide their low self-esteem behind a curtain of rationality. Like the Wizard of Oz, the superreasonable person says, in effect, "Don't notice the person behind the curtain." Indeed, the superreasonable person doesn't notice people at all, whether they're in front of or behind the curtain. Like the ostrich, the superreasonable (unconsciously) seems to say, *"If I can't see you, then you can't see me."*

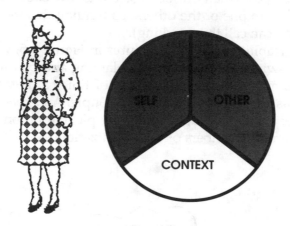

Figure 3-6.   In the superreasonable style of coping, people are entirely excluded from consideration—both the self and the other. The characteristic superreasonable posture is often stiff, unmoving, with eyes peering off into distant space, as if to say, "I'm not really here."

Here are some typical superreasonable ways of handling the same three situations:

✓   *Manager, as programmer arrives late for a meeting:* "DeMarco and Lister say that when lateness to meetings rises above thirty percent, efficiency suffers." (Actually, these two authorities didn't say anything of the kind, but the superreasonable can quote authorities on any subject, whether or not the experts ever said anything about it.)

✓   *Programmer, when asked by manager to volunteer to talk to a job applicant:* "It's always better when a professional personnel organization handles interviewing. It's even better when such an organization administers a comprehensive battery of standard psychological instruments and scales the results according to a rank-order correlation with job requirements." (Here are some "rules" that sound plausible and seem to come from an unknown, unnamed authority. Perhaps they came on stone tablets, from heaven, or by divine inspiration.)

✓   *Manager, when marketing manager asks about the possibility of revising the require-
     ments:* (Doesn't look at the marketing manager, but gazes off into space—per-
     haps seeking divine inspiration. Doesn't say anything. Doesn't acknowledge
     the request in any detectable way.)

The superreasonable stance is a good cover when you are in the company of people who are intimidated by the appearance of correctness, propriety, authority, and
profundity. The superreasonable stance says, in effect, *"It is everything; you and I are
nothing."*
     Especially in times of my own self-doubt, I'd like to believe that there are peo-
ple in the world who know the absolute Truth. Sometimes, the superreasonable
person is right, if only by chance. But nobody's right all the time, so dysfunctional
organizations are easily spotted by the number of people who believe that one of
their superreasonables is some reincarnation of Moses who will lead them to the
promised land—when in fact it's only Charlton Heston playing a role.

3.5 Loving/Hating

From the viewpoint of congruence, loving and hating relationships have the same
structure: the total exclusion of the context. The lovers in their passion can see only
each other, just like mortal enemies locked in combat. In both cases, lack of attention to the context can prove dangerous to the individuals. Lovers cross a street
holding hands, their gazes locked upon one another so they don't see the red light
or the garbage truck rushing toward them at forty miles an hour. Haters are so
intent upon making each other look bad in a meeting they don't notice that they
both look bad to the boss.

Figure 3-7.   In the loving/hating style of coping, the context is entirely excluded from considera-
                   tion as attention is focused on the other person.

Notice the loving way of handling the same three situations:

✓ *Manager, as (highly favored) programmer arrives late for a meeting:* "I'm really glad you could make it, Sarah. We really need your input." (Others in the meeting know that they wouldn't receive the same warm welcome if they were late.)

✓ *Programmer, when asked by a (favored) manager to volunteer to talk to a job applicant:* "Of course, Will." (The programmer ignores the two other commitments he has for the same time, and the fact that he knows nothing about interviewing job applicants.)

✓ *Manager, when a (favored) marketing manager asks about the possibility of revising requirements:* "No problem, Lynn. Anything else you want?" (The manager never even considers how unreasonable or unimportant the request is.)

These responses sound a bit like placating, but the principal difference is that they are always directed at the same person, and not at others. Lovers never whine, and they use the other person's name while gazing puppy-like at the love-object. Placaters, on the other hand, whine and snivel, seldom use the other person's name, and never look that person in the eye.

Now notice the hating way of handling the same three situations:

✓ *Manager, as (out-of-favor) programmer arrives late for a meeting:* "I'm *so* glad you could make it, Betty. We *really* missed your input." (Others in the meeting flinch at the extreme sarcasm in the manager's voice, which seems unreasonable given that Betty is only a minute late and the meeting hasn't even begun. Then, when George comes in ten minutes later, the manager simply smiles and says nothing.)

✓ *Programmer, when asked by (out-of-favor) manager to volunteer to talk to a job applicant:* "Get off my back!" (In reality, the programmer wants to practice interviewing skills and to influence the hiring of this applicant, but cannot miss an opportunity to attack the manager.)

✓ *Manager, when (out-of-favor) marketing manager asks about the possibility of revising requirements:* "Over my dead body!" (The manager never even considers how reasonable or important the request is.)

You can confuse these responses with blaming if you don't notice that they are always directed at the same person. Blamers look everywhere in the universe (except at themselves) for the reasons that bad things happen. Haters don't have to scour the universe; they know exactly who is responsible.

The loving/hating stance says, in effect,"*It is nothing; you and I are everything,*" which makes the loving/hating stance in some ways the opposite of the superreasonable stance. Whereas the superreasonable person has total faith in the power of abstraction, the loving/hating style has total belief in the power—either positive or negative—of one other person. The loved one can do no wrong; the hated one can do no right.

Because loving and hating relationships are so out of touch with the world, it's hard for them to be sustained at high intensity for a long time before they cause something dangerous to happen. Since they involve total focus on another person, when the relationship changes, the lover and hater often switch roles, as in this tale:

Emma was the project manager for a large software project. Charles was the owner/founder of a seven-person software contracting firm that Emma retained to design and build the operating environment for her project. Emma was the divorced mother of three grown children. Charles was single, about twenty-five years old, and charming in a shy way. Some two months into the project, it was clear to everyone except Charles that Emma had become seriously attached to him. Although he was very smart and skilled, he sometimes made poor decisions, but Emma always backed him up, to the detriment of the project.

About five months into the project, while Emma and Charles were out of town together on a vendor visit, Emma came to Charles's motel room in a nightgown and tried to seduce him. He turned her down, and by morning her love had switched to hate. Within two weeks, Emma had unilaterally canceled his company's contract, even though it cost a substantial penalty and meant the project had to be started over.

In this case, the former loved one became the enemy. More rarely, the enemy becomes the beloved friend. Neither of these relationships contributes much to quality software.

3.6 Irrelevant

Irrelevant behavior may not be as common as the other incongruent coping strategies, but because it is the most striking and difficult to handle, managers always remember it. Most people simply have little familiarity with truly irrelevant behavior, and less experience in dealing successfully with it. Do you think you could handle the following irrelevant responses?

✓ *Manager, as programmer arrives late for a meeting:* "Hey, did you catch the Giants game last night? I won the office pool and I'm looking for people to help me celebrate."

✓ *Programmer, when asked by manager to volunteer to talk to a job applicant:* "Hey, do I get to have an expense account lunch? The Garden Café is supposed to be terrific, now that they've remodeled. I hear the purple velvet seats came all the way from Florence."

✓   *Manager, when marketing manager asks about the possibility of revising the require-ments:* "Do you see that kitten up on the roof? It's a calico. I wonder how it got there? Do you want to see if we can catch it?"

Figure 3-8.   In the irrelevant style of coping, everything is missing, which leads to entirely unpre-dictable behavior. The posture can be just about anything, but typically involves a lot of movement—often right out the door—which (unconsciously) protects the person from being pinned down on anything.

You can see the power of the irrelevant posture, but notice that it is a purely nega-tive power—the power to prevent things from getting done. That's why this coping style increases in frequency in organizations where people have lost any real hope of accomplishing their goals. In effect, the irrelevant behavior says, *"Nothing counts for anything."*

That fits perfectly when people feel entirely powerless. When a project cancel-lation is impending or whenever managers are perceived as not in control of a proj-ect, the quantity of irrelevant behavior increases. With more irrelevant behavior, the project does even worse, leading to ultimate collapse.

3.7 The Role of Self-Esteem

The problem is not that these five incongruent strategies don't work. They work the same way Mark Twain's cat worked:

> **A cat that sits on a hot stove once won't do it again, but it probably won't sit on a cold one, either.**

Once upon a time, when we were young, these strategies did something useful for us, so we continue to use them, even when the stove is cold. Incongruent strategies can work in much the same way that poor-quality programs can work. They both settle for less than they could get if they worked well.

3.7.1 Internal messages

Why would I be willing to settle for less? An analogy with poor-quality programs provides a hint. We settle for a poor-quality program when we don't have much confidence that we can make it any better. Indeed, we may shout, "Don't touch the program" out of fear that attempts to make it better will only make it worse. We may justify this settling for less by arguing, "At least, it gets the daily payroll almost right, and we only have to make a few corrections, plus do the monthly summary by hand."

Incongruent coping behaviors are programs, too, though not for computers, but for human beings. They work for me because they sometimes give me some protection, so I keep using them, especially when I don't feel very good about myself or my ability to make them better without making them worse. The way they work is illustrated by the internal messages I give myself:

✓   Blaming behavior says, "At least I get the power jump on everyone."

✓   Placating behavior says, "At least I always agree and try to keep everyone happy."

✓   Superreasonable behavior says, "At least I'm smart."

✓   Loving behavior says, "At least I support the one perfect person."

✓   Hating behavior says, "At least I oppose the devil."

✓   Irrelevant behavior says, "At least I get attention."

These "at least's" might be adequate if I were working in a delicatessen slicing pastrami, but when I'm trying to maintain or build software, I need all the effectiveness I can muster. Software quality dynamics are not very forgiving of poor coping behavior. To manage software projects effectively, I must decrease the amount of time I spend settling for less by increasing the amount of time I spend being congruent.

3.7.2 A locked-on congruence/incongruence dynamic

Figure 3-9 shows one way that software managers can get locked into behaving incongruently. When I perceive that I cannot control what is important to me (regardless of whether my perception is justified by the facts), my self-esteem falls; when my self-esteem falls, I lack the confidence to cope congruently. Regardless of the incongruent coping style I choose, its ineffectiveness leads to poor control, which feeds back to my perception of poor control.

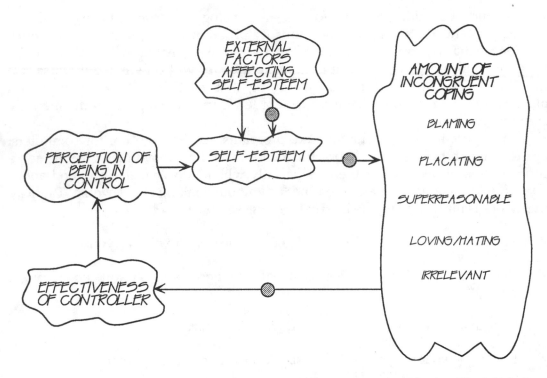

Figure 3-9.   A software manager can get locked into incongruent behavior. The initial trigger might be an external factor, such as a flu epidemic, a change in upper management, or an announcement of a competitive product. Once the low self-esteem loop starts, it becomes self-reinforcing.

The favorable side of Figure 3-9 is that the positive feedback loop can lock on in either direction. If I have high self-esteem to begin with—if I feel generally good about myself—then I won't be so likely to cope incongruently with stressful situations. My congruent actions will increase my chances of being an effective controller, so my self-esteem will rise. This dynamic suggests that if I am embarking on a management job, my first task is to do what's necessary to raise my self-esteem before I start taking actions as manager. The same principle applies if I am choosing someone else to manage: Look for someone with high self-esteem and do whatever is necessary to boost it.

     In the next chapter, then, we'll see how high self-esteem can be used to boost behavior from incongruent patterns into something more productive.

3.8 Helpful Hints and Suggestions

1.   My colleague Wayne Bailey points out that because irrelevant behavior has the power to stop things, such behavior is often a sign of something that needs stopping. For instance, irrelevant behavior is often used to shock someone else out of superreasonable behavior.

2.   Another colleague Bill Pardee thinks that irrelevant behavior may often arise as a play for affiliation or to defer or avoid confronting conflict. In general, from Wayne's and Bill's observations, irrelevant behavior is never about what it seems to be about. Indeed, another name for this behavior is distracting. So when you want to understand irrelevant behavior, look somewhere else.

3.   My colleague Norm Kerth suggests that you can learn about the congruence of an organization from listening to the nature of the jokes and the amount of laughter. Bitter jokes, or no laughter at all, are obvious signs of incongruence.

4.   Norm and another colleague Phil Fuhrer both suggest looking at congruence through the degree of truth in communications between organizational levels. For example, are status reports guarded? Are reports of management planning sessions vague?

5.   Payson Hall, a self-confessed "bit twiddler," couldn't resist pointing out that there are eight permutations of self, other, and context, but only six are accounted for by the described coping stances. I myself am a bit-twiddler, and some time ago had shown this discrepancy to Virginia Satir. Before her death, she and I had a number of discussions on the subject and were able to identify the loving/hating style as missing from her initial five stances. However, we never arrived at anything definitive about the other two ("self alone" and "other alone"). We did conclude that self alone might be hard to distinguish from irrelevant and that other alone might easily pass for an extreme of loving/hating.

3.9 Summary

✓   In order to cope effectively with the world, we must be able to take into account three areas—the self, other, and context—and balance their requirements all at the same time. To do this is to behave congruently.

✓   When feelings of self-esteem are low, they are manifest in characteristic incongruent coping styles: blaming, placating, superreasonable, loving/hating, or irrelevant.

✓   When people fail to take other people into account, they fall into a blaming posture. When blaming, a person is saying, in effect, "I am everything; you are nothing."

✓   When people forget to take themselves into account, they fall into a placating posture, and are effectively saying, "I am nothing; you are everything."

✓   A very common pattern is a blaming boss locked in a never-ending cycle with a placating employee.

✓   Another common variation of the blaming/placating dynamic is the sudden switch in roles when the placater has swallowed enough abuse, and suddenly throws it all back at the boss.

✓   In the superreasonable style of coping, people are entirely excluded from consideration. The superreasonable stance says, in effect, "It is everything; you and I are nothing."

✓   From the viewpoint of congruence, loving and hating relationships have the same structure: the total exclusion of context. The loving/hating stance says, in effect, "It is nothing; you and I are everything."

✓   In the irrelevant style of coping, everything is missing, which leads to entirely unpredictable behavior. This behavior has a purely negative power—power not to get things done, but power to prevent things from getting done. In effect, the irrelevant behavior says, "Nothing counts for anything."

✓   Incongruent coping styles each settle for less than they could get if they worked well. They do "work" to the extent that they sometimes give some protection, so they are used when self-esteem is low.

✓   Managers acting incongruently may get locked into their stance by a positive feedback loop connecting ineffectiveness and low-self esteem.

3.10 Practice

1. Give an example of how a colleague built a case against a person in your company, either an employee or a manager. This kind of case building demonstrates how the placater is actually preparing to blame, but has to save up for one big blame dump.

2. Consider the case of the executive who "rewards" a staff manager for doing a dirty job by making him manager of a group of 55 people, even though the executive admits that the manager isn't qualified to manage such a group. This is placating behavior. Explain why a more congruent way to handle this situation is to reward the manager by offering him an 18-month training program that will give him a chance to become qualified.

3. As Donald Norman observes in his invaluable book *The Design of Everyday Things*,

> It seems natural for people to blame their own misfortunes on the environment. It seems equally natural to blame other people's misfortunes on their personalities. Just the opposite attribution, by the way, is made when things go well. ... In all cases, whether a person is inappropriately accepting blame for the inability to work simple objects or attributing behavior to environment or personality, a faulty mental model is at work.[3]

Give an example of when you observed such a faulty mental model, and of how you might deal with it congruently.

4. As Figure 3-9 shows, external factors may affect my self-esteem, but many of these external factors are within my control. What are some of the techniques you use when your self-esteem needs a boost? Which ones work and which ones only make you feel worse about yourself, like gobbling down four quarts of your favorite Ben and Jerry's ice cream?

5. Reread the loving/hating story of Emma and Charles. This time, however, read it as the story of Edward and Charlene, with Edward being the project manager and divorced father of three grown children, and Charlene the twenty-five-year-old owner of a software company. Does the story sound different? Are your reactions different? Which way do you think it actually happened?

6. My colleague Norm Kerth says that the internal superreasonable message should be, "At least <u>everyone thinks</u> I'm smart." Norm argues that when he's being superreasonable, he knows deep down that he's faking it. In my own case, I'm so out of touch with myself I don't even know (at least until later) that I'm faking it. What's your own style of being superreasonable?

4

Transforming Incongruence into Congruence

The relationships that succeed can be described simply. Within the family, the adults work as a team, are open with each other, demonstrate their presence as individuals, and show their respect and esteem for each other. They treat each other as unique, are aware of and build on their sameness, and grow and learn from their differences. They model the behaviors and values they wish to teach to their children.[1]
— Virginia Satir

What better way to shift the topic from incongruence to congruence than by quoting Satir's description of congruence in a family setting. It sounds wonderful, but we are talking about organizations. So, before you read further, transform the words *family* to *office*, *adults* to *veterans*, and *children* to *new employees*. Now read it again. Does this sound like the kind of organization you would like to work in? If so, keep reading to learn how to begin transforming incongruence into congruence.

4.1 Congruent Behavior

Although congruence is ubiquitous and easy to recognize, people often fail to notice such behavior because it works so well. Or if they do notice a variety of congruent behaviors, they may fail to lump them together under the heading of "congruence." That's because congruent behaviors are not stereotyped behaviors—

quite the contrary. Congruent behaviors are original, specific behaviors that fit the context, other, and self, as required by the Law of Requisite Variety. As a result, there are many congruent behaviors for any one situation, although behavior that is congruent in one situation may be totally incongruent in another. In one situation, it may be congruent to allow an exception to the rules, while in another, it would be congruent to insist on strict adherence.

Moreover, the external behavior alone can never be congruent if it doesn't fit with the people involved. If I feel that you are doing a poor job, it would be incongruent of me to say I'm satisfied with your work, but that doesn't mean I have to blurt out that I'm dissatisfied with your work. If I'm feeling angry, it would be incongruent of me to act as if nothing's wrong. However, that doesn't mean I immediately have to scream at you that I'm angry.

4.1.1 Experiencing congruence

Many people have never worked in a congruent organization, and thus cannot recognize congruence when they see it. As a start in learning to recognize congruence, consider the three situations of Chapter 3 handled more congruently:

✓ *Manager, as programmer arrives late for a meeting:* (First waits for the meeting to be over, for a private meeting with programmer.) "I noticed you were late. Also, if I recall correctly, this was the third meeting in a row to which you were late. I feel we lose efficiency in the meeting when you aren't there. What's your take on the situation?" (Then waits for programmer to respond.)

✓ *Programmer, when asked by manager to volunteer to talk to a job applicant:* "I appreciate your asking me, and I'm flattered you think I can do a good job. If I take the time to do that, however, I'll have to let something else go. Do you have any suggestions as to which of my tasks can be delayed?" (Then waits for manager to respond.)

✓ *Manager, when marketing manager asks about the possibility of revising the requirements:* "I'm worried that if we revise the requirements at this late date, we'll disrupt the entire delivery. If I assign Helen just to consider your proposed requirement changes, I'll have to take her off other work. That would mean slipping the delivery one week minimum even if we don't actually decide to implement the changes. Would that delay be acceptable, or would you rather hold these changes for consideration in a later release?" (Then waits for marketing manager to respond.)

Because congruent behavior is not just words but the entire package of verbal and nonverbal actions, any of the above responses could be delivered incongruently.

For instance, the programmer in the second example could say the same words sarcastically, not really expecting or wanting suggestions from the manager. Therefore, it's hard to describe congruence in a book. You have to experience the total interaction in order to observe that the nonverbal part is congruent with the verbal part. That's not as hard as it sounds, however, because you instinctively *know* when the message is not congruent.

4.1.2 Recognizing congruence

Inasmuch as congruence is so important to effective management, it's vital that you can recognize congruence. One way is to watch for subtle incongruence between verbal and nonverbal responses. Another is to listen to the content of what is said aloud, because people acting incongruently can't seem to make simple statements of fact about themselves without groveling or bragging. People being congruent are able to make simple statements of fact about themselves, such as

✓ "I made a mistake."
✓ "I went too fast."
✓ "I did a good job."
✓ "My timing was poor."
✓ "I made a real contribution."
✓ "I didn't consider all the people involved."
✓ "I'm doing the best I know how."

Perhaps the most congruent thing you'll ever hear is an occasional

✓ "I don't know what more I can do."

You won't hear this when a person is acting incongruently.

4.1.3 Can real organizations operate congruently?

The idea of congruence raises a lot of questions about the realities of organizational life:

✓ Don't we have to apologize some of the time?
✓ Can't we be allowed to disagree with one another?
✓ Can't we emphasize our own contributions?
✓ Can't we be logical occasionally?
✓ Aren't we allowed to admire someone?
✓ Can't we find someone's behavior unproductive?
✓ What if we have to change the subject?

Each of these could be seen as incongruent coping postures, but real people need them to get real work done. So is a congruent organization even desirable?

Yes, we do need to get these things done, usually every day. But congruence not only feels better, it's the better way to handle each of these situations. As Satir put it,

> To apologize without placating, to disagree without blaming, to be reasonable without being inhuman and boring, and to change the subject without distracting give me greater personal satisfaction, less internal pain, and more opportunities for growth and satisfactory relationships with others, to say nothing about increased competence.[2]

If you know how to do these things and, more important, you actually do them, you are well started on the path to becoming a higher-quality manager of software engineering. We all spend a lot of energy coping incongruently, and that energy could be better spent elsewhere. To transform that energy spent on incongruent coping, we can begin by asking two questions:

- How do we learn to behave incongruently?
- Why do we continue to behave incongruently?

We learn to behave incongruently in order to survive when we are very young, often before we learn to speak. As we shall see, each incongruent behavior is based on a behavior that is actually effective in some survival situations, and may even have a genetic component. If a certain behavior were never effective, we would have dropped it from our repertoire, but its partial success leads us to continue using it. What makes it incongruent is its misapplication when survival is not at stake.

4.2 Transforming Blaming into Assertive Behavior

Blaming, for instance, is based on the survival behavior of response to an attack. For example, if you hurt or threaten a cat, the cat may attack you to protect itself. The cat, not being able to talk, makes its attack in a physical, nonverbal manner. Before actually attacking, the cat may give a number of warning sounds and gestures, and take a characteristic posture (Figure 4-1). These warnings, which save the cat a great deal of costly fighting, are what humans often express in the form of blaming.

We can often recognize blaming by the pointed finger, clearly an attacking gesture. Like the cat, the blamer often stares at the blamee, and puffs up to look as big and threatening as possible. Although the human attack may be verbal, the words don't really matter. Linguists note that blaming can be recognized in all languages by the pattern of stressed words.[3] That is, we can recognize blame if two or more words are stressed in one sentence, even if the sentence is in a foreign language we don't understand, or in a nonsense sentence in no known language at all. (Recall the underlined words in Chapter 3's blaming examples: "Why don't you do it yourself? I'm not going to do your job for you. If you were better organized, you wouldn't need to ask me such things.") This pattern of stress, independent of the language, indicates how deep the biological basis might be for blaming behavior.

Figure 4-1.   Blaming is a form of attack used for self-protection, and is related to genetically programmed behavior seen in all mammals.

Blaming has a biological basis for a very good reason. There are times when someone else's behavior is threatening, and at those times, we want to be able to say, in effect, "I am everything; you are nothing." Blaming behavior means, essentially, "If you continue to do that, I'm going to do what is necessary to stop you, no matter what the consequences are to you."

As a software engineering manager, however, I never actually found myself in real physical danger, so I didn't need to threaten physical harm as a management technique. If I toned down my response a bit to suit the situation, however, I could produce something more effective than blaming. But before I could tone down my response, I would have to transform how I felt about the situation. Otherwise, the toning down would be a fake representation of what's going on inside of me, and therefore incongruent.

What is the congruent transformation of a blaming posture? Some possibilities are being assertive, direct, honest, candid, and forthright—all useful postures in situations in which I am seriously concerned about what the other person is doing.

4.3 Transforming Placating into Caring or Yielding Behavior

What is the congruent transformation of a placating posture? Recall that placating says, in effect, "I am nothing; you are everything."

In nature, a parent may take this attitude and even sacrifice its own life for the sake of an offspring, thus ensuring the survival of the species (Figure 4-2).

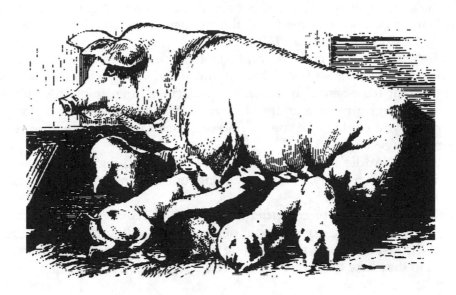

Figure 4-2.   Parents sacrifice themselves for their children to help them survive. We honor this
                 behavior and call it "caring."

Likewise, a manager may be yielding or caring to an employee because the
employee, though not performing perfectly, represents the future of the organization. Take the following example: Warner's most recent program had just wiped
out someone else's source code, which cost the project about two person-weeks of
extra labor. Jill, Warner's manager, explained the seriousness of the mistake, but
said, "Warner, I know you didn't intend to do this, and I know you feel as bad
about it as we do. I want you to know that we've all done things as bad or even
worse in our careers, so even though we're not happy it occurred, I don't hold you
responsible. What we need to do now is figure out how to prevent this in the
future. Any ideas?"

Of course, Jill's behavior would be inappropriate if this were the fifth time
Warner had done more or less the same thing. In that case, some forthright discussion would probably be in order to alert Warner to the thin ice he was on.

Another instance of placating-like behavior is in nature when one animal sub-
mits to another in a fight. Animals seldom fight to the death with members of their
own species. Instead, when one animal is clearly losing, it will submit to the other,
saying, in effect, "Okay, you can kill me if you want, but I won't try to hurt you any
more." Managers can perform the same style of damage control when they are
clearly not going to get their way. We call this "yielding to the inevitable," "giving
in gracefully," or "being a good loser." The following example illustrates one of the
most common and crucial times that both programmers and managers can use this
form of placating to great advantage.

Addie's manager was berating her about the project schedule she had submitted. "This must be done by June first," the manager shouted. "I don't want any *if*'s, *and*'s, or *but*'s; do you understand?"

Addie's instinct was either to argue or to submit to the schedule she thought was impossible, but she gathered herself and decided to yield congruently: "I do understand that it's essential to finish the project by June first. Unfortunately, I'm not a good enough project manager to have any idea how to get it done by that time. Perhaps you could teach me, or find someone more competent to replace me as project manager?"

Notice that Addie's behavior doesn't say, "I am nothing; you are everything." Instead, it says, congruently, "I am something, but I'm not up to this situation, and that's okay with me."

Both of these types of congruent transformations of placating—caring, and yielding to the inevitable—operate out of an understanding that a particular situation is not the last time we will be dealing with the person. Such behaviors are congruent when they take the future context reasonably into account.

4.4 Turning Superreasonable into Focused and Reasonable Behavior

What is the congruent transformation of a superreasonable posture? In nature, many animals freeze when threatened, for keeping absolutely still often protects them from predators that notice only moving objects (Figure 4-3). This corresponds to the managerial behavior of staying cool and reasonable or keeping your head when, as Kipling put it, "… those about you are losing theirs and blaming it on you."[4]

Figure 4-3.   Many animals freeze when threatened, as if they don't exist and the threat doesn't exist. Keeping absolutely still may protect them from harm.

Another natural survival behavior is becoming totally focused on one objective, as when a trapped animal chews its way to freedom, even if it means gnawing off its own paw. In humans, this translates into the ability to take charge and remain totally focused in an emergency situation, even if you or others may be harmed in some way. You need this kind of cool, congruent coping when the nonstop operating system has stopped, and 846 brokers are trying to buy and sell securities and earn their commissions.

4.5 Changing Lovers/Haters into Beneficial Alliances or Friendly Rivalries

What is the congruent transformation of a loving/hating posture? This stance says, in effect, "It is nothing; you and I are everything."

In nature, animals mate for life, imprint on parents, or have a deep-seated aversion to some particular plant or animal species (Figure 4-4). In humans, the bonding is represented by the ability to form alliances, while the imprinting translates into the ability to follow leaders.

Figure 4-4.   In nature, many animals have the genetic ability to imprint on their parent or anything else they perceive to be a parent.

Animals' genetic aversion to certain species translates congruently in humans to their participation in friendly rivalries or use of caution in offering trust. What is the source of the caution that keeps alliances and trust in leaders from becoming loving relationships? What keeps rivalries from turning into relationships of hate? In both cases, congruence is achieved by our always keeping one eye on the context. If the alliance becomes counterproductive, we dissolve it. If the leader proves unreliable, we shift our loyalty elsewhere. If the rivalry becomes destructive, we negotiate a new relationship with our rival, or end it.

4.6 Transforming Irrelevance into Funny or Creative Behavior

How do we transform an irrelevant posture? In effect, the irrelevant behavior says, "Nothing counts for anything."

In nature, animals display what looks like irrelevant behavior as a tactic of distraction when the situation is so desperate that no organized, rational behavior has a chance of working. Faced with danger, a trapped mouse may turn suddenly berserk, whirling around, jumping up and down, and emitting weird sounds. This behavior sometimes so confuses the attacker that the mouse escapes. It doesn't always work, but since the situation is hopeless anyway, the mouse has nothing to lose (Figure 4-5).

Figure 4-5.   A trapped mouse has nothing to lose, so totally unpredictable behavior at least has a chance to make the situation better. The mouse could seem calm and friendly one moment, then suddenly bite, or leap spinning into the air. Irrelevant behavior in humans may indicate a feeling of powerlessness.

In humans, congruently irrelevant behavior happens under the same circumstances: when nothing sensible appears to have a chance of working. For instance, in a meeting that seems hopelessly deadlocked between two blamers or two haters, someone may crack a joke or spill coffee in somebody's briefcase, which breaks the impasse before it turns really nasty. Or, in a meeting where everyone seems to have turned superreasonable, someone may say something ridiculous or paradoxical just to crack the superreasonable shell.

Figure 4-6.   Irrelevant behavior is always surprising because it cannot be related to the context. It may become diversionary, amusing, creative, or all three.

Idea-generating processes such as brainstorming can be seen as "institutionalized irrelevance"—desperate measures to be used when everything rational has been tried, or sensible measures to generate ideas before the situation becomes desperate. Consultants often use games to introduce a playful element into an organization that is seriously desperate (otherwise it never would have called upon a consultant). In some deep way, the organization realizes that it must break its patterns if it is to find a way out of some apparently hopeless situation. Behavior that might have been irrelevant in another context then becomes the most congruent thing the organization can do.

4.7 Helpful Hints and Suggestions

1. We know that blaming is fundamentally a way to make others afraid so they will stop certain behaviors. Consequently, it's particularly edifying when people blame their computers. They can't be trying to make the computer afraid of them, so they must simply be in the habit of blaming. The most congruent attitude you can have toward your computer is very close to superreasonable.

2. My colleague Naomi Karten points out that although blaming works by making others afraid, it is fundamentally a self-protective device that makes you look as if you're not afraid. All of the incongruent coping behaviors have this

quality of looking like something they're not, because they're intended (perhaps unconsciously) to deceive others. If you knew the fear behind my blame, you might attack me. If you knew that my placating hid some real feelings of superiority, you might attack me. If you knew I was really in there behind my superreasonable wall of invisibility, you might attack me. When I'm congruent, I may be terribly afraid, but at least I'm not afraid to show that I'm afraid.

3. The immediate rewards of congruence are not always obvious. My colleague Norm Kerth offers the following observation from years of consulting: "Of all the really good, natural congruent managers that I have been able to observe, all of them have been women. The organizations around them did not respect them because their group got the job done—no major hassles, no late-night burnout heroics, no turnover. Eventually the organizations split up these congruent groups, reasoning that all these senior people should be distributed across the company to help out the floundering projects. After all, the congruent team 'really didn't have any tough assignments.' Each of these women finally dropped out of the field."

At times, I observed the same phenomenon in my consulting, but I have observed some congruent male managers, and I have observed both males and females whose careers flourished because of their congruence. Often, though, they had to move to different organizations in order for their style to be appreciated. I think one moral is that there is only so much one person can do to transform a large organization. You have to act congruently, but you also have to be prepared to spend many years working for the change and the wait may not seem worth the result.

4.8 Summary

✓ Congruent behavior is not stereotyped behavior, but behavior that fits three essential components: the context, other, and self. Thus, many congruent behaviors are possible for any one situation.

✓ You must experience the total interaction to know if it's congruent. That's not as hard as it sounds, because when people experience the total interaction, they instinctively know when the message is not congruent.

✓ Congruence is so important to effective management that managers must not only know how to recognize it, but also have confidence in their recognition. One way to gain such confidence is to watch for subtle incongruence between verbal and nonverbal responses. Another is by listening to the content of a response for certain characteristic patterns.

✓ To become a higher-quality manager of software engineering, learn that the energy in incongruent coping can be transformed into something more useful.

✓   Each incongruent response is based on a behavior that is actually effective in some survival situations, and may even have a genetic component. What makes it incongruent is its application when survival is not at stake.

✓   Blaming is based on the survival response to an attack. Blaming says, in effect, "If you continue to do that, I'm going to do what is necessary to stop you, no matter what the consequences to you." The impulse to blame can be transformed into an effective coping strategy—becoming assertive, direct, honest, candid, or forthright.

✓   The urge to placate can be congruently transformed into caring, yielding to the inevitable, giving in gracefully, or being a good loser. These behaviors are congruent when they take the future context into account.

✓   The congruent transformation of the superreasonable style corresponds to the managerial behavior of staying cool, focused, and reasonable, especially in an emergency.

✓   The congruent transformation of a loving posture is the ability to form beneficial alliances. The congruent transformation of a hating posture is the ability to participate in friendly rivalries.

✓   Congruent behavior that seems irrelevant may be used as a desperate measure when everything rational has been tried. It may be diversionary, amusing, creative, or all three.

4.9 Practice

1.   Here's a way to practice detecting incongruence and to learn how sensitive you are to subtle forms. Find a partner who wants to work with you on this task. Read aloud each of the three examples of congruent responses given earlier in the chapter:

  ✓   Manager, as programmer arrives late for a meeting.

  ✓   Programmer, when asked by manager to volunteer to talk to a job applicant.

  ✓   Manager, when marketing manager asks about the possibility of revising the requirements.

  Then, take turns reading the responses aloud, with the reader trying to introduce subtle incongruence into some of the reading. The listener tries to detect incongruence between the verbal and nonverbal messages. Discuss each situation, then trade roles.

2. Here's a way to practice your blaming skills, which will help you to recognize when you are blaming. Create a nonsense sentence, like this:

    ✓ "Na na na na na."

    Working with a partner, practice saying the nonsense sentence sometimes in a matter-of-fact tone, and sometimes stressing two or more words, such as

    ✓ "<u>Na</u> na na <u>na</u> na."

    Practice until your partner can tell which utterance is blaming and which is not. Once you have perfected your nonsense blaming and nonsense-blaming recognition, switch to a sensible, factual sentence, such as

    ✓ "You've been late three times."

    ✓ "<u>You've</u> been late <u>three</u> times."

    ✓ "<u>You've</u> been <u>late</u> three times."

    Repeat the stressed and non-stressed utterances until your partner can clearly tell the difference between a blaming sentence and a statement of fact.

3. What would you deduce if people in your own organization tended to form alliances or to engage in feuds?

4. Discuss the following approaches to management in terms of incongruence, and the congruent version that they parody:

    •   The Rip van Winkle approach: You wake up after two years and demand to know, "Why is this project two years late?"
    •   The Houdini approach: You mystify them with complicated formulas and transformations, so they don't see what you're really doing.

5. What do you think the real fears behind loving, hating, and irrelevance might be?

6. Recall Norm Kerth's observation about congruent women in software engineering and how they all eventually dropped out of the field. Is building a congruent group within an incongruent organization really a good career move?

5
Moving Toward Congruence

The central problem of our age is how to act decisively in the absence of certainty.
— Bertrand Russell

Nobody can make you feel inferior without your consent.
— Eleanor Roosevelt

Author Linda Hill, in her study of new managers, found they had many problems working with what they called "problem people":

> Working with the problem subordinate was overwhelming and frustrating; new managers kept "grossly underestimating" the amount of time and energy—intellectual and emotional—needed to manage the problem employee ... Also, because they had strong emotions about managing the problem employee, an important part of the task was learning to manage their own emotions.[1]

Emotions lie behind incongruent coping. Managing emotions does not mean suppressing them or hiding them, because those are merely forms of incongruence. This chapter will develop several techniques for people to harness their emotional energy without becoming incongruent and thus ineffective.

5.1 Reframing Internal Messages

One clue to harnessing the emotional energy comes from the origins of coping stances. Behind every incongruent coping behavior is a *survival rule*, so called because we respond as if our very survival were at stake. These rules function as unconscious programs that control our behavior.

Perhaps when we were younger, following these rules was the best we could do. Even as adults, survival rules may actually guard our lives, but in the typical software engineering organization, there are few truly life-or-death situations. It only feels that way.

5.1.1 Feelings and messages

We can detect the presence of survival rules by the incongruent coping behaviors they engender. Unfortunately, by that time, it's usually too late to do anything about it. Besides, since we're usually unaware of our own incongruent coping behavior, we need a more reliable signal. One such signal is found in the internal messages we give ourselves, especially those messages that come wrapped in a strong emotional package.[2] For example, underlying our incongruent coping behavior might be fear, and that fear might come from the self-talk, "I might make a mistake."

By itself, the statement "I might make a mistake" doesn't necessarily lead to fear. One reaction might be fear, but another might be sadness, as in "Several people will be let down if that happens, and I want to please them." Or the feeling might be anger, as in "I don't want to waste any time doing this darned thing over." Or indifference, as in "Sure, and I've made lots of mistakes before, so it's no big deal." Or excitement, as in "Wow, most of my best learning has come from mistakes, so this is going to be a great opportunity."

Our feelings vary in response to the same message because we all carry different life experiences into the feeling process. When the experiences have been codified into a survival rule, then the feelings are particularly strong—generally fearful—and seem to be out of our conscious control. For instance, fear might arise from the combination of the message "I might make a mistake" and the rule "I must always be perfect."

Without this survival rule, we wouldn't expect such a strong fear and the concomitant incongruent coping. Instead, we might find the message transformed into something like "I'll do my best, but perfection isn't possible."

5.1.2 Examples of reframed messages

Internal messages give us advance warning that we are about to behave incongruently. By listening to your internal messages, then transforming them in light of high self-esteem, we can thwart incongruent action before it happens. This doesn't mean "stuffing our feelings," but, as one of my colleagues put it, "really remaking your internal landscape."

Here are some examples of low self-esteem messages, the rules that might underlie them, and how they can be reframed into more congruent messages:

Incongruent:	Someone will criticize me.
Underlying rule:	I must always be above criticism.
Congruent:	Some criticism is inevitable; I take it as a gift.
Incongruent:	I might impose.
Underlying rule:	I must always stay out of others' way.
Congruent:	Imposing goes with all communication, to some degree.
Incongruent:	They will think I'm no good.
Underlying rule:	I must always make a good impression.
Congruent:	Even if someone thinks I'm no good, I can survive.
Incongruent:	They will think I'm not perfect.
Underlying rule:	I must always be perceived as perfect.
Congruent:	Since I'm not perfect, I don't need to be seen as perfect.
Incongruent:	They might leave.
Underlying rule:	I must always maintain harmony.
Congruent:	I don't need everyone to agree all the time.
Incongruent:	They might not like me.
Underlying rule:	I must always be liked by everyone.
Congruent:	I agree or disagree because I really do.
Incongruent:	I should pretend it's important.
Underlying rule:	I must always take everything seriously.
Congruent:	I work with real problems in a real way.
Incongruent:	I might have to change (but won't unless I'm forced to).
Underlying rule:	I must always remain the way my parents taught me.
Congruent:	I'm able to change if I want to.

Although it might seem that certain rules would lead to certain coping styles, there is no necessary connection between the rules and the coping. When a rule is threatened with its violation, I can choose my favorite style of defense. For instance, consider some of my possible responses to threatened violation of my rule "They might think I'm not perfect":

- Blaming: Attack others' imperfections to give the impression that I'm perfect.
- Placating: Praise other people's perfection in hopes that they would respond by saying, "Oh, but you're perfect, too."
- Superreasonable: Try to act perfectly in everything I say and do.
- Loving: Praise the loved one's perfection, so as to be perfect in association.
- Hating: Look perfect in contrast to the evil one's imperfections.
- Irrelevant: Attempt to be the perfect clown, so as not to give them anything to criticize.

5.2 Dealing with Strong Feelings

There was a faith healer from Deal
Who said, "Although pain isn't real,
*   When I sit on a pin*
*   And it punctures my skin,*
I dislike what I fancy I feel."
— Anonymous

Unfortunately, because of the strong feelings involved, moving toward congruence is not always as easy as the previous section may imply. It's often hard to change the way you react when you have strong feelings, such as hurt, anger, or disappointment. Here are some ways to start changing the way you deal with such strong feelings, even if you believe that "pain isn't real."

5.2.1 Speak up when an issue is important to you

Whether you like them or not, your feelings are an important source of information. Feelings are nature's way of telling you what's important and what's not so important, but this information is not available to other people unless you tell them. Nobody else knows you're sitting on a pin, that you feel a design is backward, or that you think you're being treated unfairly.

You have the responsibility to use your own feelings to decide which issues are important enough to speak up about. If you stay silently bitter, resentful, or unhappy, you pay a big price—in lost time, emotional pain, or poor-quality work—and you continue to pay that price until you finally decide to speak up.

On the other hand, you also have the responsibility to draw upon your feelings to decide which issues are unimportant, and then to keep them to yourself. If you speak up frantically on every petty issue, people will learn to discount what you have to say when you truly are being chased by a wolf.

5.2.2 *Take time to clarify your position in your own mind*

To be congruent, you must set a speak-up threshold that measures your own feelings against those of others and the dictates of the context. Before you speak out, ask yourself the following questions:

- How do I know what is happening? What do I see and hear?
- What interpretation do I put on these observations?
- Are there alternative interpretations?
- What information would discriminate among these interpretations?
- What is it about the situation that makes me feel this way?
- What is the real issue here?
- Where do I stand?
- What do I want to accomplish?
- Who is responsible for what?
- What are the things I will and will not do?

5.2.3 *Speak for yourself*

Once you have asked these questions, you will find it easier to speak for yourself. Compare these incongruent and congruent ways of expressing what you think and feel:

Incongruent: Everyone wants to use this design approach.
Congruent: I want to use this design approach.

Incongruent: This is an essential function.
Congruent: I believe this is an essential function.

Incongruent: The boss thinks this is an essential function.
Congruent: I understood the boss to say that this is an essential function.

Incongruent: It's not acceptable to miss the promised schedule.
Congruent: I feel inadequate when I can't meet the promised schedule.

Incongruent: We cannot pretend to give in to their demands.
Congruent: I will not promise this result unless I believe it's possible.

Speaking for yourself increases the chances that other people will deal congruently with the issues, which increases your chances of getting a solution you can live with.

5.2.4 Speak to the right person

The context in which you speak up is particularly important. Don't use third parties, hoping the word will get back. Even if it does get back, it's likely to be transformed into a different word.

Don't claim to speak for third parties; if you have an issue, speak for yourself. If you believe a third party has an issue, get that party into the room so you can check it out. Better yet, check it out before you raise the issue in others' names. If they say they have an issue but are unwilling or unable to bring it up, don't bring it up for them. Instead, help them reach the point where they can either bring it up or drop it.

Don't gossip about third parties; gossip is a cheap, inferior relationship with someone at the expense of someone else. If your issue is with an individual, be sure you raise the issue with that person without an audience if you want to give the person a chance to save face. Then raise the issue directly:

Incongruent:	I can't stand it when people are late.
Congruent:	Jack, I can't stand it when you are late.

It's even less congruent when you send a general memo saying, "It has come to my attention that some people are being unacceptably late." If your issue is with Jack, deal with Jack. Don't be a cowardly skunk spraying the stink of blame through the ventilation system.

5.2.5 Use fair tactics

Once you are face to face with the right people, treat them with the honesty, dignity, and respect you would like for yourself. This excludes blaming, psychoanalyzing, preaching, moralizing, issuing orders, warning, interrogating, ridiculing, and lecturing.

If you are too angry or excited to control the tactics you use, then pull away until you can regain control. You can say something like, "I need a little time. I propose we get together again at <specific time>."

If even this negotiation is too difficult—perhaps making you even more troubled—then say, "We seem to be having trouble agreeing on a time, but I do need to get away for a while. I'll be in touch with you to set a time later." Then leave.

5.2.6 Strive for congruence

Blaming, placating, superreasonable, loving/hating, and irrelevant postures all make it very difficult to straighten out a wounded relationship. Congruence, on the other hand, is contagious. Congruence allows you to be creative in arriving at new ways of being in a relationship, ways that are better for both parties. So whatever else you do, strive to stay congruent, or to recover your congruence, before you try to do anything else about the situation.

Don't say, "First I'll get the job done, then I'll get congruent." The best way to get the job done is to get congruent first. Congruence doesn't always work, but it always works better than incongruence.

5.3 Steps Toward Congruence

It's easy to say, "Strive for congruence." In practice, it takes a long time and a lot of hard practice to raise your congruence batting average, and nobody ever achieves congruence a hundred percent of the time. That's why you'll need ways to recover your congruence as quickly and effectively as possible.

5.3.1 Notice the incongruence

If you're unaware that you're acting incongruently, you can hardly start a process of recovering. That's why the first step in recovering congruence is to notice your own incongruence.

Perhaps the easiest way for you to do this is to listen to your internal messages, as discussed in Section 5.1. Another powerful way to notice your incongruence is to feel it in your body. Your breath may be shallow, rapid, or irregular. Your posture may be rigid or unsteady, or you may find yourself straining to keep your balance. Pain anywhere in your body is a reliable clue to incongruence—whether the pain is cause or effect. Or, you may be experiencing nausea, dizziness, or trembling—all reliable signs of incongruence.

It takes practice to tune into your own body like this, so many people cannot rely on such physical cues.[3] The "logic" of the situation doesn't tell you much either, because incongruence is not primarily a reaction to the here-and-now situation. A more helpful clue may be that others are reacting to you in surprising ways. If you are acting incongruently, you are likely to trigger incongruent reactions in others. Rather than blaming them for incongruence, ask yourself, "What could I be doing to contribute to their behavior?" Here's how it worked for Parson, one of my students:

"I was telling one of my project managers that I had to see a plan to get her project back on schedule. As she handed me a folder containing her revised project plan, I became aware that the papers in her hand were rattling. That caught my attention, and I thought, 'How strange that the papers should rattle like that.' Looking for an explanation, I noticed she was trembling, that her face was ashen, and finally that her eyes were wet.

"My first thought was, 'Oh, she's sick!' but then I remembered the idea from class that she might be reacting to me. That seemed ridiculous, as I thought I was merely talking to her normally, but I decided to check it out.

"The first thing I noticed about myself was that I was gripping the edge of my desk as if it were a safety rail between me and the Grand Canyon. I thought I should loosen my grip, but then I realized I would probably fall on my face toward her if I did. All this while I continued talking to her about the project plan, until I noticed that I was actually shouting and banging my other fist on the desk. That's when I had my big AHA!"

5.3.2 Make adjustments

Incongruence is stereotyped behavior because it's not appropriate for the particular situation. That's why it destroys effective management. The bright side of this stereotyping is that amazingly small changes can be used to disrupt the lockstep pattern. Once you have noticed some signs of incongruence, your next move is to start a series of minuscule adjustments.

For instance, Parson thought he should loosen his grip, but he realized he would fall so he first altered his posture to bring himself into a more centered position. Postural changes are often the first small adjustment, such as

- standing up if sitting
- sitting down if standing
- moving if rigid
- stopping if moving
- getting both feet on the floor with your weight balanced
- bending your knees a bit

With the first small change, the stereotype may begin to collapse in a cascade of other tiny adjustments. Changing your posture may make you aware of how tense you are, so the next thing you may want to do is relax. You can

- take control of your breathing
- stop clutching, pressing, or gripping
- relax any tense muscles
- slow down
- stop talking

Then, when you are balanced and relaxed, give yourself a message of appreciation. Remind yourself of what a miracle it took for both of you to be here today. Tell yourself how well you've done to notice your incongruence and to make these small adjustments. You need the message of appreciation because if you don't respect yourself, you cannot respect the other person. And if you don't respect the other person, why are you here?

5.3.3 Make contact with the other person

Now that you've made contact with yourself, it's time to make contact with the other person or persons. In spite of what they may be saying, pay close attention to their body signals, because those are a more reliable indicator than their words. When you do take in the words, don't jump to your first interpretation—either good or bad—but get verbal clarification. During the clarification process, watch their body signals.

Once you feel you have understood the other person, you can comment on the present situation from your own point of view. Your comments should start with the word "I," not "You" or "It." "You" sentences tend to sound blaming; "it" sentences, superreasonable. But don't use fake "I" sentences as a way of talking about the other person, such as

Incongruent:	You always make this same mistake.
Disguised as:	I think that you always make this same mistake.
Better:	I have a hard time recovering when you make this mistake.

Stick to observations, avoid interpretations. To keep to the here-and-now, use a present tense verb. Avoid using vague, general-purpose nouns like "responsibility," "maturity," or "thoughtfulness":

Incongruent:	You acted irresponsibly.
Disguised as:	I feel that responsibility is essential to optimal performance.
Better:	From what I have heard so far, I now believe that you acted irresponsibly when you <give specifics>. Am I misinterpreting something?

This example, however, suggests another danger: becoming long-winded in an attempt to be clear. Keep it short: short words, short sentences, and not too many of them. You should, of course, be as clear as you can be, but if you have to struggle or repeat, try something like this:

Better:	I'm feeling so emotional about this I'm having a hard time speaking clearly. Am I being clear?

Again, if you can't be respectful of the other person, don't even try to make contact. Break it off and come back when it's a better time. The same is true for any other reason you can't make contact the way you'd like. Even if the other person doesn't think so, it's always okay to say,

Better:	I'm having trouble saying how I feel right now. Let's do this later.

5.3.4 Wait for the other person to respond

If you are able to stay involved with the interaction, watch out for excessive intensity, which may intimidate the other person. The best way to control your intensity is to make your statement and then wait for the other person to respond.

If you can visualize what you're saying, be sure to place a large period at the end, or perhaps a question mark. And never, never ask more than one question at a time, as in

Incongruent:	I don't want to offend anyone.
Disguised as:	Did you understand that? Was I clear? Is it responsive to what you said? Would you like me to phrase it differently? I didn't hurt your feelings, did I? Am I talking too much? Are you having trouble getting a word in edgewise?

Nobody could respond congruently to this stream of placating questions, so stop to breathe. Let the other person know by your eyes, posture, and voice tone that you have reached a full stop. If they're not getting the message, say, "I'm done." Then stop.

5.3.5 Repeat the process as often as necessary

There's one exception to the rule about repeating yourself. You can and should repeat the entire process I just described in Sections 5.3.1 through 5.3.4 as often as necessary for you to either reach congruence or leave the interaction for the time being. You know it's time to leave and regroup when nothing is changing from one repetition to the next.

5.3.6 Use the opportunity for learning

Even if the interaction doesn't work out well, you can always apply the universal lesson: You can learn from it. Afterward, sit down in a quiet place to reflect on what you did and didn't do—not blaming yourself, but emphasizing what you did well. This is how to become more congruent and also to create a congruent, learning organization, one person and one interaction at a time.

5.4 What Congruence Means to a Manager

The easiest way to recognize congruence is by asking people about their feelings. If that's hard for you or them, notice what kinds of internal messages lie behind their behavior. Incongruent messages tend to be reflected in stereotyped, repetitive behavior. Internal messages of self-worth, however, are reflected in many different external behaviors. Self-worth is at the base of congruence and gives permission to take risks—the risks required if an effective controller is to show the diversity of action required by Ashby's Law of Requisite Variety.

Most especially, self-worth gives me permission to risk behaving in a way that matches the way I feel inside—hence the term congruent. Congruence doesn't mean that I act according to some script, not even my own script. It means that

> When I feel X (angry, happy, sad, grateful, hurt, proud, or whatever)
>   I say I feel X.
>   I sound like I feel X.
>   I look like I feel X.
>   My whole body is congruent with X.
>   I share my X feeling with you.
>   Then I can ask for help if I choose to.
>   And I know I will survive if I don't get the help I ask for.

The only way to be at your best always is to be mediocre. If you're trying for high quality, sometimes you won't feel up to it. But, as Sammy Davis, Jr., said, "A professional is one who does a good job even when he doesn't feel like it." Notice that he said "good," not "best" or "excellent" or even "very good."

That's what *congruence* means: that I feel good enough about myself, even when I feel rotten, to tell you about it. That means I feel good enough to use the full variety of my action possibilities (as required by the Law of Requisite Variety) and I thus have an excellent chance to be a professional software engineering manager.

5.5 Helpful Hints and Suggestions

1. The more powerful your perceived position, the more every remark you make is magnified. Therefore, as you rise in the management hierarchy, you will have to raise your feeling threshold for speaking up. Otherwise, your offhand speculations will be mistaken as commands to action. Therefore, the grander your title, the more sensitive you need to be as to precisely what's going on inside yourself.

2. Perhaps the reason blaming is so popular among software engineering managers is the difficulty of the work, leading to a fear of losing control. Blaming is intended to provoke fear, and fear calls up survival rules and incongruent coping behavior. The hope is that the preferred coping will be placating, so that the people attacked will do exactly what managers want.

    This blaming approach might not be altogether bad if managers were perfect, so that all they needed was perfectly compliant employees. If you are perfect, you might consider employing this approach. Keep in mind, though, that not everybody prefers to placate in response to blame. Even if they don't outwardly counterattack, or freeze, or go berserk, remember that even the best placaters seem to have a finger of blame poised behind their back where you can't see it. You'll know it's there only when you become aware of their malicious compliance, which may be too late. In the end, blaming causes you to lose the very control you crave.

3. Once you succeed at being congruent more of the time, a new set of problems emerges. My friend Dan Starr put it this way after returning from the Change Shop, one of our advanced workshops:

> One of the things Change Shop didn't tell us about congruent communication is that if you get to be even fair-to-middlin' at it, other people start asking you to do it for them! They sort of say, "I notice you can tell so-and-so something that he/she really doesn't want to hear, and he/she doesn't get upset about it. I know that if I said that there'd be a big fight, so can you deliver this message?" I suppose that's a start, in that at least people are observing that healthier communication is possible, but what I really want them to do is say, "I notice you can tell so-and-so something that he/she really doesn't want to hear, and he/she doesn't get upset about it. I know that if I said that there'd be a big fight, so can you show me how to do that?" (Isn't that interesting? When I phrase the problem that way, I know what I have to do to get what I want. ...)[4]

Dan's letter made me aware of something I took for granted: the way people notice your new behavior and ask you to be congruent for them. That happens to me frequently in my consulting, and I handle it in various ways. I agree with Dan that my goal should be for me to show them how to do it, so they can learn how, but it may be too much all at once. You don't start your engineering career by designing an operating system, so don't start your congruence career with the toughest situation you can imagine.

Sometimes, I'll just take care of the situation so they can observe that someone can actually handle this "impossible" situation. More likely, I'll agree to do it, but only if they're present to watch, listen, and learn. Or I'll coach them—even if that's not what they asked for—and encourage them to try. I make the choice of actions depending on their state in their progress toward more frequent congruence.

4. To move toward congruence, you have to find your "center." Here's how my E-mail friend and colleague Sue Petersen explained *centering* to a group of software engineering managers via the CompuServe Software Engineering Management Forum: "I haven't taken judo or any of the martial arts, but I've learned centering from training animals and raising kids. I know I'm centered

when something maddening happens and I can feel myself step back and choose my response instead of going from the gut and blowing it. It only takes a fraction of a second and it's saved my life more than once. I can almost always do it with the kids, usually with the critters, and usually not with my dad or the in-laws. <sigh>"

With your own kids, either you learn centering or you're driven crazy—and that's probably true for management as well.

5.6 Summary

✓ As a new manager, you face an important challenge: learning to manage your own emotions without becoming incongruent.

✓ Beneath every incongruent coping behavior, there is a survival rule because we all respond as if our very survival were at stake. These rules function as unconscious programs that control our behavior.

✓ A reliable signal of incongruence is found in the internal messages you give yourself, especially those messages that come wrapped in a strong emotional package.

✓ By listening to these internal messages, then transforming them in the light of high self-esteem, you can thwart incongruent action before it happens.

✓ Feelings are nature's way of telling you what's important and what's less important, but this information about you is not available to other people unless you tell them.

✓ To be congruent, you must set a speak-up threshold that measures your own feelings against those of others and the dictates of the context. Speaking congruently for yourself increases your chances of getting a solution you can live with.

✓ The context in which you speak up is particularly important. Don't use third parties, hoping the word will get back. Don't claim to speak for third parties; if you have an issue, speak for yourself. Don't gossip about third parties; raise any issue with them directly. Don't issue general memos that secretly address individual cases.

✓ Always treat the other person with the honesty, dignity, and respect you desire for yourself. If you are too overwrought to control the tactics you use, pull away until you regain control.

✓   There is a step-by-step process you can use to recover your lost congruence. Roughly, you must first notice the incongruence, then make adjustments to your breathing, posture, and movement. Finally, make contact with the other person, speaking in "I-statements," and wait for the other person to respond. Repeat this process as often as necessary until you either become congruent or discover that it's not possible at the moment.

✓   Congruence means feeling good enough to use the full variety of your action possibilities. If you are congruent, you have an excellent chance to be a professional software engineering manager.

5.7 Practice

1. Working with a friend, choose a situation in which you acted incongruently. Reenact that situation, and practice, one step at a time, to move toward congruence. Run through the same situation at least three times.

2. Compare your own reaction to personal failure with the following description from an article in the *Harvard Business Review*:

    > Put simply, because many professionals are almost always successful at what they do, they rarely experience failure. And because they have rarely failed, they have never learned how to learn from failure. So whenever their single-loop learning strategies go wrong, they become defensive, screen out criticism, and put the "blame" on anyone and everyone but themselves. In short, their ability to learn shuts down precisely at the moment they need it the most.[5]

3. As suggested by Norm Kerth: Choose a survival rule, perhaps one of your own, and show how it might be defended using each of the coping styles, congruent and incongruent.

4. As suggested by Payson Hall: Observe the interactions of a senior manager you admire and respect. Does the manager appear to be congruent, consistent with the authority of the position? Is that why you respect and admire that manager?

5. Upon reading this chapter, my colleague Naomi Karten commented, "I can relate to everything in this chapter and understand it intellectually, but would have a difficult time applying it after reading it. That is, it needs to be practiced in a workshop type of setting to fully 'get' it and internalize it. In written form, it's too easy to just gloss over. I can already relate to much of this from my own background and work, but wonder about people coming to it for the first time."

I share her worry. You must find ways to practice congruence in a safe, receptive setting. Workshops are ideal, but you can do a great deal with a study group of three or more like-minded friends. Discuss the examples in this book. Gather similar examples from your daily experience. Role-play these examples several times, trying different approaches, testing how congruent they feel to all parties. Try the new behaviors and report back to the group.

Part II
Managing Others

When one does not know how to convince, one oppresses; in all power relations among governors and governed, as ability declines, usurpation increases.
— Madame de Stael

The relationship between the Lone Ranger and his "faithful Indian companion," Tonto, remains a mysterious one. We don't know what Indian language *kimosabe* comes from, nor what it means. We don't even know what the Indian sense of *companion* implies in English. What we do know is that the Lone Ranger and Tonto seemed to work well together. All their projects succeeded, and no commercial revenues were ever lost because the villains weren't delivered on time.

As we've seen, quality management requires that you manage yourself well, but that's not sufficient. To build and maintain large-scale information systems, you must also succeed in managing your relationships with others.

Poor management is not confined to software engineering, nor even to our moment in history. Poor management will always exist when managers are incongruent, for, as Madame de Stael said, "as ability declines, usurpation increases."

Thus, as you climb out of the technical tar pit onto the management ladder, your own feelings of inadequacy can make you into an oppressive manager. Oppressive managers may work alone and shoot silver bullets, but they will never become Lone Rangers.

6

Analyzing the Manager's Job

A manager is responsible for

✓   Deciding what is to be done and appointing someone to do it.

✓   Listening to why it should not be done at all, why it should be done by someone else, or why it should be done in a different way than what you've prescribed.

✓   Following up to see if the job has been done correctly, discovering that it hasn't, and listening to some of the world's worst excuses from the employee who should have done it.

✓   Following up again to see if the job has been done, only to discover that it has been done incorrectly, but deciding that you'd better leave it as it is because it's as good as you're likely to get.

✓   *Wondering if you ought to get rid of the person who can't seem to get the job done correctly, but deciding that the successor is most likely to be just as bad—maybe even worse.*

✓   *Considering how much faster and better the job would have been done if you had done it yourself; reflecting that if you had done it yourself, the job would have been completed in thirty minutes, but that instead you took three days trying to figure out why it took somebody else two weeks to do it incorrectly.*

> — from an anonymous photocopy

The above description is from a photocopy that has been circulating in offices all over the United States for at least ten years. While meant in jest, it seems to subconsciously support some negative stereotypes, without being funny enough to shatter them. The writer (I hope with tongue-in-cheek) seems to be espousing the incongruent management style that often arises from the One-Dimensional Selection Model. This is the style most prevalent in software engineering organizations, so I decided to use it as the outline for describing the manager's job.

Part I of this book deals with congruent actions and applies to everyone, whether or not they have the job of manager. Part II addresses the manager's congruence in interacting with other people. It is the nature of these interactions that defines the software engineering manager's job. That's why this first chapter in Part II attempts to define the manager's job in terms of congruent actions, using this humorous bad example as a good outline.

6.1 Deciding and Appointing

✓   *A manager is responsible for deciding what is to be done and appointing someone to do it.*

This view describes a hierarchic, autocratic Routine (Pattern 2) style of management. In contrast to this model, the more desirable Steering (Pattern 3) model says that the manager's job is to get more people involved as well as to get people more involved in decisions about what is to be done and in doing it.

6.1.1 *Piling on*

Routine (Pattern 2) organizations can be described by the nursery rhyme about the little girl with the curl in the middle of her forehead:

> *When she was good, she was very, very good,*
> *But when she was bad, she was horrid.*

The horrid part of Pattern 2 organizations is the numerous breakdowns in control. Broken-down projects run on endlessly, full of cost and frustration, producing nothing.

One sure sign of a control breakdown is to watch the rats trying to leave the sinking project ship. Unlike rats, however, most people do not actually leave their jobs until the crisis has passed, one way or the other. Instead, they sit on the edge of the deck, covering their rears and their expenses, just in case something should change to their advantage. For crisis recovery, a manager has to mobilize these sidelined people or the resources won't be adequate to keep the ship afloat. Of course, mobilizing them in advance may well prevent the crisis in the first place.

As an organization moves deeper into crisis, the best-informed people tend to become overloaded. This tendency to "pile on" is particularly strong in the work of fixing faults, because the Routine (Pattern 2) managers don't want anyone but the best-informed people to modify the critical parts of the software. Figure 6-1 shows how this innocent and reasonable appointment policy produces overload, and eventual burnout, of the most knowledgeable people.

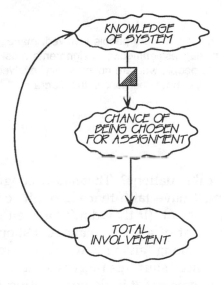

Figure 6-1.   The tendency of managers to choose the most knowledge- able people for new assign- ments leads inevitably to overload and burnout. As the gray and white box indicates, managers could choose not to do this, but they often do.

6.1.2 Reversing the appointment policy

Figure 6-2 suggests that managers can counter this piling-on effect by

- choosing the least knowledgeable people for assignments
- choosing the least-loaded people for assignments

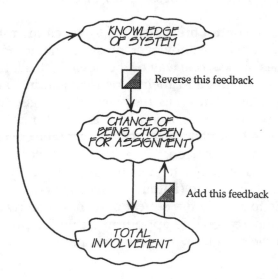

Figure 6-2.   To prevent piling on the best workers and to get more people involved, managers must resist certain temptations when making assignments. Assignments must be given to less knowledgeable people and to people who are not so totally involved—that is, managers must choose the gray half of both decisions in the diagram.

Can managers really do this when they see critical situations? That's how congruence comes into play. First of all, managers must have faith that although some workers may not have experience, they do have talent. (If they don't have either, why are they working there?) At the very first hint of a crisis, managers should start doing what they should have been doing all along: giving new people problems to solve as learning experiences. Managers must start this process as early as possible, and must be unflinching in their assignments—that is, do no placating. Of course, managers must have in place a working process for knowing what assignments are available.

Piling on the best people is not just management's tendency, but influences every person in the project. When workers have a problem, they ask themselves, "Who should I ask about this?" Then they give the answer that's modeled by their managers: "The most knowledgeable person, of course." Moreover, the technical experts themselves are delighted to be acknowledged as experts, and so collude in the process. That's why managers need to establish structures to prevent the positive feedback loop of Figure 6-1 from occurring. In effect, they need to isolate the more experienced people from the less experienced.

6.1.3 Tactics for relieving overload

Here are some actions my clients have taken to help relieve this problem of overloading their most experienced people:

- Block the telephones of the most experienced people so they cannot receive incoming calls.
- Find offices for them out of the main traffic pattern, with doors they can lock from the inside. Provide them with "Do not disturb" signs.
- Put managers near the offices of the experienced people, and post signs directing people to see the manager, rather than the overloaded person. The managers watch for violations of this directive and act to educate the violators.
- Give the experienced people a strong-willed assistant who will reroute all calls and other interruptions. A good assistant can also watch for opportunities to off-load tasks. Instruct the assistant, "Your job is to see that this person has maximum uninterrupted time to work."

Perhaps the most important action is to give the inexperienced people assignments that keep them busy but that won't require the experts' time, so they'll stay out of the way, yet become experienced people themselves.

6.2 Listening

✓ *A manager is responsible for listening to why it should not be done at all, why it should be done by someone else, or why it should be done in a different way than what you've prescribed.*

This is a perfect description of a superreasonable manager, who *listens without hearing.* Such a manager knows the answer already, and just needs to wait until the other person stops talking. This model says that managers prescribe the way things should be done (Routine or Pattern 2), rather than describe what outcomes are desired (Steering or Pattern 3).

There is a blaming undercurrent to this superreasonable manager, who perceives most of these objections to be bogus. And most of them are. Anyone who manages by prescription will hear lots of bogus objections. The objections are not to the particular prescription, but to the act of prescribing. If the manager is not in the prescription business, the need for bogus objections seldom arises.

Why would a sensible manager assume such a nonlistening, prescriptive position? Not wanting to be a manager in the first place certainly contributes to the need to retain technical direction, but that's not the whole story. Some managers, after all, are able to let go of their technical expertise and actually manage. The superreasonable tone suggests another alternative: excessive ego involvement.

Author Tom Crum relates the parable of an inventor who is so ego-involved that he cannot trust the help of others for business assistance. As a result,

> ... his invention takes on such importance that his life becomes a secret mission and he is constantly wary of everyone, thinking them potential enemies out to usurp his plans and ideas.
>
> As a result of this inability to share information, the invention is a commercial failure. In contrast, when he learns to trust others as parts of his "team," ... he is extending himself beyond his own talents and becoming richer in ability. When he perceives his support people as an extension of himself, all information gets shared.[1]

Can you apply this parable to computer programmers? A major job of the software engineering manager is to develop openness and trust among all the workers contributing to successful software. What better way to foster openness and trust than by being a model listener?

6.3 Following Up

✓   *A manager is responsible for following up to see if the job has been done correctly, discovering that it hasn't, and listening to some of the world's worst excuses from the employee who should have done it.*

"Excuses" is a blaming manager's term. Following up is done to help your workers do the job, and for this you must listen to reasons, not label them excuses. The reasons may not be correct, but so what? Right or wrong, the reasons always contain the information an effective manager needs to steer the organization. The manager who made the above statement does not understand much about how to extract such information.[2]

6.4 Evaluating Quality

✓   *A manager is responsible for following up again to see if the job has been done, only to discover that it has been done incorrectly, but deciding that you'd better leave it as it is because it's as good as you're likely to get.*

This describes a pure placating position, one that builds resentment and lowers quality. The Steering (Pattern 3) manager does not evaluate quality, but puts in place the processes, not the people, to evaluate quality. Examples of such processes are quality assurance, customer satisfaction surveys, and technical reviews.

When the manager does evaluate the quality of work, the main purpose of that evaluation is to help the employees develop their own skills. The most important feedback to your employees is actions, not words. My colleague Richard Cohen tells the following story: "At the end of a project in 1980, the project manager gave all of us 'Hero' awards and meant it when he said he thought we were all heroes. I had another manager, whom I liked a lot better and who felt that he was a failure if we had to work overtime more than a few times a month."[3]

The action that counts most is managing well in order to create the right conditions for work, rather than giving rewards for producing acceptable quality—perhaps while working under suboptimal management conditions.

6.5 Personnel Decisions

✓   *A manager is responsible for wondering if you ought to get rid of the person who can't seem to get the job done correctly, but deciding that the successor is most likely to be just as bad—maybe even worse.*

This description stems directly from the One-Dimensional Selection Model, and fits a manager who sees an all-or-none universe, one in which there are good people (like the manager, presumably) who should be retained and bad people who should be fired. This, indeed, is the typical view of newly appointed managers:

> When asked to describe what it meant to be a manager, nearly all of the managers began by discussing management's rights and privileges, not its duties. They generally began by stating explicitly that being a manager means being the boss. ... They routinely spoke of only two kinds of people-management decisions: hiring and firing subordinates.[4]

There is no room in the novice manager's repertoire for coaching, teaching, or training. Contrast this view with that expressed by a leading management consultant:

> The middle manager's job is to "grow people"—not to build a file of lifeless documents, or to spend half of each day in boring meetings. His role means walking around with an open mind toward listening and helping, and taking time to talk things over. It means being concerned about individual welfare and fostering the full potential of each person.[5]

Even when you believe the One-Dimensional Selection Model, you still have to determine who is good and who is bad—the manager or the employee. As they say in the army, "There are no bad soldiers, only bad officers." An analogy would be someone trying to get attached to a network, but the network administrator was unable to achieve the attachment. If you were going to fire someone, should you fire the person who wanted to be attached to the network, or the administrator? If the manager is unable to get a member working well with the team, doesn't the model say you should fire the manager?

6.6 Administering

✓ *A manager is responsible for considering how much faster and better the job would have been done if you had done it yourself; reflecting that if you had done it yourself, the job would have been completed in thirty minutes, but that instead you took three days trying to figure out why it took somebody else two weeks to do it incorrectly.*

Such an incongruent manager never does figure out that the reason for late, incorrect projects is poor management. Brooks's Law, of course, is the classic example explanation of managers causing the very lateness they blame others for:

Adding manpower to a late software project makes it later.[6]

Congruent managers are not locked into blaming, partly because they know that they are not passive victims doomed by Brooks's Law. Let's see how a congruent manager might deal with administering a late project.

First of all, such a manager would understand the dynamics of the law, as shown in Figure 6-3. The only feedback loop is through the manager's own actions, so that only self-blame would be appropriate. But self-blame is not necessary, because analyzing the diagram shows several ways to accelerate progress.

One observation is that although there are two paths by which adding people reduces relative progress, neither path contains a feedback loop. This makes it easier to beat the law, and the diagram suggests how. Based on the diagram, Brooks's Law could be refined as follows:

Assigning new people late in a software project to the tasks other people are already trying to do makes the project later.

When managers want to put new people on a project or to assign established people to new tasks, they must assign them to tasks not being done already. Because the project is in a schedule crisis, there will be plenty of such tasks around:

- locating faults behind lower-priority software trouble incidents (STIs)
- conducting additional independent technical reviews of code
- conducting additional independent technical reviews of test plans
- creating additional test cases
- fixing low-priority faults
- creating documentation
- updating documentation
- administering test runs when someone needs to be on-line

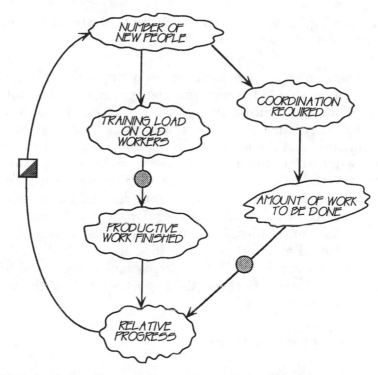

Figure 6-3.   A manager who understands the dynamics of Brooks's Law understands what it takes to beat it.

Of course, each of these tasks would be easier to do with the help of a more experienced person, but the new workers must be told that they are to operate without such help, and why they must do so. There are, however, a number of congruent steps a manager can take to improve the efficiency of their training:

- Give them a senior person as leader, taken from some area not in crisis. This gives them the advantage of experience with tools, languages, and systems, if not with the particular software in crisis.
- Give them a facilitating administrator who can get them resources and can also give them the advantage of experience in dealing with the organization.
- Use burned-out experienced people who are no longer as productive to work with them on specific understanding of the crisis software. A time-out of this kind can do double duty for the organization: teaching the new people and giving the burned-out veterans a taste of the newcomers' enthusiasm.
- Schedule an occasional meeting—once a week for an hour, for example—with the experienced people. At that time, the new people can present prepared questions for immediate feedback. Knowing there will be such

a meeting helps keep them from being desperate enough to break the rules and interrupt at other times.

This kind of sink-or-swim approach creates a stiff training regime, which some people may not be able to handle. The manager needs to monitor these people closely, to pull out those who cannot work this way, and to notice which ones have reached a level where they can make contributions to more critical problems. Not everyone will sink, and the manager will want to put the swimmers to work as quickly as possible. Unfortunately, managers may know who can handle the load emotionally, but they may not be able to tell who can handle it technically.

A good way to test people who may have reached this level is as members of error-location teams or as members of regular technical reviews. Because of the open nature of the work in these cases, the newcomers can be observed in action by the more experienced technical people. If they are contributing, it will be obvious to everybody, and soon they will find themselves being asked to handle things themselves, with salutary effects on the project. Part IV of the book will discuss managing through teams.

6.7 What Congruent Managers Do

Rather than allow the outline of this chapter to be totally dominated by an incongruent view of the manager's job, let's explore the consequences of a different model. This model says that managers are leaders, and that

> **Leadership is the ability to create an environment in which everyone is empowered to contribute creatively to solving the problems.**

Certainly the word *empowered* has been overused and debased, so I want to be specific about what this definition means. In this model, the manager's job may be evaluated by one and only one measure: *the success of the people being managed.* Note carefully that this says "success of the people," not "success of the project." Success of the project may be a component of the success of the people, but lots of sickness, broken homes, and psychological burnouts are not my idea of "success of the people."

Over the years, I have interviewed people on dozens of successful—and thus well-managed—projects. When I ask the project members how their managers contributed to their success (empowered them), here are the things they said most often:

Our managers contributed to our success by

- offering positive reinforcement
- giving precise and clear instructions, and always being willing to clarify when they're not clear

- not constraining workers any more than is essential
- letting people fully explore the possibilities
- simplifying tasks whenever possible, yet making sure the tasks aren't insultingly easy
- making the time frames clear and giving the reasoning behind them
- paying attention to people's skills
- balancing the workload among all employees
- ensuring there is some real part for everyone to play
- teaching how to be supportive by being supportive of employees and of each other
- teaching how to trust by trusting each other and the customers
- remembering what it's like to be an employee and to be managed
- answering questions correctly and honestly to build trust
- getting good consulting advice and using it
- creating a vision of the problem and communicating it clearly to every-one
- providing organizational guidance whenever employees need it
- setting things up so people can experience early success
- not asking people to do things they aren't able or willing to do
- creating an environment in which it's okay to have fun
- making their objectives clear at the beginning
- being available to workers and being generous with their time
- understanding and forgiving mistakes
- valuing creative approaches, even when the approaches are different from what they had in mind
- not forcing people to be something they're not
- finding the resources employees genuinely need to do their jobs
- changing their plans to fit environmental changes
- resisting the temptation to change the rules in the middle of the project unless it is absolutely essential
- explaining the reasons when something has to change
- always being up front with employees, even when it's embarrassing
- genuinely wanting people to succeed
- oh, yes, and occasionally making good decisions about hiring and firing subordinates

This sounds like an environment in which I'd like to work. It also sounds like the manager I'd like to be.

6.8 Helpful Hints and Suggestions

1. There is an interesting trade-off between trust and listening:

... we realized that, while understanding is an essential part of organized activity, it just is not possible for everybody to understand everything. The following is essential: We must trust one another to be accountable for our own assignments. When that kind of trust is present, it is a beautifully liberating thing. [7]

2. Because of their position in the hierarchy, managers also make implicit assignments. For instance, every time the senior management team changes one of their meetings, the change ripples down through the whole organization. One telecommunications company that is a client of mine studied this effect using scheduling data from their E-mail system. One vice president who changed the time of one meeting with her immediate staff led to an average of 670 E-mail messages being generated as the change rippled down. The study estimated an average work time per message of 12 minutes (including phone calls and personal contacts that were not recorded). This meant 670 x 12 = 134 hours of rescheduling time, at a burdened average cost of $70 per hour yielded $9,380 per vice presidential meeting change.

3. Your personal experience is never enough to manage a large project, because in one lifetime, you cannot have experienced enough different large project situations. How many five-year projects can you have completed in a twenty-year career? To be an effective manager of large projects, therefore, you must learn from others. If you don't do this well, then you must learn how to learn from others.

4. My colleague Dan Starr points out that giving the experienced people a strong-willed assistant runs afoul of the tradition that assistants are a "perk" and status symbol, not to be given to lowly techies. Thus, if you call them secretaries, you may not succeed. Ironically, you may be more successful implementing this technique by assigning a junior technical person who earns three times as much as a secretary.

5. Both Dan and another colleague Mark Manduke remind me that firing the manager of an unsuccessful team is precisely what is done in sports. Even those managers who are fondest of using sports analogies are likely to protest that this approach doesn't apply to them.

6.9 Summary

✓   In an effective software organization, the manager's job is getting more people involved, as well as getting people more involved, in decisions about what is to be done and in doing it.

✓   For example, to recover from a crisis, a manager has to mobilize sidelined peo-
     ple in order to have the resources to keep the ship afloat.

✓   As an organization moves deeper into crisis, the best-informed people tend to
     become overloaded. Managers may unknowingly contribute to this piling on,
     and can counteract it by congruent management action.

✓   In Routine (Pattern 2) organizations, managers prescribe the way things
     should be done, rather than describe what outcomes are desired (a more Steer-
     ing or Pattern 3 behavior). Prescribing managers tend to listen to employees in
     a superreasonable or blaming way without hearing them.

✓   A major job of the software engineering manager is to develop openness and
     trust among all the workers who are contributing to successful software activi-
     ties. This requires honesty and true listening.

✓   Right or wrong, the reasons given by employees always contain the informa-
     tion an effective manager needs to steer the organization.

✓   The Steering (Pattern 3) manager does not generally evaluate quality, but
     establishes the processes, not people, to evaluate quality. When the manager
     does evaluate the quality of work, the main purpose of that evaluation is to
     help employees develop their own skills.

✓   Managers who believe in the One-Dimensional Selection Model have no room
     in their repertoire for coaching, teaching, or training.

✓   Congruent managers are not locked into blaming, partly because they know
     that they are not passive victims of their employees, their bosses, or the
     dynamics of software quality. Instead, they use all of them intelligently as
     resources.

✓   Leadership is the ability to create an environment in which everyone is
     empowered to contribute creatively to solving the problems. In this model, the
     manager's job may be evaluated by one and only one measure: the success of
     the people being managed.

6.10   Practice

1.   If you are a manager, use the list in Section 6.7 to survey the people who work
     for you. Ask them if there are any other things that should be on the list of
     good things you do as their manager. Use their responses to guide your
     behavior in the future.

2.   If you have a manager or managers, use the list in Section 6.7 to study their styles. What would you add to the list of good things they do? What things missing from their list would you like them to do? How would you go about getting them to do those things?

3.   How important is software expertise in management? As we've seen, technical experience can be a handicap as can any experience in related areas that tempts you to do the work your employees should be doing. If you are a manager, get together with a few other managers who have strong technical experience and share tactics you all use to prevent the experience from getting in the way of being effective as a manager.

4.   Here are four different models of the manager's job. The manager's job is

       a.   to do the work
       b.   to make decisions about the work
       c.   to hire and train people to do the work
       d.   to hire and train people to make decisions about the work

       Which model do you think best describes a manager's job?

5.   Some management texts say that the manager's job is to make decisions, while others claim that the manager's job is to avoid reaching decision points, such as having to fire someone. What is your opinion on these descriptions? How does this issue relate to software cultural patterns?

6.   Discuss the following note of Steve Heller, a participant in the CompuServe Software Engineering Management Forum:

       I couldn't agree more that the software industry has a very poor record of selecting the people to be promoted to manager. Partly, though, the problem is the Peter Principle: if you are doing well, you get promoted to the next position, so that you eventually reach your "level of incompetence," and there you stay. My defense against that is to stay technical, even though I have done some management on occasion, and successfully at that.[8]

       How does Steve's position and career compare with your own? Have you ever experienced the Peter Principle in action?

7
Recognizing Preference Differences

The law, in its majestic equality, forbids all men to sleep under bridges, to beg in the streets, and to steal bread—the rich as well as the poor.
— Anatole France

Ashby's Law of Requisite Variety (in its majestic equality) says that an effective manager must be able to match the variety in the actions of the environment to be controlled. In most managers' environments, a large part of the variety comes from the people. Ineffective managers tend to deal with the great variations among people by pretending they don't exist, but effective managers recognize differences and know how to deal with them.

7.1 Same or Equal?

Here's a story of one of those ineffective managers told by a human resources professional at a client's office: "I was helping a manager work with problems of getting his management team to work well together. I had been called in because there were complaints of sexism. During one meeting, although he had two American women plus one Pakistani man and one Danish man on his team, he was making liberal use of baseball terms and metaphors. Finally, when he said that their project plan would be a 'delayed squeeze,' I observed that communication might be improved if he avoided American baseball idioms. When I suggested some alternative ways of dealing with the situation, he replied, proudly, 'I manage everyone the same.' Someone in the group whispered loudly, 'Uh, huh. Badly.'"

As the French novelist and satirist Anatole France suggested, treating everyone the same does not mean treating everyone equally. When this manager said, "I manage everyone the same," he probably meant, "I manage everyone equally"—a management philosophy with which I could heartily agree. Because equal does not mean same and an astute manager notices the differences among people and knows how to use them to manage effectively—equally, but not unfairly. Employees appreciate this style of management, as evidenced by a number of items in our list of good management behaviors from Chapter 6:

- not constraining workers any more than is essential
- letting people fully explore the possibilities
- paying attention to people's skills
- not asking people to do things they aren't able or willing to do
- valuing creative approaches, even when the approaches are different from what they had in mind
- not forcing people to be something they're not

7.2 Preferences

It's hard enough to work with software when conditions are optimal, but software engineering organizations are put to the test when a project comes under great stress. Under the pressure of a looming delivery date, for example, emotions can run so high that sound engineering practices are replaced by incongruent coping behaviors. To understand how to deal with such incongruence, let's first look at how people choose their behaviors under mild stress.

Although we tend to think of all software work as being logical, many actions are chosen on the basis of emotion. Emotions can run the gamut from the extremely powerful to the mildest. One of the mildest yet most important emotions is preference. People who believe that all emotions are strong and "negative" may have trouble with the idea of preference as an emotion. They can understand someone acting emotionally (strongly and negatively) when urged to respond counter to their preference, but they may not appreciate the little feeling that says, "Oh, I like this better than that."

Most of us are capable of using either hand to open a jar, but we unthinkingly choose our preferred hand. When we operate at this unthinking level, which is a great part of the time, our behavior is guided by our preferences.

Obviously, the preference for opening jars with one hand or the other is not critical to the success of a software engineering manager, but other preferences may have a much greater influence. For instance, a manager who prefers that all key decision-making positions be filled by women may tend to exclude the contribution of a competent man. If such behavior reduces choices, this management team will have a tougher time with the Law of Requisite Variety.

The same loss of variety could occur if the preference were for all men, or all white men, or all left-handed, blonde women under five feet tall. Yet just because there is a *preference*, such a loss of variety need not occur because we need not act on our preferences. Just because I prefer pistachio ice cream, I need not eat only pistachio. For instance, if my dinner host offers a choice of vanilla and chocolate, I may decide that under the circumstances, insisting on pistachio is incongruent. Although it satisfies my preferences, it ignores my host's, and it also ignores the context—it's close to midnight and there's no pistachio in the house.

In the same way, I may prefer to have all older people on my management team, but I can consider other factors when actually making appointments. If I do find a younger person who is the best qualified for the context, I set my preference aside to get a more congruent selection. At the same time, I note that I have gone against my preference, so that I may have to guard against unconsciously obstructing my young manager.

7.3 The Myers-Briggs Preferences

The preference in ice cream flavors, like many of the thousands of possible preferences, is not terribly significant for managing people. One set of preferences that managers should understand, however, is the four dimensions described in the Myers-Briggs Type Indicator (MBTI).[1] These four dimensions are significant in the workplace because they capture four elements that determine much of a person's working style. The dimensions are how a person prefers to get energy, obtain information, make decisions, and take action.

A person's preference on each of the four dimensions is represented by a single letter. In my case, for example, a selection of the four letters INFP abbreviate my own description of the four components of my working style. For each dimension, there is a pair of letters to choose from:

- E or I, according to how I prefer to get energy
- S or N, according to how I prefer to obtain information
- T or F, according to how I prefer to make decisions
- J or P, according to how I prefer to take action

So my INFP is a shorthand way of saying that I *prefer* to get my energy from inside (I), find information intuitively (N), make decisions on the basis of values (F), and take action that keeps possibilities open (P). ESTJ, by contrast, means I would prefer to get my energy from others (E), obtain information through facts (S), make decisions using logic (T), and take action to have things settled (J). Managers who understand this system find it a valuable way to start understanding the people whom they manage and with whom they work, so they can manage better, be managed better, and be a better team member.

Take careful note that the description INFP does not say that I cannot get energy from outside, find information through my senses, make decisions on the basis of logical thought, or take action that closes possibilities. It merely says that when simple or unconscious preference determines my choices, I'll tend to do certain things and not do other things. With that caution in mind, let's examine these four dimensions of preference.

7.4 Getting Energy

The first dimension describes how people prefer to get the energy to do things or how they recharge the batteries. In an organization, you can see people's *Internal/External* (I/E) preference very clearly in meetings and especially at breaks. External Processors tend to use breaks to socialize; Internal Processors use breaks to be alone and regenerate. About one-quarter of the people in the United States are Internal Processors, and the other three-quarters tend to feel that there's something socially wrong with this minority.[2]

Failure to take the I/E difference into account leads to underperformance by one group or the other. At technical review meetings, for example, Internals prefer to study the material carefully in advance, but this style tends to bore the Externals. Externals prefer walkthroughs so they can study the material through group interaction, but this forum makes it difficult for Internals to contribute.

One of the manager's jobs is to assure that meetings are designed to accommodate the environmental preferences of both Internals and Externals. Just by random choice, the most common meeting will involve a mixture of the two preferences; but even when all participants have the same preference, there can be trouble. One of my colleagues wrote me the following note:

"I was asked to facilitate a meeting of the maintenance management group, because they were 'having meeting problems.' I had worked with each of the five managers before, and knew that they were all Internal processors. After observing them for an hour or so, I commented that their meeting format seemed designed for Externals—lots of brainstorming and give-and-take interaction.

"They told me they had learned this format in a workshop their manager had sent them to in order to 'improve their productivity.' I suggested that they design their own format, including such elements as periods of silence while people prepared to respond to presentations, more written documents given out in advance, and out-of-the-room breaks to read documents passed out in the meeting.

"When I returned a month later, their meetings were entirely different—and entirely more productive. My only concern now is what will happen if an External Processor joins the team."

This dimension also affects one-on-one interactions. External managers are often puzzled when Internal employees cannot respond to rapid-fire questions about their projects. If they are not aware of the E/I difference, they may mistakenly interpret the difficulty as a sign that the Internal is uncertain or is trying to cover up some trouble in the project.

Internal managers are often puzzled when External employees immediately give answers to questions that they expected to be answered in a written report. The managers may mistakenly interpret the speedy response as a sign that the External employee is overconfident or is not taking the request seriously.

7.5 Obtaining Information

Once I am motivated to do something, I must get the information required to do it. The second dimension describes how I prefer to get the information I need to do things. Within an organization, you can see also the *Sensing/Intuitive* (S/N—N for "iNtuitive." I is already used for Internal) preference in meetings, especially during presentations. Sensors want the facts, lots of facts, while Intuitives want the big picture.

When a Sensor is giving the facts, the Intuitives become bored out of their underwear. When an Intuitive is painting the big picture, the Sensors itch for some real data, such as the percentages given in Figure 7-1.

Dimensions	%
Internal/External	25/75
Sensing/Intuitive	75/25
Thinking/Feeling	50/50
Judging/Perceiving	50/50

Figure 7-1.   Approximate distribution of the MBTI preferences in the United States, expressed as percentages of each dimension.[3]

The Sensors would study Figure 7-1, while the Intuitives would probably give it only a brief glance and dismiss it as "mere data." The Sensors would be interested to know that they comprise three-quarters of the United States population; the Intuitives wouldn't be interested unless they were given some reason for the distribution.

A manager who is having "communication problems" with employees would be well-advised to explore this difference as a prime candidate for the root cause. Intuitives working for Sensors tend to believe they are being over-managed. They think that a manager should

- create a vision of the problem and communicate it clearly to everyone

Sensors working for Intuitives cannot seem to figure out what they're being asked to do. They think that a manager should

- give precise and clear instructions and always be willing to clarify when they're not clear

Practical applications of the S/N difference are easy to find in organizations, and some of them are so dramatic as to appear magical, as in the following narrative by a manager who had recently attended a workshop on the MBTI:

"The information systems team (of which I was head) was meeting with human resources (HR) management to discuss a proposal for a new information system for HR. Melissa, the IS team's designer, had sketched the new system, and everyone was responding positively to her presentation—everyone, that is, except Norris, the HR vice president. While the others continued to heap laurels on Melissa and her design, Norris sat cross-armed, close-mouthed, and looking puzzled and annoyed.

"Melissa apparently noticed the VP's reaction, because she began to try to win his favor, but all her efforts seemed to make him look even more puzzled. Recalling our recent workshop, I called for a break. When we were alone, I said, simply, 'Norris is an S,' and Melissa gasped, 'Oh!'

"While the others were out on break, Melissa quickly sketched five foils giving very specific (though totally hypothetical) examples of how the new design would handle transactions involving specific employees. When the meeting resumed, she presented the foils, and with each example, Norris visibly relaxed and brightened. When she turned off the overhead, he smiled and said his first words of the meeting, 'This looks great! Let's do it!'

"Three months later, I happened to be at a senior executive briefing at which Norris presented the new system. I was fascinated to observe that his entire presentation consisted of five examples taken word for word from Melissa's presentation, though dressed up to executive quality by the graphic arts department."

7.6 Making Decisions

Once I am motivated and have the information required to do something, I have to *make decisions*. The third MBTI dimension describes how I prefer to make decisions: using logic (thinking) or values (feeling). Raymond Chandler, the detective writer, has beautifully described the *Thinking/Feeling* (T/F) distinction:

> There are two kinds of truth: the truth that lights the way and the truth that warms the heart. The first of these is science, and the second is art. Neither is independent of the other or more important than the other. Without art science

would be as useless as a pair of high forceps in the hands of a plumber. Without science art would become a crude mess of folklore and emotional quackery. The truth of art keeps science from becoming inhuman, and the truth of science keeps art from becoming ridiculous.

Although Chandler says one style of truth would be useless without the other, Thinkers and Feelers are often intolerant of each other's preferred style. In an organization, you can see the T/F preference in action whenever decisions are to be made. Both types want good decisions, but they differ in what attributes make a decision good. Thinkers want objectivity, logic, and impersonality; while Feelers want humanity, values, and cooperation. In arriving at decisions, neither type objects to consideration of the other's attributes, but merely considers them of low priority.

In the United States, although the overall population is divided fifty-fifty between Thinkers and Feelers, the educational system is skewed toward F values in the lower grades (where most of the teachers are Feelers), but moves toward T values as the grade level advances. At the university level, the great majority of teachers are Thinkers. In an organization, this skewing may give the Feelers a curious advantage. Because they have been better trained in T decision making, Feelers have more access to a balance of styles than the Thinkers, who have not been as well-trained in F decision making.

Here's an example from a management training session of how the T/F difference leads to entirely different solutions for what appears to be the same problem. In a discussion entitled "My Most Difficult Problem," both Callie and Dennis named "handling customer requests for system modifications" as their choice of most difficult problem. Further analysis, however, revealed great differences between them.

Callie's response to customer requests was based on her T preference combined with her strong preference for Internal processing. She didn't want to refuse anybody anything they asked, but she wanted time off the phone to use her strong thinking process to determine whether the request made sense before agreeing to it. The customers, however, wanted to keep her on the phone until she committed to something, and she didn't know how to deal with them.

Dennis, in contrast, had an F preference for decision making along with a preference for External processing. He handled telephone requests very well, but couldn't cope with E-mail requests (the E in E-mail certainly doesn't stand for "External processing"). Many of the E-mail requests were for features that Dennis didn't feel were right to implement, but he often agreed anyway. His problem was that he wanted face-to-face contact to explain why he wasn't really a bad person for refusing to give the customers what they thought they wanted.

The source of both problems was an environment that didn't match their preferences. Callie preferred off-line time to think about changes, so we taught her to ask the customers for written documentation. If they refused to send any, she had no trouble turning them down, because the lack of documentation was clear evidence (to her way of thinking) that they hadn't given enough thought to their request (which was the worst possible sin).

Dennis preferred on-line time, because it was important to him that he not let anyone think badly of him. He solved his problem by responding with a request for a face-to-face meeting, which was exactly Callie's worst nightmare of a setting for an interaction.

Many management problems can be solved in just this way, by designing the correct environment for decision making. What makes this a difficult approach for some managers is that they must be willing and able to tailor the working environment for each person, and that requires knowing the people they manage.

7.7 Taking Action

The fourth MBTI dimension describes my preferred mode of taking action. The *Judging* (J) preference is to have things settled, while the *Perceiving* (P) preference is to keep my options open on the chance that more information will affect the choice.

The terminology of this dimension seems to cause a great deal of confusion. Judging refers not to the tendency to be judgmental, but to the preference for making decisions (hence the word, *judging,* which I think would have been better expressed as *deciding*). Perceiving refers not to the tendency to be perceptive, but to the preference for taking in information (hence the word *perceiving*). My own preference, with twenty/twenty hindsight, would have been the words *closure-seeking* (for *judging*) and *information-seeking* (for *perceiving*). But those of us in software engineering have lots of experience using confusing terminology, so we'll live with Judging and Perceiving just as we've lived with *floating point* and *fixed point* all these years.

Here is a description of how the Perceivers are sometimes seen by the Judgers: "A friend of mine described a colleague as great at running the 'ninety-five-yard dash.' That is a distinction I can do without. Lacking the last five yards makes the first ninety-five pointless."[4]

When I showed this description to one of my Perceiving friends, he laughed and gave the following description of how he sees Judgers: "They run a great hundred-yard dash. Once in a while they even run it in the right direction."

Judging/Perceiving differences are often the source of great conflict, but they can also be the source of great attraction because each needs the other. For instance, married couples are more often J/P mixes than would be predicted if this attraction were not a factor. From a working point of view, teams without any Judgers at all tend never to finish anything; while teams without any Perceivers finish things only to find they aren't really finished because some factor has been omitted.

You can't necessarily tell about a J/P preference by watching what people do, because they can arrive at the same action by way of different preferences. One example is the delivery of software before it's been adequately tested. Judging developers may finish quickly because they simply·need to be finished. Perceiving developers may finish quickly because they want to work on another module that presents more interesting challenges.

The actions and results are the same—quick, superficial testing—but the motivation is different, so the two situations should be managed differently. For instance, the Perceiving developer's behavior may change if the manager makes clear that no new module can be started until the developer can demonstrate that the old one has been thoroughly tested. The Judging developer's behavior may change if the manager simply gives very explicit measures, such as path coverage, that must be met before the case is closed.

My colleague Lynne Nix has an interesting way of relating the J/P dimension to software cultural patterns.[5] She places the patterns on a preference scale from Anarchy (Perceiving) to Bureaucracy (Judging), as shown in Figure 7-2. A Variable (Pattern 1) organization prefers complete anarchy, while a Routine (Pattern 2) organization prefers complete bureaucracy. A Steering (Pattern 3) organization compensates for Pattern 2's overenthusiam for routine by moving left, but a little too far left. An Anticipating (Pattern 4) organization moves back to the right, but overreacts to the possibility of anarchy. A Congruent (Pattern 5) organization moves to the center, exactly balancing anarchy and bureaucracy with the ability to respond congruently as the situation requires.

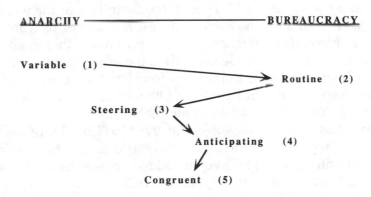

Figure 7-2.   Lynne Nix's way of relating the J/P dimension to the five software cultural patterns.

According to this model, all other things being equal, Perceivers will be more comfortable in Patterns 1 and 3, while Judgers will be more comfortable in Patterns 2 and 4. This may explain why I have found it easier to move a Pattern 1 organization directly to Pattern 3. The Perceivers in the Pattern 1 organization shudder when I describe Pattern 2. The Judgers who have managed to survive in a Pattern 1 organization at least see Pattern 3 as more comfortable than the complete anarchy under which they suffer.

7.8 Why MBTI?

Naomi Karten is the author of several ground-breaking books,[6] and I consider us to be great friends and colleagues. We help each other enormously in reading each other's manuscripts, which benefit from the differences between us. I believe her MBTI type is INTJ, which you will notice is the same as my INFP in two dimensions and different in two others. Some of our interactions provide clear illustrations of the benefits and pitfalls of differences as described by the MBTI.

Virginia Satir used to comment that we connect through our sameness and grow through our differentness. One of the ways I've been trying to grow is by better understanding the Thinkers of the world, and Naomi Karten gave me a big boost when she commented on a draft of this chapter: "I don't prefer to use my left hand. I'm left-handed so I use my left hand. I would actually prefer to do many things with my right hand. It would require me to make many fewer adjustments in interacting with a right-handed world."

Her comment taught me something about the difference between the Feelers like me and the Thinkers like her. To me, preference is (ideally) determined by emotional reactions, while to her it is determined by logic. My learning demonstrates how the T/F difference, properly managed, can be a colossal resource to a team, and not simply a source of conflict and misunderstanding.

But Naomi went on to say, "If it's unthinking, then it's at a subconscious level. Preferences are at a conscious level." Though the definition of the word preference applies to both conscious and unconscious decisions, each of us leans toward our own (may I say it, Naomi?) preference. But she and I agree that in an ideal world, choices should be on the conscious level. In fact, the whole point of learning about preferences is to help raise them to the conscious level, where Naomi and I both prefer managers to spend most of their time. Otherwise, they will do things, as she says, "because they simply aren't aware of alternatives."

That's why I have raised the subject of the MBTI model of preferences: to make you more aware of some important dimensions of what you're choosing when you interact with others. I believe this added consciousness will make you a better manager. Of course, as with any model, there are dangers with the MBTI model. I've chosen the MBTI model over many other personality models because it's the least dangerous in terms of use against people. It is self-descriptive, and doesn't require the interpretation of mental health professionals. Whereas many other personality models arose from attempts to find out what is wrong with people, the MBTI model was designed to discover each of our special, but differing, gifts. However, the innocence of its origins doesn't prevent a tool from being abused by mean-spirited or ignorant people.

I cannot protect against the mean-spirited, but ignorance is curable. One of the dangers is that this chapter and other discussions in this book are merely the briefest introduction to the MBTI model, and an introduction from the point of view of one type among sixteen. My Thinking colleagues, particularly, object to the way I approach this subject, and of course they're right to object. Each of us has to approach our own personality in our own way.

For me, it took a good deal of study and experimentation even to discover my own type and understand some of its implications. When first introduced to the MBTI system, I believed I was an ENTP (External, Intuitive, Thinking Perceiver). After a year or so of study and practice, I realized I was an ENFP, but then further understanding led me to believe I'm an INFP. That's where I've stayed for a number of years, but who knows where self-discovery might eventually lead. If I can make several mistakes about my own type, you can see that it would be easy to abuse the MBTI model. If it seems a valuable tool to you, please make the effort to study it more deeply. Here's the way an INFP would do it:

- Practice first on yourself, not on others.
- When you are ready to move out into the world, find a partner or partners (as I have found Naomi and many other wonderful friends) who differ from you in one or two dimensions.
- Connect with your sameness as you explore your differentness with, not on, your partner.
- Share your own gifts and let your partner teach you about gifts that are less familiar to you.
- Do all this practice with much more humor than judgment.

7.9 Helpful Hints and Suggestions

1. The real leverage for a manager is in managing emotions, because from what I've observed, most people and organizations spend only ten percent of their time and energy on rational problem solving. The rest goes to physical maintenance and emotional matters. If emotional matters take fifty percent of their time and energy, then a ten percent reduction leads to a fifty percent improvement in the time and energy for rational stuff. A ten percent increase in time spent on emotional matters leads to a fifty percent reduction in time spent on rational matters.

2. A basic law of perception is that we tend to minimize small differences (tendency toward assimilation) and to exaggerate appreciable differences (tendency toward contrast). Thus, our perceptions make the world more sharply differentiated than it is, and we're a lot more alike than we are different.

3. Never forget that the MBTI letters indicate preferences, not skills or aptitudes. A good example from this chapter is Lynne Nix, who provided the model in Figure 7-2. To the best of my memory, Lynne is a Sensor, but she happens to have a terrific aptitude for abstract models. I don't know if she likes them as much as I (an Intuitive) do, but she certainly knows how to use them.

7.10 Summary

✓   Poor managers tend to deal with variations among people by pretending that they don't exist. Effective managers recognize differences and know how to deal with them congruently.

✓   Treating everyone the same does not mean treating everyone equally. The astute manager notices the differences among people and knows how to use them to manage effectively—equally, but not unfairly.

✓   Although we tend to think of all software work as logical, many actions are done on the basis of emotion. One of the mildest yet most important emotions is preference.

✓   When an unconscious preference reduces choices, we have a tougher time with Ashby's Law of Requisite Variety. Just because there is a preference, however, such a loss of variety needn't occur, for we don't have to act on our preferences.

✓   The four dimensions of the Myers-Briggs Type Indicator (MBTI) are significant in the workplace because they describe four elements that determine much of a person's working style.

✓   For each dimension of the MBTI model, there is a pair of letters to choose from:

  • Internal or External, according to how I prefer to get energy
  • Sensing or iNtuitive, according to how I prefer to obtain information
  • Thinking or Feeling, according to how I prefer to make decisions
  • Judging or Perceiving, according to how I prefer to take action

✓   Failure to take the I/E difference into account leads to underperformance by one group or the other. One of the manager's jobs is to assure that meetings are designed to accommodate the environmental preferences of both Internals and Externals.

✓   Sensors want the facts, lots of facts, while Intuitives want the big picture. A manager who has communication problems with employees should explore this difference as a prime candidate for the root cause.

✓   Thinkers and Feelers are often intolerant of each others' preferred style. In an organization, you can see the T/F preference in action whenever decisions are to be made. Both types want good decisions, but they differ in what attributes make a decision good. Many T/F problems can be solved by designing the correct environment for decision making.

✓   The Judging (J) preference is to have things settled, while the Perceiving (P) preference is to keep options open on the chance that more information will affect the choice. Judging/Perceiving differences are often the source of great conflict, as well as the source of great attraction, because each needs the other.

7.11 Practice

1.   The place to start understanding others' preferences is with your own. For instance, here are my own INFP feelings about working in the various software cultural patterns:

Variable (Pattern 1): I would like this pattern if I didn't care about the larger picture. It's fun.

Routine (Pattern 2): I wouldn't like this pattern: too stifling.

Steering (Pattern 3): I could like this: fun teamwork, though I might get impatient with not being challenged.

Anticipating (Pattern 4): I would like the challenge here.

Congruent (Pattern 5): I would like this environment if I wanted to do something that nobody has ever done before, like when I worked on Project Mercury and the space tracking network.

What are your preferences with respect to these different patterns? Can you see how your preferences might influence your efforts to achieve a certain pattern?

2.   There are a number of ways you can discover your own MBTI preferences. You may already know simply from reading this chapter, but more likely you'll have to work on it. One way is to take a self-test such as that found in *Please Understand Me*.[7] Or else you can take a workshop on the MBTI and be tested there, learning more about practical applications in the process. Find the method that works for you and do it.

3.   Once you have your own MBTI type pretty well established, move out into your community to start learning about other types. You can follow my INFP process given in the chapter, or create your own approach.

8

Temperament Differences

Thus spoke the Master Ninjei:
"To program a million-line operating
system is easy;
to change a man's temperament
is more difficult."[1]
— Geoffrey James

The dimensions of the MBTI model are useful to a manager in and of themselves, but when they are combined, they produce sixteen identifiable personality types. Kiersey and Bates have given archetypal vocations to the sixteen types, and they are arranged below to help you remember them:[2]

INTP	(Architect)	ESFJ	(Seller)
ENTP	(Inventor)	ISFJ	(Conservator)
INTJ	(Scientist)	ESFP	(Entertainer)
ENTJ	(Field marshal)	ISFP	(Artist)
INFP	(Questor)	ESTJ	(Administrator)
ENFP	(Journalist)	ISTJ	(Trustee)
INFJ	(Author)	ESTP	(Promoter)
ENFJ	(Pedagogue)	ISTP	(Artisan)

If you don't take these vocations too seriously, they can be helpful, but this is probably too much detail for the working manager to recall on the spot. Much more practical are Kiersey and Bates's reduction of the sixteen types to four "temperaments": the NT Visionary, the NF Catalyst, the SJ Organizer, and the SP Troubleshooter.[3] This chapter will relate those temperaments to the job of controlling software.

8.1 Four Kinds of Control

When we speak of controlling software development, we can conveniently identify four different kinds of control:

- intellectual control
- physical control
- emergency control
- emotional control

8.1.1 Intellectual control

Intellectual control is what we used to think of as the whole ball game in software, as in the claim "Software is pure intellect." Most of the major innovations in software have been in the area of improving intellectual control—innovations such as higher-level languages, structured programming, various pictorial aids to programming, relational databases, and object-oriented design. Although you may not agree that these have been the major innovations in software, at least they have been the innovations that have received the most attention.

8.1.2 Physical control

Physical control is necessary because even the intellect resides in the blooming, buzzing confusion of the real physical world. Eventually, this real world imposes itself on the pleasant fantasy that software is pure intellect. Someone wipes out the only copy of the source code. Someone else changes "just one line of comment" and through a typing error causes a million dollars' worth of damage. Someone steals the source code and produces a competitive version of a major product. A fire destroys all copies of the system documentation.

Physical control is introduced into software to deal with just such real-world deviations from the pure intellect model of software, either by prevention or by detection and correction. Examples of physical control include configuration management systems, source code and data security, backup and repository procedures, and error detection and correction schemes. Notice that innovations in these areas have not generally received the hullaballoo of the intellectual innovations.

One notable exception is the hardware topic of fault tolerance, which for some systems has been a high-profile topic.

8.1.3 Emergency control

In spite of the best intellectual effort and the best physical control, sometimes more is needed. In software development, things can happen at a slow rate and often need unsticking, as when one blocking fault stops progress on an entire project for a month. In software maintenance, things happen at a fast rate and often need something to get them moving again, as when a customer is screaming on the phone for a quick fix so the payroll can get out.

As we improve our ability to control the physical and intellectual parts of the software business, we encounter a paradox. More and more situations are handled routinely, even automatically, so our productivity increases. This means we can handle more work with the same resources, but more work means more situations in which the routine doesn't work. So, as we develop routines to handle intellectual and physical problems, we find that our ability to manage well depends not on our ability to handle routine situations, but on our ability to handle exceptional situations—emergencies, in other words.

8.1.4 Emotional control

In a perfectly rational world—perhaps in a world where software was developed and supported entirely by machines—intellectual, physical, and emergency controls would be sufficient. Over the past forty years, I have heard many pundits predict that completely automated software development (software pundits usually don't speak of support) was just a few years off. Never having seen much progress in this direction, I have come to regard such "predictions" as mere wishful thinking.

What is the wish that these prognosticators are fulfilling? I believe it is the wish for perfection, which leads to the wish that people would entirely disappear from the software business because people are not, and cannot ever be, perfect. People are not perfect thinkers, nor can they carry out routine tasks infallibly. In emergency situations, their imperfections may be magnified. Even worse, sometimes the situation is physically and intellectually simple with no emergency conditions, yet people still fail to perform perfectly.

We have many possible explanations for such imperfect performance:

- He wasn't motivated.
- She was depressed.
- They were afraid to do it that way.
- He was being stubborn.

- She was distracted.
- They weren't serious.

Each of these explanations—motivation, depression, fear, stubbornness, distraction, or lack of seriousness—is in terms of the emotional system. That's why underlying all the other three forms of control is *emotional control.* Under the influence of strong emotions, people are unable to think clearly and rationally, to follow simple procedures, or to apply their creativity in solving emergency problems. Strong emotions have a tendency to produce stereotyped behavior, which means that behavioral variety is reduced. When a manager who is responsible for controlling the system falls prey to emotions and acts without a full repertoire of choices, how can control be effective, let alone perfect?

Emotional control does not mean eliminating emotions, any more than physical control means eliminating the physical world. That's impossible. Emotional control does not mean suppressing emotions either, or pretending they don't exist. Emotional control means having the emotions, acknowledging them for the information they convey, and coping with them congruently.

8.2 Understanding the Four Temperaments

Each of Kiersey and Bates's temperaments tends to react to out-of-control situations in characteristic ways, each one favoring one of the four types of control. Each temperament can also be characterized by the kind of situation in which it gets trapped, and this trap is always the temperament's greatest strength carried to excess. Let's look at the four temperaments in turn, and especially at aspects of their style as managers, as well as what they each like in their own managers.

8.2.1 The NT Visionary

The Visionary (NT, or Intuitive Thinker in the Myers-Briggs system) likes working with ideas. NT Visionaries are most interested in designing, rather than implementing, things. Their strength is captured in the saying "Nothing is more dangerous than an idea whose time has come." NT Visionaries are dangerous to the established order, because they lead the rest of us out of our complacency into their brave new worlds. Without them, we'd still be shivering in caves, waiting for someone to invent fire.

You can trap an NT Visionary by saying, "Capture the essence," for the NT Visionary easily gets caught in oversimplifying complex details into a unified theory. In other words, "Nothing is more dangerous than an idea when it is the only one you have."

From Chapter 6's list of desirable managerial actions, the NT Visionary would probably exhibit and value these:

- not constraining workers any more than is essential
- letting people fully explore the possibilities
- making the time frames clear and giving the reasoning behind them
- simplifying tasks whenever possible, yet making sure the tasks aren't insultingly easy (Of course, the NT Visionary's idea of simplification may not fit yours.)
- creating a vision of the problem and communicating it clearly to everyone
- valuing creative approaches, even when the approaches are different from what they had in mind
- explaining the reasons when something has to change

Although NT Visionaries represent only about twelve percent of the population in the United States,[4] they are much more highly represented in the software industry. In many of my client organizations, they form the majority of the technical staff. Despite their immense contributions and before I understood this particular temperament, I had a hard time being in the same room with them. I always thought the NT Visionaries were having an argument, when all they were doing was having a discussion. Once I realized that I was simply seeing them through my own INFP glasses, I really came to love and appreciate them not just for their contributions, but for who they are as people.

8.2.2 The NF Catalyst

People who are Catalysts (NF, or Intuitive Feelers) like working with people to help themselves grow, but they are concerned that people not suffer. (That's why I couldn't stand to watch the NT Visionaries "arguing.") NF Catalysts are needed to keep everybody working together through the rough times, and to support individuals going through tough emotional times.

You can trap an NF Catalyst by saying, "Make sure everyone agrees," for the NF Catalyst values harmony above all else. There are many circumstances when it's unnecessary for everyone to agree, but the NF Catalyst has a hard time recognizing them. I've heard more than one NF facilitator ask, "Does anyone object to our taking a bathroom break?"

This question perfectly characterizes the most common and destructive NF management mistake. If one person doesn't want a bathroom break, are all the rest of us to sit in pain and misery? NF Catalysts, in their passion for taking care of everybody, often harm a great number of people in an overly focused effort to save one. An NF manager, for instance, may bend over backward to defend a lower-level manager from charges of abusive behavior. By protecting this manager, the NF Catalyst allows the continued abuse of many other employees.

From our list of desirable managerial actions, the NF Catalyst would approve of these:

- offering positive reinforcement
- paying attention to people's skills
- ensuring there is some real part for everyone to play
- teaching how to be supportive by being supportive of employees and of each other
- teaching how to trust by trusting each other and the customers
- remembering what it's like to be an employee and to be managed
- answering questions correctly and honestly to build trust
- not asking people to do things they aren't able or willing to do
- understanding and forgiving mistakes
- always being up front with employees, even when it's embarrassing
- genuinely wanting people to succeed

8.2.3 The SJ Organizer

The Organizer (SJ, or Sensory Judge) likes order and system. The important thing to an SJ Organizer is not just doing it, but doing it right. Most SJ Organizers would heartily agree with the slogan "Anything worth doing is worth doing right."

You can trap an SJ Organizer by saying, "Do it right" or "Do it on time," for they value order over everything else. They have a hard time understanding that other slogan: "Anything not worth doing is not worth doing right." There are many occasions when things need not be in perfect order, but the SJ Organizers have a hard time recognizing them. For instance, one SJ Organizer who was assigned to report the conclusions of a strategic planning meeting put the agreed items of the company's vision statement in alphabetical order. The NT Visionaries accused the SJ Organizer of not taking their work seriously, but they failed to understand that the SJ Organizer was giving the list the best possible care.

From our list of desirable managerial actions, the SJ Organizer would approve of these:

- giving precise and clear instructions, and always being willing to clarify when they're not clear
- simplifying tasks whenever possible, yet making sure the tasks aren't insultingly easy
- making the time frames clear and giving the reasoning behind them
- balancing the workload among all employees
- answering questions correctly and honestly to build trust
- getting good consulting advice and using it
- providing organizational guidance whenever employees need it
- not asking people to do things they aren't able or willing to do
- making their objectives clear at the beginning
- being available to workers and being generous with their time

- not forcing people to be something they're not.
- finding the resources employees genuinely need to do their jobs
- resisting the temptation to change the rules in the middle of the project unless it is absolutely essential

Notice that some of these items are also on the NT Visionary's list, even though NT Visionaries and SJ Organizers are often at each other's throat. For instance, both will agree with the phrase "making the time frames clear and giving the reasoning behind them," but their reasons will be quite different. The SJ Organizers favor setting clear goals, so that they can be met by organized action. They agree with the phrase "time frames clear." The NT Visionaries don't really care about the particular times; give them the reasoning behind the time frames and they will figure out the schedules for themselves, though not necessarily the times anyone else thinks are scheduled.

The SJ Organizers, bless them, are probably the least appreciated of the temperaments. They just take care of things, whether they're fun or not, and they do it so well that we others tend not to notice them except when they go a little overboard and try to do everything for everybody.

8.2.4 *The SP Troubleshooter*

Troubleshooters (SP, or Sensing Perceiver) like getting the job done and want quick fixes, not elaborate plans. They say, "If it ain't broke, don't fix it." They also say, "If I can't fix it, it ain't broke."

The way to spot an SP Troubleshooter is to ask for, and get, a quick-and-dirty solution, for an SP values results above all else. In some circumstances, the SP's quick-and-dirty solution is more dirty than quick, if you add the clean-up time that will be required. When it comes to software, the SP's favorite word seems to be *zap*, and SP Troubleshooters often see configuration management systems as the devil's own invention.

From our list of desirable managerial actions, the SP Troubleshooter would probably approve of these:

- not constraining workers any more than is essential
- ensuring there is some real part for everyone to play
- setting things up so people can experience early success
- creating an environment in which it's okay to have fun
- understanding and forgiving mistakes
- changing their plans to fit environmental changes

Again, the SP Troubleshooters can agree with the same statements that the other temperaments approve, but for different reasons. When the NT Visionaries applaud a manager for "not constraining workers any more than is essential," they are thinking about not constraining ideas. The SP Troubleshooter is much more concerned with not constraining actions.

Or the NF Catalysts value a manager's "understanding and forgiving mistakes," because that is the decent way to treat people. The SP Troubleshooters value the same characteristic, but for a different reason: Not allowing them to make mistakes is like tying their hands behind their back.

Actions, too, may be the same for different temperaments, but for different reasons. My partner, Dani, tells the following story from one of her workshops: "I was teaching about temperaments and asserted that SP Troubleshooters are the type of people who jump out of airplanes just for the fun of it. Cora, the one SP in the class, nodded her head vigorously, so I asked her to tell about her experience. She said she had done it 'just to see what it was like.' I asked if she was going to do it again, and she said, 'Probably not. It was fun, but now I've done it already.'

"I was very pleased with myself, until Jerry asked if anyone else in the class had ever jumped out of an airplane. To my chagrin, Stuart, an SJ Organizer, raised his hand, seemingly contradicting my theory. Trying to put a good face on things, I asked Stuart why he had jumped. His answer was simple and direct as only an SJ Organizer's answer can be: 'Because the sergeant ordered me to.'"

8.3 Temperaments in Action

Temperament shows itself best in action—the way people prefer to handle situations. These preferences affect the way they try to control situations, the kinds of situations in which they are most comfortable, and the ones they find uncomfortable or even intolerable.

8.3.1 Kind of control

There's an obvious relationship between the four temperaments and the four different kinds of control: intellectual, physical, emergency, and emotional. The NT Visionaries, of course, tend to think of intellectual ways to control a situation, while the NF Catalysts prefer to work on the emotional plane. The SJ Organizers favor physical control that systematizes everything, while the SP Troubleshooters like to handle emergencies so much that they may create them even when they don't exist. Here's an experience I had with an SP Troubleshooter that filled me with awe:

I was working on a systems design project with an airline whose reservation system tended to fail whenever there was some sort of weather emergency. As part of the project, I was given a tour of one of their hubs. The tour guide was one of those people who run around the airport in gold or red jackets helping passengers who have missed flights, lost baggage or children, or need some other sort of special handling. After the tour, I thanked my host, who shook my hand enthusiastically and said, "Well, it was okay, but you should try to come back when there's a blizzard. That's when it's really interesting around here, because the computer system always breaks down!" If any SJ Organizers had overheard this comment, they would have called the SP Troubleshooter "irresponsible."

Because temperaments indicate only preferences, they don't necessarily guide a person to the kind of control that's most appropriate for the situation. The manager's job is to rise above simple type preferences and consciously consider all control possibilities. One way to do this, if there's time, is to consult someone from each of the four temperaments before deciding the best way to handle the situation. Although preference does not necessarily imply competence—there are plenty of cruel NF Catalysts and disorganized SJ Organizers—each temperament does tend to have more experience, both good and bad, with its preferred type of control.

8.3.2 Cultural patterns

Because each software cultural pattern favors different kinds of control, each temperament tends to react differently to each pattern.

In Variable (Pattern 1) organizations, the NT Visionaries revel in their independence; the NF Catalysts try to form small teams; the SJ Organizers go nuts; and the SP Troubleshooters are like pigs in mud.

In Routine (Pattern 2) organizations, the NFs work hardest to protect against unfeeling management, while the SPs move to the Help Desk or volunteer for tiger teams to patch the many faults. The SJs are turned loose to indulge their deepest fantasies of control, causing the NTs to rebel—or move to management.

In Steering (Pattern 3) organizations, the NFs happily steer by providing feedback to and about people. The NTs move into planning, where they envision new destinations for the NFs. The SPs are not too happy much of the time, because there are fewer breakdowns, or emergencies. The SJs are happy, but nervous about it because they can't figure out where the orderliness is coming from or what the rules are. In particular, they enjoy the teamwork, but worry about just who should get rewarded for the team's success.

8.3.3 Cost and schedule overruns

Software projects often overrun their cost and schedule estimates and team members do not hesitate to name someone or something as the sole culprit. But there may be many culprits, since a project is staffed with many people, and each temperament if unchecked will contribute to overruns in characteristic ways.

The NT Visionaries characteristically ignore the details of what it really takes to do something. Their visions wouldn't be useful without this ability to ignore details, but their estimates may omit essential tasks, thus making their underestimates look like overruns. One way to balance this tendency is to have the SJ Organizers check the estimates, although this effort will prove maddening to the NT Visionaries.

The NF Catalysts' obsession that everybody agree on everything tends to allow unreasonable or impractical objections to slow down the project. A good way to balance this tendency is to get the NF Catalysts to agree on reasonable decision processes early, before any particular person is being considered. Then the project members must follow these processes, reminding the NF Catalysts that they agreed in advance.

The SJ Organizers' concern with following procedures strictly tends to waste time on procedures that aren't really necessary in each particular circumstance. To counteract this tendency, be sure any written procedures specify not just what, but when. Reminding the SJ Organizers of the extra costs and delays doesn't hurt either.

The SP Troubleshooters' quick-and-dirty solutions may result in quality problems that take a long time to fix. To balance this tendency, insist on change control and technical reviews of all changes. Be careful, though: The SP Troubleshooters can be charmingly persuasive.

8.3.4 Reaction to error

People of all temperaments react to errors, but their reactions differ. Managers can use these reactions to motivate people of each temperament to prevent errors.

The NT Visionaries detest any error because they want their vision to be perfectly realized. Remind them of this when they get impatient with details.

The NF Catalysts detest errors because they don't want anyone to suffer from the system's faults. Remind them of this when they don't want to hurt anyone by pointing out mistakes.

The SJ Organizers see failures as wasteful. They can be great allies in your fight against error, but they sometimes miss the forest for the trees. Remind them that error prevention is not just a matter of getting the commas and semicolons right, and that too much attention to detail may make them miss something really big and costly.

The SP Troubleshooters are not disturbed by errors in the same way the other temperaments are. They see failures as (short-term) problems to solve, which is an acceptable viewpoint unless they get careless. Remind them that it is more clever to prevent error than to fix it, and that it is boring to fix the same errors over and over. Teaming them with SJ Organizers can slow them down a bit, but don't expect them to like it.

8.3.5 Observation

Volume 2 deals with the topic of observation as a requirement for control, but does not discuss the influence of the observer's personality on project control. Let's update that topic here.

Of all the MBTI dimensions, the S/N (Sensing/Intuitive) dimension obviously affects observational style the most. The Sensors want directly observable or measurable facts; the Intuitives want principles that save them the trouble of having to observe or measure anything. In arguments, they will have radically different ideas of what constitutes evidence, but they will have to learn patience with the others' views.

Volume 2 also discusses observer positions: Whenever you act as an observer, you have a choice of where to "stand" to make your observations: the self, other, or context positions. Obviously, a congruent position is no single one of these positions, but moves among them as required by the situation. Each temperament, however, tends to prefer a specific position.

The SJ Organizers and SP Troubleshooters easily take the self position, inside themselves (the *insider* position). This position gives them the ability to realize what their own interests are, why they are behaving the way they are, and what they might be contributing to the situation. From this position, however, an SJ Organizer or SP Troubleshooter may fail to notice how others could be involved, and also fail to notice big-picture consequences.

The NF Catalysts easily take the other position, inside another person, observing from that point of view (the *other* or *empathic* position). This position gives them the ability to understand why other people are reacting the way they do. The NF Catalysts, however, often fail to notice that they are not actually inside the other person, but only imagining that they are. They may then "know" what other people want, which gets them in a heap of trouble.

The NT Visionaries favor the context position, outside, looking at themselves and at others (the *outsider* position). This position gives them the ability to understand and place things in context not only in space, but in time as well. From this distant position, however, they may forget that those little specks on the horizon are human beings.

8.3.6 Interaction

Temperaments also describe some of the characteristic ways people interact. *Volume* 2 uses the Satir Interaction Model (Figure 8-1) as an overall framework for discussing the way people observe and take action.[5] Each of the four temperaments has a characteristic type of mistake people make when interacting.

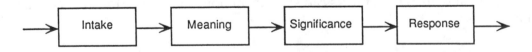

Figure 8-1.   The four basic parts of the Satir Interaction Model.

The NT visionaries and NF catalysts, both being Intuitive, skip quickly over the Intake step. After all, they believe "that's only data." The NTs tend to go instantly to Meaning, while the NFs tend to jump immediately to Significance. Seeing a design flaw, an NT might exclaim, "It won't work," leaving others in the room to wonder what "it" is. An NF, seeing the same flaw, might say, ominously, "We're in a lot of trouble," leaving even the NTs to wonder why. To counteract these tendencies to omit observations and skip immediately to conclusions, a manager can use the Data Question: "What did you see or hear that led you to that conclusion?"[6]

The Sensors, however, have very different reactions. The SJ Organizers tend to stay in Intake mode too long, gathering fact after fact after fact, long after there is more than sufficient data to come to a practical conclusion (at least for us Intuitives). You may be able to help the SJ by setting time-limited checkpoints at which you ask, "What can we conclude from the data we have so far?"

The SP Troubleshooters actually use the whole process rather well, but tend to go so fast that it looks to others as if they are jumping instantly to Response. Moreover, SPs may grow impatient when asked to explain the steps of how they arrived at their response. In that case, you can appeal to their desire to be clever, and ask them to teach you how they did it.

8.4 Temperaments As Tools for Understanding

Let me conclude this abbreviated discussion of temperament with some advice from my colleague Dan Starr. In Dan's words, the main values of any "typing" scheme (not just the MBTI model and Kiersey and Bates's Temperament system) can be summarized as follows:

- They remind me that people are different—in a lot of ways.
- They give me some models of the areas in which people are different.
- They invite me to ask what I prefer in a number of areas—and allow me to get a better understanding of who I prefer to be.
- They remind me, when I'm having trouble understanding some other person, that it just might be because we prefer to approach the world differently.
- They give me some models of approaches to the world other than mine, which may allow me to solve communication problems ...
- ... or which may remind me of other ways in which I might approach a problem at hand.

Dan sums this all up by saying, "I try to use the temperament/type models as tools for understanding and influencing myself, not for labeling others." We would all do well to follow his example.

8.5 Helpful Hints and Suggestions

1. Although understanding types and temperaments is useful, don't try to apply them too widely. For example, high drama, which we characteristically find in Variable (Pattern 1) and Routine (Pattern 2) organizations, attracts certain people and turns off others. Part of this may be attributed to type, but there are

other important factors. Those attracted to dramatic situations at work tend to have few outside connections or interests. You can generally tell from their conversations that all that interests them in life is the drama of software development.

2. One of my INFP tendencies is to tease my NT Visionary and SJ Organizer friends when I think they're taking things too seriously. The NFs know how to tease, but our teasing can also be felt as cruelty to NTs and SJs. My colleague Judy Noe read a draft of this chapter and told me she was disappointed that I hadn't given the NT point of view a fair representation. She said that she, as an NT, has a hard time speaking on her own behalf, and hoped that I, an NF Catalyst, would do it for her. I revised the chapter, and I hope that my caricature of the NT comes across as a more lovable person. Though some people see NTs as stiff and aloof, it's sometimes more useful to see them as soft, cuddly bunnies hiding their sensitivity in a protective layer.

3. Here's Dan Starr's hint on another way we NFs use the other position: Sometimes, when I'm having a hard time solving what would seem to be a straightforward problem, I try to take another temperament—like the time I had a real short-term, quick-and-dirty issue to deal with, so I asked myself "How would an SP handle this?" It worked, and I came up with a solution I don't think I would have discovered had I stayed in my "preferred" NF position.

4. As they come to understand types and temperaments, many people wonder why Kiersey and Bates chose just the four combinations they did. Kiersey and Bates's book is the best place to find that explanation, but I can give my own explanation of why I think they made a good choice. I immediately discovered that the four temperaments precisely matched my own MOI model[7] of successful leadership. (MOI stands for motivation, organization, and information as the three ingredients of being a successful technical leader.) When it comes to acts of leadership, the NFs lean toward Motivation, the SJs prefer Organization, and the NTs thrive on Information. Kiersey and Bates also showed me that I was missing one component: the troubleshooter role played by the SP. Since then, I've always found this model useful in understanding how people behave, both individually and in groups.

8.6 Summary

✓   The combination of MBTI dimensions produces sixteen identifiable personality types. Subcombinations produce other useful views of personality, such as the four temperaments of Kiersey and Bates.

✓   There are four different kinds of control involved in controlling software development: intellectual, physical, emergency, and emotional, which can be related to the four temperaments.

✓ Most of the major innovations in software have been in the area of improving intellectual control, at least they were the innovations that received the most attention.

✓ Physical control is introduced into software to deal with real-world deviations from the pure intellect model of software, either by prevention or detection and correction.

✓ As we develop routines to handle intellectual and physical problems, we find that our ability to manage well depends not on our ability to handle routine situations, but on our ability to handle exceptional situations.

✓ Sometimes, the situation is physically and intellectually simple with no emergency conditions, yet people still fail to perform perfectly. As long as people are involved, the other three types of control become meaningless without emotional control.

✓ Strong emotions produce stereotyped behavior, which means that behavioral variety is reduced. Anything that reduces variety reduces the manager's ability to control.

✓ The NT Visionary likes working with ideas. The NF Catalyst likes working with people to help them grow, and is concerned that people not suffer. The SJ Organizer likes order. The SP Troubleshooter likes getting the job done. Because each software cultural pattern favors different kinds of control, each temperament reacts differently to each pattern. Each temperament, if unchecked, will contribute to overruns in characteristic ways.

✓ People of all temperaments react to errors, but they tend to react in different ways. Managers can use these reactions to motivate people to prevent errors.

✓ When observing, the SJ Organizers and SP Troubleshooters easily take the self position; the NF Catalysts easily take the other position; and the NT Visionaries favor the context position.

✓ In interactions with other people, the NTs tend to bypass the Intake step and go instantly to Meaning, while the NFs tend to jump immediately to Significance. The SJs tend to stay in Intake too long, gathering too many facts; while the SPs actually use the whole process rather well, but tend to go so fast that it looks to others as if they leap instantly to Response.

8.7 Practice

1.   The descriptions in this chapter are all from the point of view of one INFP, and are therefore only a small part of the picture. Describe the temperaments from your point of view, then share your descriptions with friends of each temperament. If you don't have friends of each temperament, make some.

2.   Choose some problem that you've recently solved (or failed to solve) and try looking at it from the point of view of the three temperaments that aren't your own.

3.   As suggested by Payson Hall: Based on the simple descriptions in this chapter, which of the temperaments seems most compatible with you? Remembering that they are generalizations and tendencies, try to determine which you identify with most strongly, then take the MBTI and compare the results.

4.   Again, suggested by Payson Hall: Have someone you trust and work with read this chapter. Ask that person which of these temperaments best describes who you are.

9

Recognizing Differences As Assets

Women who seek to be equal with men lack ambition.
— Timothy Leary

The dimensions of the MBTI model certainly point out important differences among people for the manager to understand and work with, but they are no more important than many other human differences. Indeed, any difference can become important when it is not understood, accepted, or handled well. This chapter will touch on several other dimensions of differences that interfere with some managers' ability to be effective controllers.

Each difference in this chapter merits at least an entire book of its own, so consider these sections as mere introductions. If you want to learn more, please consult one or more of the excellent references cited in this chapter.

9.1 Why Differences Are Assets

Ashby's Law of Requisite Variety says that variety is important for effective managerial control. It does not say that the control has to be hierarchical. The software business, being so complex, is unlikely to be controlled effectively by one manager telling a whole lot of technical people exactly what to do. Control must reside within every person involved, and ordinarily that will require a great many differences among those people. So two questions managers often want to answer are, "Which sort of person is right for this job?" and "Which differences will affect performance?"

The Association for Psychological Type[1] is the principal resource center for information on the MBTI model. Their *Journal of Psychological Type* regularly publishes research articles, many of which report studies of type distributions in different occupational groups. One lesson of these studies is that there is generally no right answer to the question "Which sort is right for this job?"

The tables in these articles generally show that people of all personality types can do almost any job, although there are preferences for certain types in certain kinds of work. The only exception was an article about tax preparers for H&R Block in which every one of 31 preparers were ISTJs, or the "trustee" archetype. Given my image of the job of tax preparer, an ISTJ trustee is a perfect match for the job: the person who wants to prepare my return and the person I want to prepare my return.

I can't imagine what it would be like to enjoy preparing my own tax return, let alone the returns for hundreds of other people. Still, I know intellectually that some people relish this job, and I know emotionally that I'm very happy there are such people. Otherwise, I would have to do my own tax return, and I'm sure I wouldn't do a very good job of it—not because of incompetence, but because of distaste for the job.

The same is true for the software business, although software work seems far more varied than tax preparation. At least that's my perception, perhaps because I know so much more about software work than tax return preparation. Because software work consists of so many varied tasks, it's unlikely that any one personality type, one set of skills, or one viewpoint would be best suited to all parts of the job. That's why we need differences among software people, no matter how much grief these differences may cause the software engineering manager.

To gain an idea of the power to be harnessed by exploiting differences among software workers, we'll first consider two contrasting models of how a manager could use variability: Management by Selection and Management by Systematic Improvement.

9.2 Management by Selection Model

The Management by Selection Model is a variety-reducing approach that is based on the One-Dimensional Selection Model applied to the technical staff. This approach produces two faulty assumptions:

- Programmers (analysts, testers, writers, or whoever) are born, not made.

- Technical people can be ranked on a one-dimensional scale.

Here is the way this model is applied:

1.   Identify the bad programmers (or any other technical workers).

2.   Get rid of the worst ones.

3.   Repeat this process; each time you do so, the average ability rises.

As suggested by the dynamic shown in Figure 9-1, this selection process can be effective. If the average quality of the programmers is too low, remove some poor ones, thus raising the average.

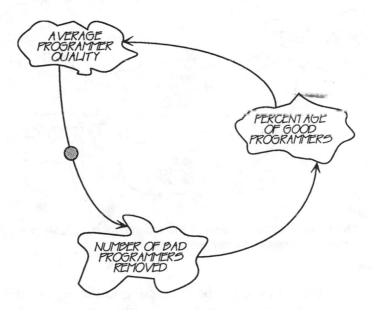

Figure 9-1.   The dynamic idea behind the Management by Selection Model of improving technical capability.

This process, however, is slow to show improvement. In order for it to work correctly, there must be enough time on the job to demonstrate who is good and who isn't. Another problem is that it produces only mediocre results, because there's no way the average performance can improve above the best programmer in the bunch unless you add new programmers from a fresh source.

Yet another problem is the need for a continuing supply of new programmers, at least some of whom are above your current average. On the one hand, best may attract best, so morale may go up as long as you're in the phase of getting rid of the real stinkers. But as you continue to apply this method, your organization may get a reputation for summarily firing even good people, which may drain the pool of applicants. Moreover, your best performers may leave because this method doesn't really focus on their performance. In that case, the method may reduce the variance in programmer performance, but not actually raise the mean. Figure 9-2 shows a more complete dynamic that takes such effects into account.

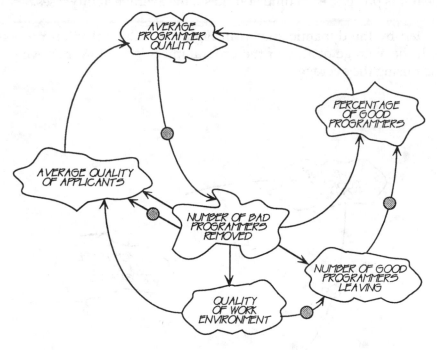

Figure 9-2.   The potential improvements of the Management by Selection approach may be diminished by second-order effects.

Removing poor performers need not be depressing to the organization. If someone is truly a detriment to the team, other team members may welcome that person's removal. But swooping in from above and removing people—no matter how welcome or fair—will frighten those who remain: "Could I be next?" they have to wonder.

Figure 9-2 suggests that the Selection Model works best if the removal of the worst performers is done without disturbing the rest of the organization, but that's not easy to do. Any manager skilled enough to fire people without upsetting the rest of the organization is skilled enough to use a much more promising model of improving technical quality.

9.3 Management by Systematic Improvement Model

The Selection Model says that technical people can be ranked on a one-dimensional scale. The Management by Systematic Improvement Model, in contrast, is based on multi-dimensional thinking:

- People differ in many dimensions that can affect performance.
- Programmers (analysts, testers, writers, or whoever) can learn.

Here is the way this model is applied:

1. Identify the good programmers (or any other technical workers).

2. Analyze the performance of the best to determine why they are doing so well.

3. Develop systems (training, technical reviews, teams, mentoring, or modeling) for passing these best processes on to large numbers of people.

The underlying dynamic of the Management by Systematic Improvement Model is diagrammed in Figure 9-3. Like the previous model, it is based on selection—not on the selection of people, but the selection of processes. Even more, it's based on communication and learning and is a living, not a dead, model.

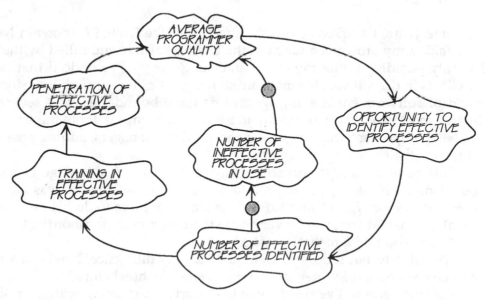

Figure 9-3.   The Systematic Improvement Model is based on the selection of processes, not people.

The model says

1.   Attention to process increases the awareness of what's effective.

2.   Training increases the penetration of existing effective processes.

3.   Identifying effective processes leads to abandoning the ineffective processes.

The training, of course, takes many forms. For one thing, simply going through the identification process tends to train everyone involved, so a group effort will have better results than an isolated team of experts. Second, much of the training will be invisible, as many ineffective processes will simply disappear once they have been identified. Third, the training will be more effective if it's safe, particularly if it's not used to identify "bad" people and blame or fire them.

For instance, some people think that the purpose of technical reviews is to catch people doing bad things, but their greatest benefit is catching people doing good things. If I'm reviewing your work and see something good, I can safely incorporate it into my own work without ever admitting I was bad.

In the Systematic Improvement approach, one of the manager's most important jobs is to create and maintain this atmosphere of safety in technical reviews, in personnel reviews, and in any other normal activity. In particular, it must always be safe to be different.

9.4 Cultures

For some years, I worked across the street from the United Nations in New York City. Taking my brown-bag lunch in the UN park, I was enthralled by the cultural diversity parading by for my entertainment. Recently, I've noticed that several of my clients in the software business are showing a similar cultural diversity. Today's world of software engineering ignores national boundaries, and several of my clients export their wares to more than a hundred countries. From these same countries, they import software engineers and product managers, adding greatly to the richness of their working environment.

This cultural richness doesn't always seem like an advantage to their managers. One such manager asked me to consult on a problem he was having with Chou, a developer from Hong Kong. "He simply refuses to do his assigned work, no matter what I do or say. I'm very close to firing him for insubordination."

"Have you told him that?" I asked.

"Absolutely, but it doesn't seem to make any difference. I've been a manager for twelve years, and I've never run into anyone like him before."

Perhaps because I've spent more than thirty years living with an anthropologist, the phrase "anyone like him" touched a sensitive spot in my mind. I arranged to interview Chou, calling upon what little I knew about Chinese culture[2] and especially Hong Kong Chinese culture.[3] Here's what I discovered, as best an American can communicate the situation:

Chou had been a brilliant student in a doctoral program in computer science at a top university, but had dropped out for financial reasons. Like many Hong Kong Chinese working overseas, he was sending a good part of his salary back home to contribute to the family's savings so that if necessary they could leave Hong Kong when the People's Republic of China takes over in 1997.

He really wanted to continue his studies and eventually become a professor, but family obligations came first, even though the family now had enough money to escape if necessary. He could not even think of asking the family's permission to leave work and return to school. They would certainly tell him to do so, because his becoming a scholar would bring great honor to the family. But seeming to beg off of his family obligations would bring him personal dishonor, so he was caught in a bind—one that was incomprehensible to his American manager.

Chou was refusing to do assignments in the hope that he would indeed be fired. Then he could write his family and say he had lost his job because he lacked a Ph.D. This sounds ridiculous to an American, but Chou's family knew that nobody could order a scholar to do anything he didn't want to do, nor would fire him for refusing such an order. Having been fired, he could honorably return to school to earn his doctorate—not for selfish reasons, but for the sake of the family honor.

Chou's American manager was astonished to discover Chou's "reasoning." Once he had some understanding, the manager could work out a plan whereby Chou could take advantage of the company's tuition benefit program, return to school while working part-time, and complete his doctorate in less than three years, using some company-related work as his thesis topic. Chou became a model employee, able and willing to contribute from his unique cultural viewpoint.

9.5 Females and Males

Your own culture often gets in the way of being an effective manager. Here are two value statements from American culture that can reduce the variety of your responses:

- Reason, logic, numbers, utility, and practicality are good.
- Feeling, intuition, qualitative judgments, and pleasure are bad.

These are especially harmful when combined with two other American cultural values:

- Men should be rational, logical, facile with numbers, and practical.
- Women should be feeling, intuitive, qualitative, and pleasure-oriented.

Managers who subscribe to these cultural values may find themselves cut off from half the best information and ideas available to them. On the other hand, managers who pretend that these are not American cultural ideas will fail to see others operating as if they held these values. For whatever reason, men and women of most cultures typically operate differently in some areas.

For example, American men and women tend to use language differently. I was recently working with a puzzling conflict among several subproject managers who were part of a team building a distributed network for price quotations. Before I arrived on the scene, Adrian had accused Opal and Harriet of gossiping about another member of the team. In the meeting I attended, Adrian was describing some of his customer's foibles. Harriet exploded. "When I talk about our colleague to try to understand him better, you call it gossip. So what do you call it now, when you're tearing down your customer behind his back?"

Adrian shrugged his shoulders as if to say, "What can I do?" and turned to me to help him out. I was tempted to hide my confusion by quoting Nietzche, who said, "Woman was God's second mistake." Being a male myself, I was just as puzzled as Adrian. I remembered a book I had seen—*Everything That Men Know About Women.* The problem was that every page of the book was blank!

Some months later, I was reading Deborah Tannen's book *You Just Don't Understand: Women and Men in Conversation.* Tannen's pages were not blank, and on one of them I read the following:

> The relatively positive or negative value on talking about personal details—of one's own life or others'—is reflected in the positive and negative views of gossip. One man commented that he and I seemed to have different definitions of gossip. He said, "To you, it seems to be a discussion of personal details about people known to the conversationalists. To men, it's a discussion about the weaknesses, character flaws, and failures of third persons, so that participants in the conversation can feel superior to them. This seems unworthy, hence gossip is bad."[4]

Tannen goes on to explain the difference between talking-*about*—which is a way of establishing connection with an absent person—and talking-*against*—which is a way of redressing an imbalance of power. Opal and Harriet felt they were talking about their teammate, but Adrian felt they were talking against him. This would have been okay with Adrian—witness his talking about his customer—to bring an arrogant fool down to size, but it was inappropriate with a teammate. The women, on the other hand, clearly saw Adrian putting down his customer, and that kind of gossip was not okay with them, nor was his perceived hypocrisy.

Had I known Tannen's work at the time, I might have been able to apply her sage advice:

> What is the solution, then, if women and men are talking at cross-purposes, about gossip as about other matters? How are we to open lines of communica-

tion? The answer is for men and women to try to take each other on their own terms rather than applying the standard of one group to the behavior of the other. This is not a "natural" thing to do, because we tend to look for a single "right" way of doing things.[5]

You would do well to follow this advice, and even to generalize it to any two groups possessing different cultures. To do that, however, you will have to learn about the other cultures, and that will take much work. Certainly, you won't learn all you need to know by just reading this book or this chapter. Indeed, each of these sections merits a few books, at least. Of course, the subject of females and males merits its own library.

9.6 Other Significant Differences

One of the great cultural treasures we Americans have is the Declaration of Independence, which states, "All men [which now includes women and descendants of former slaves] are created equal." This doesn't mean that all people are created the *same*. As I discussed earlier, the manager's job is to employ people's differences to best advantage for the task at hand, while treating all people as equals, with respect and dignity.

9.6.1 Sensory modalities

Volume 2 of this series discusses some different ways people use their brains and sensory abilities. For instance, people differ greatly in what neurolinguistic programming calls their "strategies." These are the programs by which people order the ways they take in information—their internal and external pictures, sounds, smells, tastes, and feelings—when they solve a problem.

Some strategies are effective in one situation and not in another. For example, programmers often use their personal sequence in locating faults. Here, for example, is my preferred sequence:

1.   First, I scan a program visually for any breaks in the pattern.

2.   If that reveals nothing, I imagine myself being the computer, and sense what it feels like to run this program.

3.   If either step 1 or step 2 turns up something funny, I read the curious segment out loud to myself.

If these steps fail, I usually turn to someone else for help, but I am generally adept at finding faults in programs (not so adept at preventing them, however).

Suppose I am now a manager, trying to guide others in how to be an effective locator of faults. Is my strategy going to be effective for other people? Not likely, because people differ greatly. Yet managers often impose their own strategies unknowingly on a programmer for whom those strategies are neither familiar nor effective.

A more fruitful management approach is to learn about differences in strategy,[6] then apply them to determine what strategy the other person is using. If it's not working, the manager can then suggest minor modifications to adapt the strategy to the current situation.

9.6.2 Ability

Another difference is ability. Most software people want to believe that it's okay to treat people differently if they have different abilities, but do we know how to recognize ability? For example, managers often want to hire superprogrammers, but do they actually know how to recognize them? One of my E-mail colleagues, Tom Bragg, questioned some of the statements that I make in *Volume 1* about superprogrammers,[7] which has led me to try to frame a more accurate statement:

Typical shops (generally Variable or Pattern 1 organizations) that make the mistake of picking someone to be a superprogrammer do so for one of several reasons (I use the masculine pronoun, because this is almost never done for females):

1.   Someone claims to be a superprogrammer, and there is little evidence one way or the other on the matter (as when he is new to the organization), and the managers are sufficiently desperate to believe anything not directly contradicted by any facts at their disposal.

2.   Someone has done a superior job on one or two other projects (usually much smaller, and perhaps by luck), and the managers are sufficiently desperate to believe anything not directly contradicted by any facts at their disposal.

3.   Someone has actually done consistently superior work on a number of similar projects and has a sufficient sense of duty (or pity for the poor people involved in the project). This is the one method that works, but note that the superprogrammer will *not* accept jobs that he really cannot do. A big (but often unnoticed) part of the superprogrammer's prowess is the ability to say no to projects that really are hopeless. Often, this ability comes from an early experience of burning out or suffering some personal loss, such as getting divorced (that's what happened to me, more than thirty years ago, and it's a lesson I'll never forget).

This superprogrammer approach works well enough in Variable (Pattern 1) organizations, but it has several problems. The two most common ones are these:

1.   Nobody knows how to create superprogrammers, and the ones that have been created have been made at great expense (a lot of it personal and of a kind you don't want to ask of anyone; I can assure you that no project is worth losing your kids over). So the method is not easily extended to a large number of people, although with the right environment and the right pay, some organizations can keep a couple of superprogrammers on staff.

2.   The dwarfs may not like it, and they are keeping the mines going after all. We need a new category, ultra-superprogrammer, to characterize those even rarer individuals who are superprogrammers yet work in such a way that everyone loves to have them around because they learn from them. (Well, almost everybody. There's no accounting for envy.)

9.6.3 Physical capacity

Nowadays, the term *handicapped* is not politically correct, the currently favored term being *differently advantaged*. This doesn't exactly trip off the tongue, but it does touch on a great truth. Over the years, I have worked with a number of blind or deaf programmers and managers, and, without exception, I learned startling new things from each of them.

I've also noticed that groups with a blind or deaf member communicate much better because their differently advantaged member forces them to keep communication in the forefront. Similarly, when the group has a member lacking the ability to move about freely on two legs, the group members pay attention to the physical aspects of their processes, which results in more efficiency even among the bipeds.

9.6.4 Age

We all say it's wrong to discriminate against people because they are unable to do things physically. But do we really act on this belief? In many of the Variable (Pattern 1) organizations I've worked with—especially software startups—the corporate culture is based on a seven-day week of fourteen-hour days. This is great for the young and healthy, but what about the old or the not-so-healthy? Doesn't this culture discriminate against them?

Each age brings its own advantages. The young have energy; the old have experience. After three-score years, I find it harder to code all night, but I've also learned things that allow me to create lots more high-quality code in a normal working day. Of course, though experience is the best teacher, the best teacher doesn't necessarily teach anything to an inept student. Similarly, though youth has energy, it does seem to take more than randomly directed energy to create high-quality code.

Each age also brings its own typical crises that managers would rather not have to deal with. The twenty-year-old man may spend all his time romancing the co-workers in the office. The thirty-year-old man may be fretting over being unmarried, or being married to a woman whose career is surpassing his. The forty-year-old man in a moody mid-life crisis may lose many working hours daydreaming about escaping to Fiji and writing a great novel, or wearing flannel shirts and living in the woods.

Yet incongruent managers may be even more distressed by employees who can deal with age-related situations. For instance, the science-fiction author Ursula LeGuin observed in one of her novels, "But old women are different from everybody else, they say what they think."[8] Among incongruent managers, saying what you think is not a prized employee attribute; and these managers may notice that this attribute increases with age, even in some men. In general, older employees won't put up with the same things that younger employees will, and that can be either good or bad, depending on your management style.

9.7 Helpful Hints and Suggestions

1.   If you don't have much experience with other cultures, there are many paths for getting some. Travel, of course, can be helpful, but not if you sit on a tour bus listening to the official explanation of things. You would do better to spend an evening or two reading a good book of advice for the intercultural traveller.[9]

2.   If your group is not so fortunate as to have a differently advantaged member, you can gain some of the advantages by taking turns being the member with a special point of view. Spend a day at the office blindfolded. Wear ear plugs. Rent a wheelchair. I guarantee that you will learn important things, your work will be better, and your group will become a more cohesive team.

3.   Some managers fantasize that life was easier when they had to deal only with people like themselves, because they then didn't have many differences to contend with. But the modern view of the brain is that we each are multiple selves, as different as different individuals.[10] So becoming aware of your own multiple intelligences can help you understand how to deal with the diversity on your staff.

4.   When selecting the attributes of people to work with, remember that intellect is great, but character is more important.

5.   A common practice in our society is to set up one-dimensional rating systems that hide individual differences. Three common examples are IQ tests, grades in training courses, and personnel rankings, all of which are detrimental to an organizational goal to improve quality.

6.   Wayne Bailey, who reviewed an early draft of this book, warns that the cloud labeled "Quality of Work Environment" in Figure 9-2 doesn't refer to the physical work environment: "In one organization, they provide you with a great private office with windows, and constantly reward you for working harder and longer, but [they] practice the variety-reducing style of management. As we used to say, developers were treated like 'coding cattle.' If you weren't a good producer, they would get rid of you."

Presumably, you were transformed into meatballs for serving with spaghetti code.

9.8 Summary

✓   Any difference can become important when it is not understood, accepted, or handled well.

✓   The software business is unlikely to be controlled effectively by one manager telling a whole lot of technical people exactly what to do. Control must reside within every person involved, and that ordinarily will mean a great many individual differences in the way things are handled.

✓   One lesson of the MBTI studies published in the *Journal of Psychological Type* is that there is generally no perfect answer to the question "Which type is right for this job?" Generally, the studies show that people of all types can do almost any job, although there are preferences for certain types in certain kinds of work.

✓   Because software work consists of so many varied tasks, it's unlikely that any one personality type, one set of skills, or one point of view would be best suited to all parts of the total software job. That's why we need differences among software people.

✓   The Management by Selection Model is based on the One-Dimensional Selection Model applied to the technical staff. This approach advises managers to identify the "bad" programmers (or any other technical workers), get rid of the worst ones, and repeat this process so that the average ability rises.

✓   The Selection approach is slow to show improvement, and produces only mediocre results. The approach requires a continuing supply of new programmers, and may damage your organization's reputation among job applicants. Your best performers may leave because this method doesn't really focus on their performance.

✓   The Management by Systematic Improvement Model is based on multi-dimensional thinking. The model is applied by identifying the "good" programmers (or any other technical workers), analyzing the performance of the best to determine why they are doing so well, and developing systems (training, technical reviews, teams, mentoring, and modeling) for passing these best processes on to large numbers of people.

✓   The Systematic Improvement approach says that attention to the process will increase awareness of what's effective; training increases penetration of existing effective processes; and identifying effective processes leads to abandoning the ineffective processes.

✓   Organizations that import technical and managerial staff from other cultures add greatly to the richness of their working environment. This cultural richness, however, doesn't always seem like an advantage to the managers, who seldom have the training or experience to deal with it.

✓   For whatever reason, men and women of most cultures operate—on average—differently in some areas. Managers who favor "male" or "female" values may find themselves cut off from half the best information and ideas available to them.

✓   People differ greatly in what neurolinguistic programming calls their strategies. These are the programs by which people order the ways they take in information—their internal and external pictures, sounds, smells, tastes, and feelings—when they solve a problem. A toolkit of different strategies can be a great asset in difficult aspects of software work.

✓   Most software people believe that it's okay to treat people differently if they have different abilities, but they don't know how to recognize ability. Most also believe it's wrong to treat people differently if they are differently advantaged, but they fail to use what they could learn from them. Finally, discrimination based on age (either favoring young or old) is so universal in software that we seldom notice it, let alone take advantage of what lessons age differences can provide.

9.9 Practice

1.   Here are some more ideas from American culture that can reduce the variety of your responses:

  •   Fantasy and reflection are a waste of time, even crazy.
  •   Playfulness is for children only.

- Managing is serious business, and humor is out of place.
- Any problem can be solved by scientific thinking, training, or money.
- Fast is better than slow; time equals money.
- There is one solution to every problem.
- There are two sides to every question—not three, and not overlapping.

Pick one of these cultural "rules" that influences your own management style and find someone from another culture who is willing to discuss alternative ways of thinking.

2. In one organization, upper management established five different ranking systems based on different weights of the same productivity factors. Every worker was ranked according to all five systems. In their annual performance review, workers were rated based on the one scale by which they each performed the worst. Discuss what you think the managers were trying to accomplish, as opposed to what they probably accomplished. Can you see any possible good to having five separate rating scales, if they were used differently?

3. Discuss how you might combine the Selection and the Systematic Improvement models to produce an even more effective policy for upgrading technical quality.

4. Americans have a wonderful way of adopting people, artifacts, and practices as their own, then failing to notice that they aren't as American as apple pie. For instance, Lee Copeland, a Mormon friend from Salt Lake City, wrote me that he "got a real chuckle at home the other night. My daughter, who was born in India, was wearing her African T-shirt, eating Chinese food, and practicing her Spanish."

    Lee's chuckle presumably came from recognizing normally invisible multicultural origins. Look around you right now to see how many people, artifacts, and practices you can identify from cultures other than American culture, whatever that is.

5. After reviewing this chapter, my colleague Bill Pardee writes: "Since we work only on the problems we know about, the problems we don't know about have the best opportunity to grow out of control. Diversity, whether on a development team or among book reviewers, reduces the unrecognized problems. Diversity in activity, like not working on the weekend, also helps uncover problems and opportunities. Diversity in perspective (screen, paper, table of contents, outline) also helps."

    Try something diverse in your activities, such as not working on the weekend if that's your habit, or working then if it's not. Take notes on the previously unknown problems you discover. Take notes on the previously unknown solutions you notice.

10

Patterns of Incongruence

*Why is it we never have enough time
to do it right,
but always have enough time
to do it over?*
— Anonymous

This message, posted in many software organizations, tells us that a lack of time seems characteristic of our curious trade. If the technical staff is always hungry for time, their management seems literally starved. In many organizations, managers lack time because they aren't able to deal congruently with incongruence in others. Different cultural patterns have their characteristic patterns of incongruence, so that each pattern puts a different load on its managers.

10.1 Where Does the Time Go?

Author Linda Hill, in her brilliant study of recently promoted managers, notes that none of the managers seem to have enough time:

> Above all, they were struck by the unrelenting workload and pace of being a
> manager. When asked what advice he would give to someone considering a

management job, one of the managers commented: "This job is much harder than you think. It is 40 to 50 percent more work than being a producer! Who would ever have guessed?"[1]

Moreover, Hill cites many other studies that confirm what all of us have observed: Experienced managers never seem to have enough time either. In many software organizations, this management time frenzy is added to the endemic software schedule frenzy.

In *Volume 1* of this series, the Controller Fallacy[2] suggests that managers who are very busy are not generally doing a good job of control. If they're not doing a good job, where does all the time go?

To be effective, a manager or any other person acting as controller must not only take in data, but also consider all the intake, come to some sort of decision, and take action. Inasmuch as everybody in an organization is responsible for controlling something, it's possible to measure an organization's health through the people's characteristic decision-making styles. That's because people's inner feelings translate into characteristic styles of coping, which then translate into effective or ineffective controller actions.

Ineffective actions resulting from incongruence leave problems unresolved, so one effect of incongruence is an increase in the number of problems someone other than the originator must deal with. Thus, more incongruence creates the need for more problem-solving or fire-fighting time (Figure 10-1). In a recent conversation I had with Elaine Yarbrough, president of the Yarbrough Group of consultants and mediators, she said that her client managers report that more than a quarter of their time is spent managing conflict, much of which involves problems that seem to be solved yet return again.[3]

Figure 10-1.   One factor influencing the amount of time spent on a certain type of problem is how frequently that problem recurs, which for some problems depends directly on the amount of incongruent coping.

Such problems, you may think, must be nontechnical in nature, but that's not necessarily so. For example, consider debugging expertise, which most people think of as technical in nature, but skilled observers T.R. Riedl and his co-authors reported otherwise at a recent SEI conference:

> ... we are struck by the extent to which expertise in debugging is social and psychological expertise. Moreover, it is likely that much of this skill is used by developers in other applications than debugging. Debugging requires interpersonal skills because software systems are social products; given the ever-increasing size and complexity of software systems, these skills become more and more necessary.[4]

A major task of the software engineering manager is to help people in the organization develop their social skills, not just because the workplace is better when people are polite, but because social skills influence more and more the effectiveness of technical skills. Teaching social skills is an investment in problem resolution, but even more in problem prevention. As the organization learns to be congruent more frequently, the amount of time spent dealing with incongruence decreases. (See Figure 10-2.)

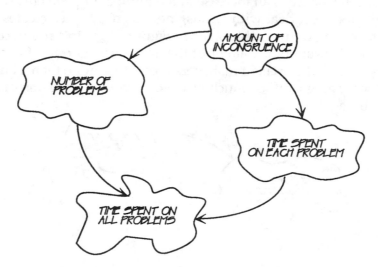

Figure 10-2.   The less congruent we are when dealing with a type of problem, the more time we'll spend on each problem, and the more problems we'll have, so our total time spent increases nonlinearly with the multiplication of these two causes.

The self-reinforcing loop of Figure 10-3 shows how an organization or individual locks onto a pattern of incongruent behavior. The same loop, however, describes how an organization can lock onto a pattern of congruence. What makes the difference is the quality of managers' decisions, as reflected in the behavior they display—behavior that others can use as a model.

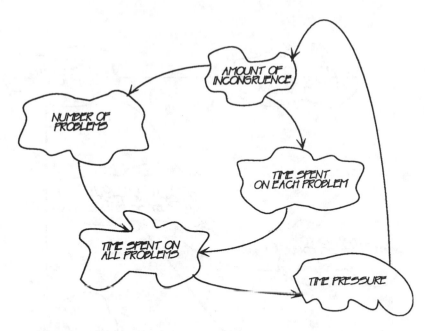

Figure 10-3.   As time pressure grows, incongruent behavior grows, which leads to more prob-
                lems and more time spent on each problem, which increases time pressure and
                completes a self-reinforcing loop.

This self-reinforcing loop exists in any industry, but it is especially prevalent in software engineering work because of the conflict between stiff quality and schedule demands. Feeling unable to trade off either quality or schedule goals, managers are too often tempted to sacrifice the quality of human interaction, for which they soon pay the price in both quality and schedule.

10.2 The Placating Pattern

In order to meet these demands, managers do many things that they know are harmful. To placate customers, they allow programmers to use shortcuts that go against all standards of good practice. The programmers themselves may beg to be allowed to omit technical reviews, tests, and other quality procedures, and the managers are all too willing to placate them by yielding. This placating pattern is especially common in Variable (Pattern 1) cultures, which goes a long way toward explaining why they are called variable cultures.

Placating, of course, is not a conscious choice, but comes out of the managers' feelings of low self-worth when facing customers and programmers. However, simply becoming conscious of the placating and its ill effects may not eradicate the placating pattern. To understand why not, study the dynamic in Figure 10-4.

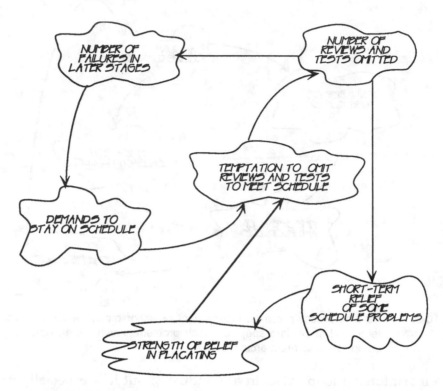

Figure 10-4.   Some success at placating programmers and customers by omitting reviews and tests can lead to an increased belief that reviewing and testing only delay the project, which leads to more problems with the schedule in the long run, which leads to the omission of more reviews and tests.

As a project falls slightly behind schedule, the manager is pressured by customers to get back on track, as well as by programmers to find quick-and-dirty solutions. Technical reviews may not seem to add a great value, and may even find problems that will slow down the project. This kind of thinking tempts the manager to allow the programmers to omit one of the initial reviews, or perhaps the second review of a product that didn't pass its initial review, especially since they are begging for this easy way out. The project now seems back on schedule, thus reinforcing the belief that placating both customers and programmers worked. In the long run, though, more failures show up, and now the faults behind them are harder to locate and harder to resolve, so the project falls further behind schedule.

At first, the temptation to skip a review is not very great because the manager knows better. With each "success," however, the temptation to skip a tough review gets less and less resistible, while at the same time each schedule slippage lowers the manager's feeling of self-worth. Eventually, the review system falls by the wayside, or exists in name only. Without an effective review system in place, the project finds faults at the latest, most costly time, with maximum impact on the schedule.

Managers use this delay in schedule to justify the omission of further reviews and tests, feeling worse and worse about themselves with each cycle and further delay.

10.3 The Blame Chain

One reaction to the effects of the placating pattern is to switch to blaming: managers acting abusively in the hope of getting employees to perform better. This unconscious pseudo-reasoning is the most frequent motivation for an organization to attempt to move from Variable (Pattern 1) to Routine (Pattern 2) cultures. Having a routine way of doing all projects makes it easier to identify the culprit when things go wrong: Just look for someone who didn't follow the routine. Using blaming behavior to try to fix employees has the dynamic illustrated in Figure 10-5, and is characteristic of many Routine (Pattern 2) organizations.

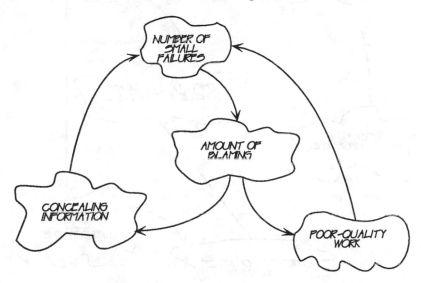

Figure 10-5.   Failures lead to blaming, and blaming leads to concealing information and to poor-quality work, perhaps intentionally to escape the abuse or perhaps explicitly to undermine the blaming manager.

When an employee or group makes a mistake or doesn't meet a schedule, the manager has extra problems to solve. Yielding to the temptation to blame the offenders soon leads to a lot of extra effort by the target to escape the abuse. On the other hand, the employees slowly build up resentment for the abusive manager. They find more and more ways to be unresponsive or even to sabotage that manager, which then leads to more failures.[5]

Why would an intelligent manager continue to blame? One possibility is ignorance of the dynamic of Figure 10-5, but that explains only a few cases. More frequently, managers continue to blame because of the dynamic of Figure 10-6.

At first, the temptation to blame may not be very great, perhaps because the manager doesn't really believe very strongly in the efficacy of blaming. With each "success," however, the belief grows stronger and the temptation to abuse gets less and less resistible. Eventually, everyone receives abuse from the manager without the slightest provocation, often because of something somebody else did. Although productivity may have initially increased, productivity eventually drops as more and more people come under fire from the abuse. Once the cycle starts, productivity continues to drop until the manager is in a continuous rage and becomes entirely ineffective.

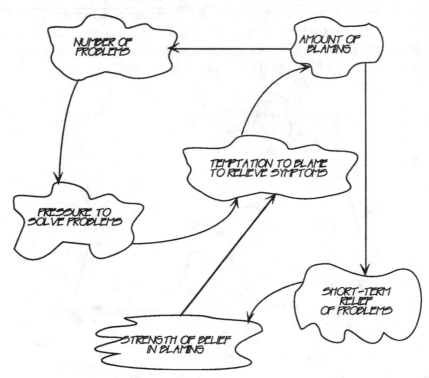

Figure 10-6.   Initial success at blaming employees can lead to an increased belief in the efficacy of a blaming management style, which leads to more problems with employees in the long run, which leads to more blaming.

10.4 The Addiction Cycle

Notice the similarity in dynamic structure between Figures 10-4 and 10-6, which has been generalized in Figure 10-7 and works like this:

1.   There is a short cycle in which doing X relieves symptoms.

2.   There is a longer cycle in which doing X makes those very symptoms worse.

3. The short cycle of addiction influences the strength of belief in X, so that the strength of belief in X grows the more that X is used, although in the long cycle, X leads to a worse situation.

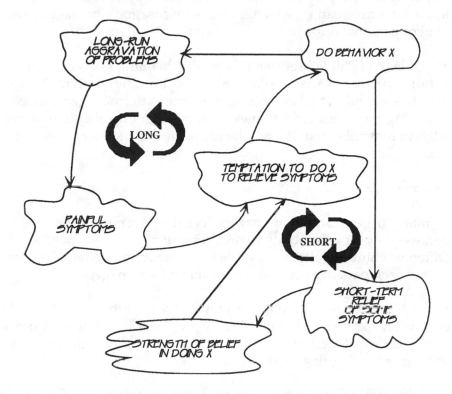

Figure 10-7. The generalized addiction cycle is composed of a process of short-term relief and a process of long-term worsening of symptoms, which work together to create a false belief that the addictive behavior is the only way to relieve symptoms.

This combination of short and longer cycles creates the addiction dynamic, regardless of whether X is placating by skipping processes, blaming employees, smoking cigarettes, or shooting heroin. At the heart of the addiction dynamic is the strength of belief in doing X.

The full name of the cloud shown at the bottom of Figure 10-7 should be "the strength of belief that doing X is the *only* way to relieve the symptoms." Addiction is, at its core, a belief that there is only one way to do something and that it must be done that way. If you understand this key to addiction, you can spot addicts very easily, and you also have a clue for curing the addiction. After Chapter 11 gathers all our models of human behavior into one unifying model, subsequent chapters will apply the model to curing addictions to various forms of incongruence.

10.5 Helpful Hints and Suggestions

1.   Since nobody in a Routine (Pattern 2) organization ever actually follows the routine exactly, you can always find a reason to arbitrarily hold any victim responsible for a project's trouble. Thus, one way to identify this pattern is to listen for scapegoating, which is also an excuse for a manager to exercise any kind of personal prejudice.

2.   My colleague Phil Fuhrer reminds me that blaming takes its own form in each cultural pattern. Variable (Pattern 1) and Routine (Pattern 2) organizations tend to seek individual culprits, while some Pattern 2 organizations seeking to reach higher levels tend to elevate their blame to the "single root cause." Always remember that it's not the name but the incongruence that creates the blaming behavior.

10.6 Summary

✓   In many organizations, managers feel they lack the time to do their jobs because they lack the ability to deal congruently with incongruence in others. Different cultural patterns have their characteristic patterns of incongruence, so that each pattern puts a different load on its managers.

✓   Ineffective actions leave problems unresolved, so that one effect of incongruence is an increase in the number of problems that someone other than the originator must deal with. Thus, more incongruence means more problem-solving or fire-fighting time.

✓   A major task of the software engineering manager is to help people in the organization develop their social skills, not just because it's better when people are nice to each other, but because social skills are becoming more and more important as a basis for effective technical skills.

✓   Organizations tend to lock onto either a pattern of incongruent behavior or a pattern of congruence. What makes the difference is the decisions of the managers, which influence their behavior and become an example for others.

✓   Feeling unable to trade off either quality or schedule, software managers are too often tempted to sacrifice the quality of human interaction, for which they soon pay the price in both quality and schedule deficiencies.

✓   The placating pattern is especially common in Pattern 1 cultures, which largely explains why they are called Variable cultures. For example, a project that has no review system in place finds faults at the latest, most costly time, with maximum impact on schedule. Managers use this delay in schedule to justify the omission of further reviews and tests.

✓ In blaming cultures, especially in Routine (Pattern 2) organizations, yielding to the temptation to punish the offenders for failures soon leads to a lot of extra effort to escape the abuse. On the other hand, the workers increasingly resent the abusive manager and find more ways to be unresponsive or even to sabotage the manager, which then leads to more failures.

✓ The addiction cycle works like this: There is a short cycle in which doing X relieves symptoms. There is a longer cycle in which doing X makes those very symptoms worse. The short cycle of addiction contains the strength of belief in X, so that the strength of belief in X grows the more that X is used, although in the long cycle, X leads to a worse situation.

✓ Addiction is, at its core, a belief that there is only one way to do something and that it must be done that way.

10.7 Practice

1. In a blaming culture, criticism isn't really effective. It simply motivates people to avoid getting criticized, as by not getting caught. Think of a situation when you were evaluated in a blaming way, and recall your reactions. Think of a situation when you blamed somebody else. Do you know what his (her) reactions were? If not, can you guess? If you can't guess, are you able to ask him (her)? If so, ask the person and see what you learn.

2. As suggested by Dan Starr: The application of the addiction dynamic to blaming and placating organizations can be extended to a lot of other counterproductive behaviors as well, such as the hero mentality. Discuss the addiction to heroism, and give examples from your own experience. What other addictive behaviors have you observed?

3. Again, as suggested by Dan Starr: The addiction dynamic can be tied back to the idea of first-order measurement. In what ways are we better at measuring the short-term pain relief of the addictive behavior than we are at measuring the long-term harm it creates?

11

The Technology of Human Behavior

When I was five, I decided that when I grew up I'd be a "children's detective on parents." I didn't quite know what I would look for, but I realized a lot went on in families that didn't meet the eye. There were a lot of puzzles I did not know how to understand.[1]

— Virginia Satir

To become more congruent, you'll need a map to guide you in your journey. The cybernetic control model in Figure 11-1 provides such a map.

To control the system, you must choose appropriate actions from a diverse set of possible actions, ranging from taking a deep breath to responding openly to deferring action. Your observations range from awareness of your own body to the business situation to the unexpected reactions of others. Your process model includes several models of human behavior, including a lot of behavior that goes on in organizations beneath the surface.

In order to work with people on a practical level, the working manager, just like the working family therapist, needs a process model that's more than an unrelated collection of models. This chapter assembles all of these isolated models into a larger model that can be used as a day-to-day guide to achieving more congruent management. Then, the chapters in Part III will apply this model to numerous common situations from software engineering management.

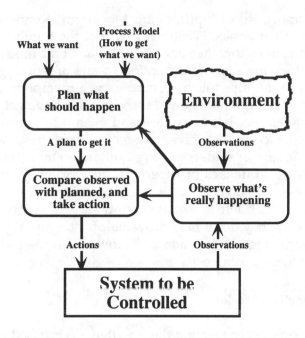

Figure 11-1.   The cybernetic model of what must be done to control a system can be used as a guide to achieving congruent management.

11.1 The Search for a Model

No matter our chosen profession, all of us share Satir's search for answers to the puzzles of our childhood. Some inquiring minds search in the tabloids, others in their own families. Most of us carry on this search every day in our work, and although the work may differ, the search is the same.

Let me tell you a bit about my own search, which I have learned is much like that of others who went into the computer field. When I was a young boy, computers first appeared in the popular press. At that time, they were often referred to as "giant brains" or "thinking machines." Although I had been labeled a very bright young boy, I wasn't happy. People in my family kept doing things to me that seemed unfair, irrational, and often totally random. Computers seemed simpler. Perhaps, I thought, I would first learn to understand computers, and that learning would help me understand why people acted in such mysterious ways. I didn't know the term then, but I decided I would become a programmer/analyst, first for giant brains, then for human beings.

That's why I got started in computing, and mastering the art of programming computers. As it turned out, mastering giant brains didn't help enormously with mastering the small ones. Eventually, I gathered my courage and started seeking out a few special people who worked directly with people—among them W. Ross

Ashby, Anatol Rapoport, Ron Lippitt, Doug McGregor, Kenneth Boulding, and many others through their books. When I finally met the family therapist Virginia Satir, we became detectives together and shared clues and models. Five years of working with her helped me a lot more than forty years of working with machines.

Still, I haven't lost my love for the computer as a metaphor. It has helped me put many other learnings into models, and these models have helped take some of the mystery out of other people's behavior—and even a bit out of mine. I believe that the ability to use such models gives those of us with a software engineering background an advantage in understanding human systems, an advantage that partially compensates for our lack of experience in working with people. To use this advantage, however, we do need to be aware of its limitations.[2]

Although there's much left to explain, I now have a technological model of why people act the way they do. It may prove helpful to you, if you are willing to put the computer technology to one side and move on to the technology of those smaller, but more intriguing, brains.

11.2 The Satir Interaction Model

My model of why people act or respond the way they do is based on the Satir Interaction Model.[3] Figure 11-2 shows the bare skeleton of Satir's model. *Volume 2* discusses the first three boxes in some detail. Since this volume is concerned with congruent action, its task is to explain the Response box, which chooses our actions. To do that, I'll also delve a bit deeper into the other three boxes.

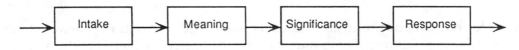

Figure 11-2.   The four basic parts of the Satir Interaction Model.

11.2.1 Intake

The first thing in understanding this model is to recognize that Response is not limited to the last step in the model. Even the manner in which I take data from the world (Intake) is not merely composed of passive looking, listening, and feeling. I take in some data, then respond by deciding whether to open up for more, reduce the data by filtering, or proceed with making meaning of what I already have. Figure 11-3 suggests a more complete picture of Intake as a responsive process.

To see this process at work, notice what happens next time you talk to someone and you become aware that the person isn't listening. Then say something that totally shifts the context, or change modalities by touching, or singing, or standing up and drawing a picture. Notice how the listener's response to your input changes.

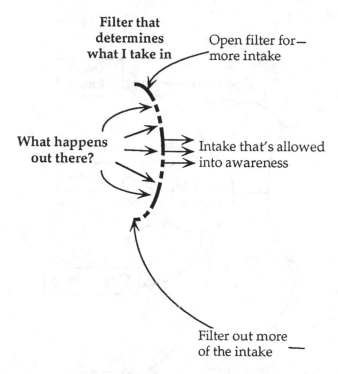

Filter that determines what I take in

Open filter for—more intake

What happens out there?

Intake that's allowed into awareness

Filter out more of the intake —

Figure 11-3.   Intake is an active, responsive process, filtering out some of what happens in the world and allowing other events to come into awareness

11.2.2 Meaning

The Meaning step contains a response as well. All of the many meanings I can make from my Intake can be broken down into four major categories in answer to the question, "What does this intake mean?" Each of these categories leads to a general type of response that is partly universal and partly unique to each person, as shown in Figure 11-4. For me, the possible responses are, roughly

- "don't know," which leads to a desire for more data to clarify
- "not relevant," which leads to my shutting off some of the intake, turning my attention elsewhere
- "threat," which leads me initially at least to stop thinking and go into an automatic mode in which I lose conscious control of my responses
- "opportunity," which leads to more thinking, to clarify what external response to give next

Each person's responses are unique. Somebody else may respond to "don't know" by shutting off intake. My response labels me as a "curious" person who is attracted to things I don't understand.

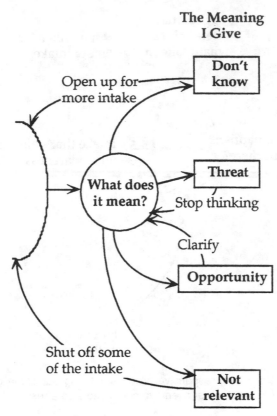

Figure 11-4.   The second step, making Meaning, is also a responsive process. Some of my possible responses control the filtering of further data from the world.

My "stop thinking" response to "threat" is not a characteristic I value in myself. I
prefer that "threat" would lead me to take in more data and think more clearly, but
my initial instinctive response is to shut down. I don't think I can change my basic
pattern, but I can change my reaction by shortening the shutdown period. On the
outside, it may now look as if I instantly move to take in more data and think more
clearly, but there's an internal struggle hidden beneath it.

11.2.3 Significance

The significance of each possible meaning can be considered in terms of the possible consequences to me, as shown in Figure 11-5. Of course, this is only a simplification of the thousands of possible consequences I may perceive, but my first
response at this stage is to group into some broad but important categories of what
might happen to me as a result of this interaction: learning, death, illness, play, creating, nothing, and so forth. It is the category I choose that determines the general
pattern of my response.

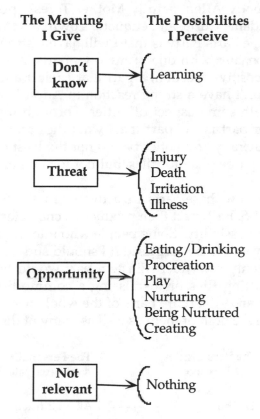

The Meaning I Give | The Possibilities I Perceive

- **Don't know** → Learning
- **Threat** → Injury / Death / Irritation / Illness
- **Opportunity** → Eating/Drinking / Procreation / Play / Nurturing / Being Nurtured / Creating
- **Not relevant** → Nothing

Figure 11-5.   Each meaning suggests certain possible consequences for me, and these consequences determine the significance to me.

11.2.4 Who's in charge of the response?

One of the reasons that "small brain" technology is so complex is that the human brain seems to operate not as one mind, but as a "multimind,"[4] or team of minds. If I am coping well, I have many different minds to put in charge for different situations. This, of course, is precisely what Ashby's Law of Requisite Variety says I must do if I am to be an effective controller of complex systems. This decision is sometimes conscious and sometimes unconscious.

Virginia Satir helped people access their different minds through an exercise called a "Parts Party."[5] At the start of a Parts Party, the participants think of a variety of real or fictional people to whom they have a strong emotional reaction—about half positive and half negative. For instance, during one Parts Party, I selected physicist Albert Einstein, mountaineer Sir Edmund Hillary, fictional Rambo, Nazi Adolf Hitler, Verdi's tubercular heroine Mimi, Rasputin (the "Mad Monk" who aided the downfall of the last Russian tsar), tennis star Billy Jean King, movie director and actor Woody Allen, saintly Mother Teresa, poet Elizabeth Barrett Browning, chemist Madame Curie, and etiquette's own Miss Manners.

The idea behind the Parts Party is that I will have a strong emotional reaction to a character who resonates with one of my own parts. A part that I accept and value will produce a positive reaction; a part that I reject and despise, a negative reaction. Thus, I wouldn't have a strong reaction to Adolf Hitler if I didn't have a part that I identify with some aspect of Hitler. Through my own Parts Party, I learned that my Hitler part is the part that swats flies and generally rids me of external irritations. Generally, my Hitler part is not the least concerned about how the fly feels, which might be okay for flies, but not for human beings who are irritating me.

Figure 11-6 shows how these parts are activated by the possible consequences I perceived in Figure 11-5. Each part then produces a characteristic style, or personality, for handling each possibility. Some people who interact with me see only one of these parts, and they would be surprised if I should suddenly bring out another. Someone who knows only my Albert Einstein part would be shocked to see my Adolf Hitler part swatting flies or dismissing a commodities salesman on the phone. Yet, both Adolf and Albert are parts of the whole me, and if you work with me long enough, you'll see both of them as well as many of the rest of the cast.

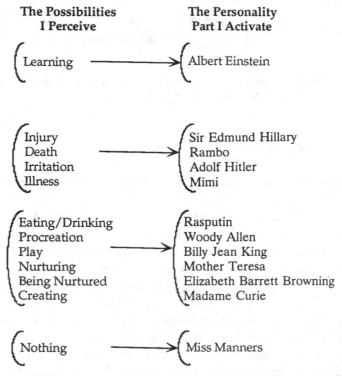

Figure 11-6.   Each possibility activates a different part, or sub-personality, of myself.

11.3 How Meaning Is Developed

Where do all these meanings come from to drive my interactions? To answer this question, imagine a tree whose branches lead to the various possible meanings in a given situation (Figure 11-7).

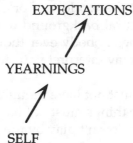

EXPECTATIONS

YEARNINGS

SELF

Figure 11-7.   The root and lower branches of the tree leading to the meanings that I make in a given situation.

The root of the tree is my *self*—the essential part, the way I connect with the world around me. This is what some religions call the soul, or the inner light, or the spirit. Sometimes we meet people who don't seem to have one of these, but that's because it's buried under the higher branches of the tree.

The main trunk is formed by my *yearnings*—the natural or innate energy that translates my self into types of action. Some common yearnings are

- to propagate the species
- to survive as an individual
- to be loved
- to be taken care of and nurtured
- to be healthy
- to be in harmony with nature
- to be valued
- to be whole

From each yearning branches one or more *expectations*—the translation of universal yearnings into specific ideas about how the world works to produce or withhold what is yearned for. For example, different people who all want to be valued may try to satisfy this yearning in very different ways:

- to work very hard and do exactly what they are told
- to entertain everybody with clownish antics
- to produce and rear many babies
- to think of things nobody ever thought of before
- to acquire lots of money

Expectations are often held in the form of rules,[6] such as one of mine that drives me to write books:

If I think of things nobody ever thought of before, I will be valued.

The rule expresses the way I expect the world to work. The expectations combine with perceptions as well as my cultural background to produce meanings (Figure 11-8). Suppose I think of lots of things nobody ever thought of before, but you tell me you don't like what I've done. I may interpret your feedback to mean

- You don't value me, so I must not have thought of enough things.
- You don't value me, so the things must not have been original.
- You are a bad person, who doesn't play by the rules.

Notice how it never occurs to me that my rules may not be applicable to this situation. My rules contain valuable information from my earliest experiences about how to survive, in order to achieve my deepest yearnings. No wonder I don't easily let go of rules.[7]

Cultural learnings, which also influence meaning, are similar to rules in that they are deeply buried and rarely questioned. My partner, Dani, recalls a day in the Swiss Alps watching Marguerite knitting a pink sweater for her expected grandchild and remarking, "Oh, you think it will be a girl?" Marguerite looked puzzled, so Dani explained that pink was for girls. "No," came the reply. "Pink is for boys. Blue is for girls." When Dani explained that the meanings were opposite in American culture—pink for girls, blue for boys—Marguerite replied, "Oh, that's *funny*."

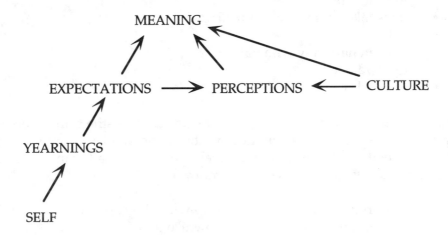

Figure 11-8.   Expectations and culture influence perceptions, and all three combine to make meaning from a particular situation.

A more serious situation arose when I was participating in a seminar with my friend Ben Brown Bear of the Sioux Nation. Some group members complained that Ben wasn't listening to them, which they had inferred from his not looking at them when they talked. Ben explained that among his people, making eye contact in that situation was a hostile sign, like a challenge to fight.

11.4 Style versus Intent

Ben's avoidance of eye contact didn't match my cultural expectations of someone who was actually listening intently, and I felt annoyed with Ben even though I understood the cultural difference intellectually. As *Volume 2* discusses, feelings are an information system that tell me about the *significance* of the match or mismatch between my expectations and my perceptions. The feelings drive my actions, so if you can reach me at any level underlying my feelings, you have a chance to change my response to you.

Standing in the way of your recognizing those feelings, let alone what lies beneath, is my personal *style* (Figure 11-9). My style includes

- my typical sequence of coping styles when my self-esteem is low
- my preferences, especially my personality preferences
- my conscious learnings (like technical knowledge or knowledge of you)
- my habits, such as gestures or verbal expressions
- my addictions, such as to abusive behavior
- my culture, which may influence all of the above

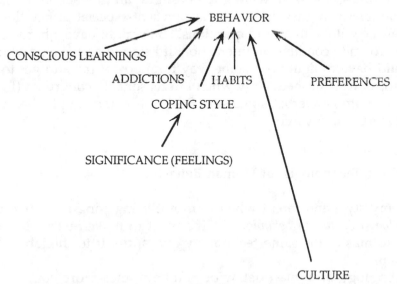

Figure 11-9.   The deeper parts of what I really want are covered by a surface style that includes my conscious learnings, my coping style, and a number of less-than-conscious learnings, such as preferences, habits, and addictions.

With all these intervening facets of style, the same intent may produce a very different output from different people, or even from the same person at different times. Suppose my intent is to help Sue, one of my staff, learn to figure out technical problems for herself. Here are some ways that this intent might be wrapped in different styles in reaction to her request for help on a problem:

A: "Don't bother me with your stupid questions!"

B: "When the student is ready, the teacher appears."

C: "What do you think is the answer?"

D: "I recall a time, when I was in graduate school at Berkeley, and I had a question that I brought to my professor: Dr. Clausen, I believe he was, the inventor of the semi-automatic cosmic ray analyzer. He was a very busy man—though he never did win the Nobel Prize he thought he was going to get for his invention. ... " (and on, and on, and on)

E: "Sue, it would be a lot easier for me and perhaps better for you if you learned how to answer such questions for yourself. If I answer it now, you won't learn much about that. Are you willing to sit here and work through the process with me?"

Clearly, in some of these cases, Sue wouldn't have a prayer of deducing my intent from my style unless she were willing to enter into an interaction. In some cases, that would be relatively easy, but each case presents special difficulties. If I said, "Don't bother me with your stupid questions!" Sue might have a hard time simply staying in the room to continue an interaction. If I started on the long-winded story (D), she would have to figure out some way to interrupt me and get to the point before the project was finished. Only when I'm reasonably congruent (E, accompanied by appropriate nonverbal signals) is Sue's job made simple, because I have matched my style with my intent.

11.5 The Skilled Technologist of Human Behavior

To untangle my style and intent when I am not being congruent, Sue must be a *skilled technologist of human behavior*. Or, if I want to make Sue's job easier, I too would have to master the same technology and apply it to the job of becoming more congruent.

The technology of human behavior is many times more complex than the technology of software. Engineers sometimes express disdain for the study of human behavior, saying it is a soft science, not a hard science like electrical engineering or computer science. Well, software may be a hard technology, but human behavior is a difficult technology. Compared to you or me, an operating system is a piece of trivia.

In my interactions as a manager, as I try to understand or influence another person, I am modifying the other person's program, or stimulating that program to get certain responses and not others. For people who have survived to adulthood and hold jobs, most programs are 99 percent functional. But one bit wrong can produce total or very large dysfunction that can destroy any software project, no matter how well managed elsewhere. Thus, the size of my control intervention is not the issue. The issue is the *precision*.

In order to be capable of precise interventions, I need understanding and tools at all levels of Figure 11-10. This includes practice, not just theoretical knowledge. To work at level N, I need to know a lot about N-1, N-2, and so on down to the bottom of the hierarchy. For example, preferences and coping style are strong influences, but they are often masked by the linguistic surface. Thus, I must understand linguistic habits to obtain access to coping style and preferences. When I am able to see through these levels to deeper levels, I can achieve a more complete rapport and to manage people (myself and others) with minimal energy and disruption.

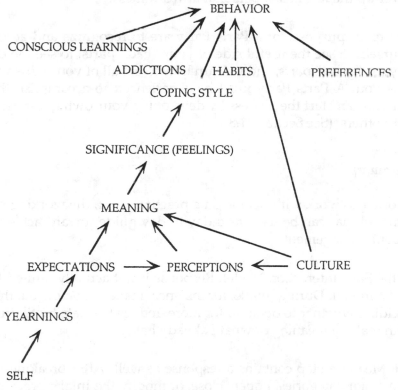

Figure 11-10.   There are many layers underlying behavior, and each layer has a technology of its own, which effective managers must master.

The chapters that follow as Part III will explore some of these levels, to start you on your way to becoming a skilled technologist of human behavior yourself.

11.6 Helpful Hints and Suggestions

1.   When trying to decipher a puzzling interaction, try doing it the same way you would work through a program that produces a puzzling output. Start with the output (the Hitler or the Einstein) and work backward; start at the top of the hidden part (the feelings) and work down to the deepest roots.

2.   As you trace through interactions, remember that low self-esteem is always at the root of incongruent behavior. But don't confuse self-esteem with self-importance. Self-important behavior—such as insisting on executive privileges, making other people wait for scheduled meetings or perhaps cancelling at the last minute, or refusing to attend leadership training because "I know all the material"—is always a *symptom of low self-esteem*. It is one of the disguises that blaming takes—I am everything; you are nothing—precisely in order to cover up the feelings of personal unworthiness.

3.   The main purposes of a Parts Party are to recognize and accept all parts of yourself, to see the useful side of your "bad" parts, to see the dangerous side of your "good" parts, and to learn how to get all of your parts working to support you. A Parts Party must be experienced to accomplish these purposes, but you can start the process by developing your own guest list and sharing it with others. (See Section 11.8.)

11.7 Summary

✓   In order to work with people on a practical level, the working manager needs a model that can be used as a day-to-day guide toward achieving more congruent management.

✓   In the Satir Interaction Model, Response is not actually limited to the last step in the model. During Intake, for instance, I take in some data, then respond by deciding whether to open up for more, reduce the data by filtering, or proceed with making meaning of what I already have.

✓   The Meaning step contains a response as well. After breaking the data down into major categories, I open, close, or modify the Intake process to fit the perceived meaning according to my personal style.

✓ The significance of each possible meaning can be considered in terms of the possible consequences to me, and the possibility chosen determines the general pattern of my response.

✓ The human brain seems to operate not as one mind, but as a team of minds. If I am coping well, I have many different minds to put in charge of different situations, as Ashby's Law of Requisite Variety says I must do if am to be an effective controller of complex systems.

✓ The many members of my "team" can be thought of as distinct personalities, and (half seriously) identified with well-known characters. All characters, good and bad, are parts of the whole me, and if you work with me long enough, you'll eventually see most of the cast.

✓ Underlying the Satir Interaction Model is a tree-like structure whose branches lead to the various meanings that I may make in a given situation. The root of the tree is my self. The main trunk is formed by my yearnings, each of which branches into one or more expectations.

✓ Expectations are the translation of universal yearnings into specific ideas about how the world works to produce or withhold what is yearned for. Expectations are often held in the form of rules that express the way I expect the world to work. Even though a rule may not apply to the present situation, I do not easily relinquish it, because it contains valuable information from my earliest experiences about how to survive in order to achieve my deepest yearnings.

✓ Standing in the way of your recognizing my intent in an interaction is my personal style, the surface formed by my coping style, preferences, conscious learnings, habits, addictions, and culture. To reach my intent, you can use a model of human behavior to penetrate that style and find what lies beneath it.

✓ The technology of human behavior is many times more complex than the technology of software. When I am able to see through this complexity to deeper levels, I am able to achieve a more complete rapport, and to manage people (myself and others) with minimal energy and disruption. This is what I mean by becoming a skilled technologist of human behavior.

11.8 Practice

1. Construct some diagrams like Figures 11-2 through 11-6 for yourself, showing how your different parts are activated. Explain them to at least three other people. Have them construct their own diagrams and explain them to you.

2. Construct a diagram like Figure 11-10 showing what underlies the way you make meaning of events. Explain it to at least three other people. Have them construct their own diagrams and explain them to you.

3. Take each of the five responses to Sue (A through E) and connect them to my interaction model. Start by trying to figure out which part made the response, and work backward from there to possible feelings and meanings.

4. Prepare a guest list for your own Parts Party. Identify eight to ten characters to whom you have a strong reaction, about half positive and half negative. With each one of the characters, associate one or more adjectives. For instance, with Elizabeth Barrett Browning, I might associate "sensitive" and "loving," while with Rambo, I might associate "powerful" and "crude." Share your list with some of your friends, and ask them if they ever see these parts of you and how they interpret them.

Part III
Achieving Congruent Management

Keep good natured ... no matter what you find ... you did not invent life, so do not hold yourself responsible for what life does to you; decline to lay blame on anyone.

— Hugh Mearns

"Who was that masked man?" The townspeople never knew who the Lone Ranger was, but fans of the show knew that his career as the masked defender of justice began in tragedy. He and his fellow Texas Rangers were ambushed by a gang of outlaws, and he was the only one to escape with his life. He could have spent the rest of his life playing the victim, but instead he responded by building a new and more effective role for himself. The rest is (fictional) history: how the Wild West was tamed.

The Lone Ranger possessed no secret weapon. The technology available to him was precisely what was available to the guys in the black hats. The difference was in the way he used—and didn't use—his technology. The typical bad guy had only one way to solve problems of control—namely, to gun somebody down. In remarkably few episodes did the Masked Man ever use his hardware, and if he did, it wasn't to kill, but to disable the hardware of his opponent.

The Lone Ranger won the battle of Good over Evil because he had many behaviors at his disposal. He was clever, skilled with his hardware, persuasive, and, most of all, congruent. He never fired his gun in anger, or hatred, or revenge.

When the history of software engineering is written, the story will be the same: Thousands of individuals will respond to failure by playing victim, by pouring on hardware, or by attacking others. Only a few will respond congruently, creating new and more effective roles, and taming the Wild Profession.

12

Curing the Addiction
to Incongruence

*An ounce of application is worth
a ton of abstraction.*
— Booker T. Washington

Addictions are notoriously difficult to cure because most people don't recognize an addiction in the first place and they fail to understand its dynamic in the second. These failures lead to the belief in several ineffective methods of curing the addiction. This chapter examines those failures and offers a practical method of cure.

12.1 Forcing the Addict to Stop

The simplest idea about curing addiction is to stop the use of X, under the belief that X causes the addiction. X does not cause the addiction; the addiction dynamic causes the addiction. We know that's true because not everyone who is exposed to X becomes an addict. Take morphine addiction, for instance. Many people are exposed to morphine in hospitals and don't become addicted because they have other ways of dealing with the various pains in their life. Only those people who are inclined to believe (for personal, economic, cultural, or other reasons) that there is only one magical way to cure life's problems are likely to become morphine addicts.

The same is true for the addiction to omitting technical reviews to push the schedule. The only managers who become addicted to this practice are those who don't understand what the review does for them and who have no effective alternate ways of dealing with a schedule delay.

There's no evidence that prohibition works, and lots of evidence that it doesn't. Sometimes, it doesn't work because it's impossible to enforce the prohibition, as the entire population of the United States saw when alcohol was prohibited in the 1920s. As Figure 12-1 shows, prohibition leads the addict to make greater and greater attempts to do X. If the prohibition is strong enough, the addict may not succeed in doing X, but the strength of the belief is unchanged. This means that the addict is still addicted, and that as soon as a crack in the prohibition appears, the addict will do X again.

Prohibition, then, cannot stop addiction, though at best it may stop new people from becoming addicts. Nevertheless, in a work situation, we may not care if the person or persons stay addicted as long as they cannot practice the behavior. For example, the prohibition of code patching can be absolutely enforced with an appropriate configuration management system. When such a system is first introduced, programmers who are addicted to patching invariably try dozens of ingenious ways to beat it. If there's a crack, they will surely find it. If not, they'll eventually find that they may as well work within the system, albeit grudgingly. Their belief system remains unchanged, though, and given any chance, they'll slip right back into the old behaviors.

Because the existing addicts will try harder and harder to beat the prohibition, the cost of this way of stopping the behavior is at least an increase in policing activity, with the accompanying deterioration in the general climate. Nevertheless, in circumstances like patch prevention with configuration management, the benefit can be worth the cost.

In other circumstances, however, it's simply not possible to obtain such absolute prevention. For instance, many software engineers are addicted to fiddling with software tools to the point at which it interferes with their productive work. However, they are not addicted to the tools, but to the overuse of tools. But because tools are a necessity for programming, there's no conceivable way management can stop these tool addicts from having access to their addiction.

At its worst, prohibition creates a class of people who profit from helping addicts beat the prohibition, and this class of people grows and recruits more addicts. A case in point is the tool vendors, who have a legitimate function, but who also may have no scruples about pandering to tool-based addictions. Why else would we find that seventy percent of purchased software tools are never used productively, yet few vendors will give their customers a refund for a returned tool?

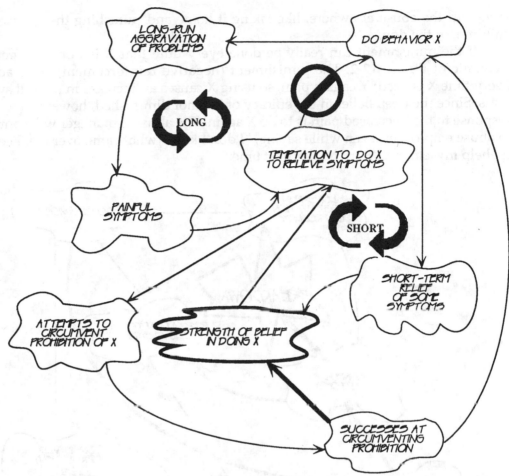

Figure 12-1. The simplest idea for stopping an addiction to X is prohibiting the use of X. This may lead to success or failure, but it always leads the addict to increasing efforts to do X because nothing is done about the long-range pain. If the prohibition works, the addiction may not grow stronger, but neither does it grow weaker. If it doesn't work, the addiction grows stronger, and new methods of getting X have now been learned.

12.2 Punishment

Some people believe that they can cure an addiction by punishing the addict each time X is used. For example, upper management may criticize a middle manager for abusing employees. In this case, of course, the punishment must not be done in an abusive way, lest it simply reinforce the behavior it's designed to stop. Abuse only confirms the model and makes the abuser more abusive. The abuser simply tries harder not to get caught the next time—to do the abuse in private, accompanied by threats to employees if they inform upper management. Another approach is to shift the abuse elsewhere, like taking it home and punishing the spouse, the children, or the dog.

If the punishment can really be done every time that X is done, we get the dynamic of Figure 12-2. The punishment (negative reinforcement), Y, is added every time X is used; Y causes pain, so using X causes an increase in painful symptoms. Since the deep belief in the efficacy of X is not diminished, however, the only response to this increased pain is to do X again. The abusive manager will continue to abuse employees, even while saying, "I don't know what came over me. I couldn't help myself, but I'll try harder next time."

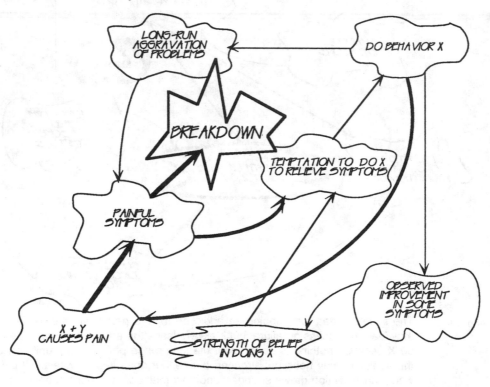

Figure 12-2.   Another way to try to cure the addiction is to attach a punishment (negative reinforcement), Y, to X in such a way that it cannot be avoided any time X is used. In this case, the addiction doesn't grow stronger, but it doesn't grow weaker either, as the conviction remains strong that if only I could get X with Y removed, I would feel better. Also, if Y is painful, it may add to the existing misery, thus increasing the temptation to do X, and eventually leading to enough pain to cause a breakdown.

The manager keeps abusing, thus being punished by upper managers. The short cycle of pain continues to build up until something breaks down. Upper managers may give up, turn irrelevant, and fire the manager. Or they may stop punishing and become superreasonable, saying, "That's just the way some people are. Besides, it's not that bad, and we are getting results, after all."

If high-level managers stick with Y and the manager's abuse grows stronger, then perhaps the abused employees will all leave, and the work will fail. More likely, though, only a few of the employees will actually quit. Most of them will simply continue to undermine the abusive manager. Eventually, the manager will suffer some sort of physical, mental, or social breakdown, like getting ulcers or a heart attack, suffering a nervous breakdown, or suddenly resigning.

12.3 Rescue

Because the pain of the addict is so visibly part of the dynamic, some people believe an addiction can be cured by relieving the pain—a placating or rescuing strategy. Unfortunately, because X itself is causing the pain, regardless of the original cause, this rescuing strategy cannot be used on the cause but only on the symptoms. The rescuer attempts to provide symptomatic relief, but can only succeed if the relief is generated from a dynamic that's more powerful than the long-range cycle of the addiction.

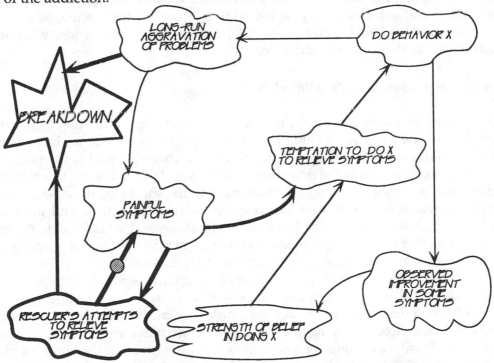

Figure 12-3. The rescuer tries to help the addict by relieving the pain generated in the long-term cycle. This intervention can succeed if the dynamic of the rescuer is more powerful than the long-term cycle's dynamic, but then the addict can become addicted to the rescuer. Usually, though, the rescuer or the addict breaks down because the rescuer cannot continue to match the escalating pain from the long-term cycle.

Sometimes, it is actually possible to create a relief dynamic that's more powerful. In the nineteenth century, for example, heroin was put into use as a "cure" for morphine addiction. It was successful at ending morphine addiction so long as heroin was available because heroin was more powerful. Of course, the morphine addiction then became a heroin addiction, which wasn't much progress. This replacement dynamic is being repeated in the twentieth century with the use of methadone. And, oh yes, morphine itself was thought to be a "cure" for opium addiction.

In the software world, FORTRAN was put forth as a cure for the addiction to assembly language. COBOL was designed to eliminate the dependence on programmers, since executives would be able to write their own code. Spreadsheets were going to replace COBOL, but now many executives spend more time fiddling with their spreadsheets than doing executive-type work. Indeed, weren't PCs going to cure the addiction to mainframes?

In most cases, however, replacement does not occur because the rescuer cannot develop a stronger relief dynamic. The rescue attempts only hold down the painful symptoms in the short run, but require greater and greater efforts until something breaks down. It may be the addict, it may be the rescuer, or it may be the entire system. This is a very common result in alcohol addiction, wherein the spouse may break down before the alcoholic.

12.4 Co-Dependency or Co-Addiction

If the rescuer is a strong person, the addict can replace the addiction to X with an addiction to the rescuer. For this to happen, the rescuer must be locked into a dynamic that is also an addiction dynamic: an addiction to rescuing. A spouse puts up with the abuse, lies to the police about who was driving the car in an accident, and nurses the alcoholic through the hangover. In the short run, these rescue efforts produce rewards for the spouse, because the alcoholic is contrite and grateful. In the long run, however, they lead to even more abuse and worse accidents, so the rescuer is locked into a long-run, short-run dynamic. In the alcohol literature, this relationship is called co-dependency, but it is really co-addiction.

Co-addictions are very common in work situations, particularly between managers and employees, but also between co-workers. Abusive managers are often effusively apologetic and kind to abused employees later on. To certain people, this kindness is the closest they have ever known to genuine respect and good treatment. They easily lock into a co-addiction with the abusive manager—a classic blaming/placating dance. Upper management cannot understand why, if the manager is so abusive, the employee doesn't complain and in fact says how wonderful the manager is.

A frequent co-worker co-addiction develops when one worker cannot do a job and the other rescues him (her) by covering up and doing the work for both. The rescuer gets a lot of gratitude for this behavior, but the first worker doesn't have to improve performance. I have often found situations in which one programmer was doing the work of two, unbeknownst to their manager, until one of them was moved. Managers who don't understand this dynamic may believe that it is an inevitable consequence of teamwork. True teamwork, as we'll see in Part IV, is not based on an addiction dynamic, but on behaviors that genuinely solve long-run problems, rather than merely relieve short-run symptoms.

12.5 A Successful Cure

Another tempting idea for a cure is to use the Principle of Addition. If you offer an alternative solution (Z) that's superior to X, wouldn't the addict simply stop using X and start using Z? Such an approach can prevent addiction, but by itself cannot stop an addiction because the addiction is based on a firmly rooted belief. To change the addiction, you'll have to use something more powerful than logic. You'll have to build another belief that's stronger. In other words, lecturing about bad software engineering management practices without offering other ways is just another form of a short-cut cure, with more or less the same results as all the other solutions.

In order to get an addict to accept an alternative way, you must do three things to the addiction dynamic (Figure 12-4):

1.   Prohibit X.

2.   Provide an alternative solution (Z) that really works.

3.   Soften the short-term pain if necessary, but not with X.

Here's why this strategy can work. Prohibiting X breaks the two cycles that form the addiction dynamic so that the addiction doesn't get worse. Providing an alternative that really works creates two new cycles; these don't create an addiction because Z doesn't aggravate problems in the long-run, but instead relieves them.

Softening the short-term pain is usually necessary in order to allow time for the long-range success of Z to be appreciated. In effect, using Z does relieve the short-term pain because the addict who uses Z is given relief. You can see that in order for this strategy to work, the relief of symptoms must invariably accompany Z in the early stages, and must not aggravate problems in the long run so that it won't create another addiction dynamic. For instance, if you're going to install unbreakable change control to cure the addiction to patching, you must allow a long and safe grace period in which project delays are not punished, and you must also reward all attempts to use the new systems, even when they aren't entirely successful.

The following chapters will show how to do these things for some of the most common counterproductive management addictions to incongruence.

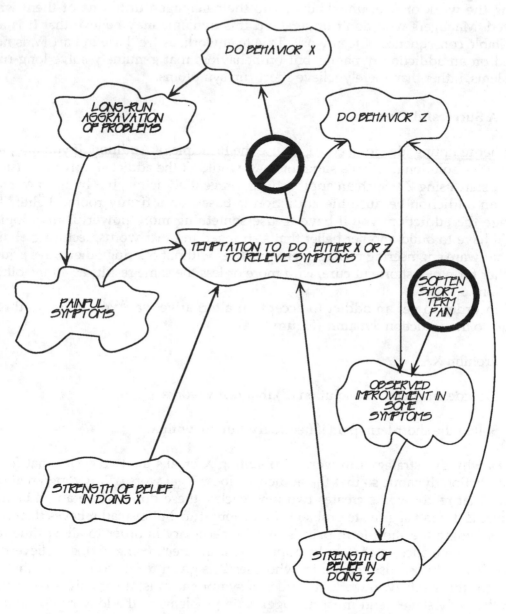

Figure 12-4.   A successful method for dealing with an addiction to X is to prohibit X, provide an alternative (Z) that really works, and soften the short-term pain if necessary, but not with X. This strategy makes both long and short feedback loops into negative feedback, thus stabilizing the system. It works provided X is prohibited long enough for the belief in Z to grow stronger than the belief in X. Notice that the belief in X is not changed, so the addiction remains, but is overridden by the stronger belief in the efficacy of Z.

12.6 Helpful Hints and Suggestions

1. The reason prohibition can sometimes work is that there is a substitution taking place, although not necessarily one specifically provided or even noticed by the prescriber. For example, code patching is prohibited by a configuration management system. In one team, the addiction stays, but in another it fades away because the team members discover a way to run a job with a small change without having to run a three-hour recompilation and rebuild.

2. An even more simple-minded version of forcing the addict to stop is instructing the addict to "just say no." If the addicts could say no to their magical cure for all of life's problems, they wouldn't be addicts. "Just saying no" works, but only for non-addicts.

3. My colleague Wayne Bailey makes the following interesting point about the dynamic of negative reinforcement shown in Figure 12-2: "If management punishes based upon observing the painful symptoms and not the behavior X, then the punishment will be delayed and thus reinforce the addiction cycle." This is precisely what managers do when they don't understand the connection between the behavior and the painful symptoms—that is, when their models are inadequate.

4. Wayne Bailey continues with this comment on Figure 12-4: "Since the belief in Z will be based on improvement in the long-term situation, the improvement may not be easy to observe. In this case, a fourth step may be needed: take action to make the improvements observable, and observable as early as possible." His fourth step is one of the major reasons for creating a measurement program based on effects that can be observed early, when they are still small.

5. Another colleague Phil Fuhrer reminds me of the importance of knowing the true goal of your attempts to change an addiction. For instance, the true goal may be to get patching under control, not necessarily to eliminate it entirely, because patching may be needed, though only in real emergencies. If managers lack confidence in their ability to handle emergencies congruently, they may substitute complete prohibition for their true goal. This rigid position will encourage clever addicts to create emergencies in which the managers themselves will be forced to approve of bypassing the configuration management system. *Volume 4* of this series will consider what it takes to create a reasonable configuration management system.

12.7 Summary

✓ Addictions are notoriously difficult to cure because most people don't recognize an addiction in the first place, and don't understand its dynamic in the second. These failures lead to the belief in several ineffective methods of curing the addiction.

✓ The simplest idea for curing an addiction is to prohibit the use of X, under the belief that X causes the addiction. But X does not cause the addiction; the addiction dynamic "causes" the addiction. There's no evidence that simple prohibition works, and lots of evidence that it doesn't.

✓ In a work situation, we may not care if people stay addicted as long as they cannot practice the behavior. For example, the prohibition of code patching can be absolutely enforced with an appropriate configuration management system. The addicts may struggle to find a way around the system, but at least new people never get a chance to become addicted.

✓ The negative reinforcement model suggests that you can cure an addiction by punishing the addict each time X is used. If done perfectly, negative reinforcement doesn't cure the addiction, but eventually leads to something breaking down, and not always the addict.

✓ Some people believe you can cure addiction by relieving the pain—a placating, or rescuing, strategy. In most cases, the rescue attempts only hold down the painful symptoms in the short run, but require greater and greater efforts until something eventually breaks down.

✓ In other cases, the rescue attempt leads the addict to replace the addiction to X with an addiction to the rescuer. The rescuer then becomes locked into an addiction to rescuing, sometimes called co-dependency.

✓ A cure that works is to use the Principle of Addition: Offer an alternative solution (Z) that's superior to X. In order to get the alternative way accepted by an addict, you must do three things: Prohibit X; provide an alternative (Z) that really works; and soften the short-term pain, if necessary, but not with X.

12.8 Practice

1. Which of Kiersey and Bates's temperaments do you think would be attracted to each of the supposed cures for addiction? Why?

2. As suggested by my reviewer Mark Manduke: Prohibition may lead to compliance, but it doesn't lead to commitment. Can you recall a circumstance in which the technical staff complied with management's prohibitions, but they were not sufficiently committed to get a difficult job done?

3. As suggested by Wayne Bailey: Diagram the dynamics arising from the punishment approach of Figure 12-2 concerning who leaves and who stays. Workers who leave first are those who have a healthy sense of self-worth and those who also tend to be the most productive. The employees who stay have their self-worth eroded over time, and that further reduces their productivity.

4. As contributed by Phil Fuhrer: How would a rescuing manager attempt to deal with an organization addicted to code patching? How would a punishing manager? How would you apply the Principle of Addition method to a code-patching addiction?

13
Ending
the Placating
Addiction

President: I'm really interested in knowing how long it's going to take to develop this software.

Manager: This is a really ambitious undertaking. It's going to take X months and Y people.

President: What? It can't possibly take that long to develop software. Have it done by Z. Just be creative.

Manager: Well, okay. We can get it done by Z, but only if we cut the functionality in half.

President: What? We can't possibly make money on a product like that. Keep all the features, and get it done by Z. Our market window is fixed; our required functionality is fixed; we can't hire any more people. You'll think of something. Otherwise, we'll be out of business and out of jobs.

Manager: Well, okay.[1]

This hypothetical but typical dialogue gives us a chance to practice applying our technology of human behavior. Is Morie, the president, blaming or being superreasonable? Is Charlene, the manager, placating or blaming? Naturally, without probing behind the style of each, we can't answer, but let's make some guesses.

My first guess, based on MBTI statistics, is that Morie is an extrovert and Charlene is an introvert. Thus, Morie is comfortable working out problems "online" with one of his managers. Charlene, on the other hand, carefully works out her estimates before meeting with the president, and has difficulty changing them on the fly.

Why would Charlene agree to keep all features and get done by Z? This could be either blaming or placating behavior. The blaming behavior may not be obvious, but imagine her saying to herself (stressing the underlined words), "This bozo doesn't know a thing about software. Rather than waste my time arguing with him, I'll agree to everything. When we deliver late, with less than the function he wants, there's nothing he can do. Besides, I know better what he really needs." That would be blaming behavior, a subject discussed in Chapter 14. This chapter deals with the placating organization, and what to do about it.

13.1 The Placating Organization

Charlene is placating if she defers her judgment to Morie, even when she's more competent. He doesn't have to be blaming in order for her to placate; he may indeed be just discussing in his extroverted style. She placates when her self-esteem is so low that she's willing to say, "I am nothing; he is everything."

Let me tell an embarrassing personal story that will make this point clear: Some mornings, when I go to my closet to choose a shirt, I notice a shirt that I haven't worn in a long time, generally because it doesn't fit well or I don't like it. When I'm not feeling so great about myself, I'll often wear that ill-fitting, miserable-looking shirt, reasoning, "That poor shirt must feel so bad because it thinks I don't like it any more."

Logically—congruently—I should send the shirt on to its next life with the Salvation Army, but I say, in effect, "I am nothing; you are everything" to a shirt! Now that's placating! There's no blamer—not even another person—in sight.

13.1.1 Deming's Point Eight

Although it is possible for any cultural pattern to be effective, many Variable (Pattern 1) cultures are not. Most of the ineffective Variable cultures are placating cultures, with the management described precisely by Deming in explaining his Point Eight, "Drive Out Fear":

> Most people on a job, especially people in management positions, do not understand what the job is, nor what is right or wrong. Moreover, it is not clear to

them how to find out. Many of them are afraid to ask questions or to take a position.[2]

In software engineering, this common pattern is a remnant of the earliest days of computing. Then the machines had a very high minimum entry price, so if you weren't ready to commit millions of dollars to a single decision, you couldn't play. They were also seen as being so incomprehensible that only geniuses could program them, and so inflexible that each decision locked the buyer into an architecture for years. That kind of situation created an environment that encouraged incongruent coping behavior (Figure 13-1). In such an environment, technicians had job security, and customers and managers feared any technician who seemed to be able to make the machine obey.

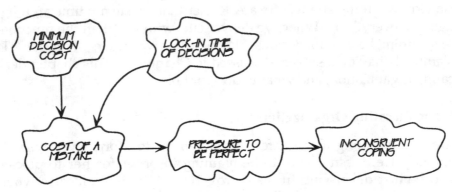

Figure 13-1.   When decisions must be made in costly chunks that will affect the organization for a long time, pressure mounts to make perfect decisions, which can lead to incongruent decision processes.

13.1.2 Technical arrogance

This is the kind of environment Charlene would be counting on had she said to herself, "When we deliver late with less than the function he wants, there's <u>nothing</u> he can do." If she thinks this way, she's counting on Morie to placate her and the other technical staff.

Power corrupts and, in that respect, technical power is no different from any other kind. I was a programmer in those early days, and can attest that with one-tenth of the computing power in the world under my fingers, it was hard to resist being a snot. Of course, I didn't think of myself that way, but here's how one of my typical interactions probably went:

Customer: I wonder if you can fix this problem.

Jerry: Don't you understand anything? That's just the way computers work.

Manager: Do you think you could try to do something?

Jerry: I have more important things to do if you want me to keep this system running.

Customer: Of course. We don't want to bother you.

Jerry: Yes, if you would just leave me alone, I can do great things for you. Just leave it to me. After all, I understand computers, and you don't, so that means I understand your business better than you do.

Manager: We're very sorry we bothered you. Is there anything else you need?

Jerry: I'll let you know.

Here, I was blaming, and both the customer and manager were placating. But even if I had been behaving congruently, they would have placated because they felt powerless in the face of technology.

13.1.3 Placating the developers

Figure 13-2 shows a typical coping style of such an organization with both managers and customers placating the programmers, and perhaps the customers placating the managers as well. Such an organization produces low quality because customers are afraid to ask for what they want for fear of offending the programmer or the entire information systems (IS) organization.

Manager

Programmer

Customer

Figure 13-2.   The typical coping style of some Variable (Pattern 1) organizations.

In the early days of computing, the high cost of monolithic hardware forced customers to depend on their internal IS department, and many were not permitted by upper management to seek alternatives, if there even had been any. No wonder customers started to rebel as soon as a few cheap alternatives arrived on the scene. Nevertheless, a great many IS organizations are still trapped in this Variable (Pattern 1) placating style.

13.1.4 Placating the maintainers

Now that many possibilities exist for computer solutions, organizations are trapped in a placating pattern for a different reason. For example, their entire business may be balanced on the shoulders of one or a few maintenance programmers, and nobody else knows enough about a few critical systems to risk offending them. This combination generates the pattern shown in Figure 13-3. The customer blames the IS organization, and the manager stands between the customer and the maintainer lest the maintainer feel the blame and quit. In this case, the manager placates in both directions at once, while the maintainer remains superreasonably oblivious.

Customer   **Manager**   Maintainer

Figure 13-3.   Some organizations are supported by one or more maintainers who the managers feel must be protected from the customers, lest they take offense and depart, taking all knowledge of critical systems with them.

13.2 Transforming the Placating Organization

How can we transform such placating organizations? According to our model for ending addictions, we must do three things:

1.   Prohibit placating.
2.   Provide an alternative to placating that really works.
3.   Soften the short-term pain, if necessary, but not by placating.

The next sections explore each of these actions.

13.3 Making Placating Less Attractive

The first action is to prohibit placating, but how can this be done? Of course, no organization can hope to eliminate placating entirely; when self-esteem is low enough, people can placate in any context. It is possible, however, to create conditions so that the probability of placating is reduced. In this type of case, people feel good about themselves and their work—with reason—and this good feeling is contagious.

13.3.1 Blaming is not the opposite of placating

First, I must mention a popular idea that doesn't work. Many people have tried to replace placating with blaming, but that leads to a rigid Routine (Pattern 2) organization, as we'll see in Chapter 14. The advocates of this model warn against praising people, lest it be taken as a sign of weakness:

> Acts of praise should be few and far between, otherwise it cheapens the value of the praise and dulls that little sharp needle of dissatisfaction. Keep them guessing as to whether you are going to praise them or shoot them down. Guessing keeps them on their toes.[3]

This kind of misguided management comes in several other forms, such as restricting initiative and failing to respond as promised:

> When someone has tried to make an improvement and has not been heard—sent back to the job and told, "You do the work; I'll do the thinking"—he is not apt to return soon with another idea. Worse yet, to give the vague answer, "I'll get back to you," (which often never happens) leaves the worker demoralized.[4]

Managing in these inhuman styles doesn't make people feel good about themselves, and so can hardly be expected to cure an addiction to placating. At best, it will reorient the placating toward the managers, rather than away from them. Yet so many managers employ this style that I have become convinced they *want* to have a placating organization, one that says to them, "You are everything; we are nothing." I know of companies in which the number of habitual placaters is so great that low self-esteem must have been a primary factor in their selection of employees.

13.3.2 Choice prevents placating

Placating occurs when self-esteem is low. Raising self-esteem—through management style, training, and affirming feedback—can help to block placating, but in itself cannot prevent it. For instance, IS customers often have high self-esteem, but not in the context of computers. Feeling technically incompetent, they must humble themselves to the sole source of technical help.

To understand their situation, picture yourself stranded in a remote hotel, and suppose that each meal offers a menu with only one selection. Having no other choice if you don't want to go hungry, you eat what the chef has prepared. If the chef is rude to you, you are polite to him. If he is rigid, you are accommodating. If he demands a high price, you bite your tongue and pay.

This no-choice restaurant more or less describes the situation of the captive customer of an in-house software organization. Of course, the restaurant may be excellent, and the chef's choices invariably pleasing to your palate. Those of us who have eaten many meals in hotel restaurants know that this happy situation is possible, though extremely rare. Moreover, there is no particular reason for a restaurant with a captive clientele to maintain its excellence, which leads to the following principle:

To prohibit placating, give customers alternative sources of services.

Although this principle is the foundation of American capitalism, it seems to unhinge the mightiest managers of internal IS organizations. They certainly agree with the principles of capitalism, but always for the other guy. They know (extending the dining metaphor) that if the customer ever has an alternative, she may try to retaliate for the rude chef.

In the IS world, when the customer finally decides to retaliate, she pronounces the dreaded word *outsourcing*. Outsourcing is to IS managers what a silver crucifix is to Count Dracula. But contrary to the internal manager's trepidations, outsourcing may be the best thing that ever happened and customer alternatives need not be limited to outsourcing.

13.3.3 Outsourcing

Outsourcing not only frees the customer from the tyranny of the internal IS organization, but also frees the internal organization. One sort of freedom is illustrated by this analyst's story: "I used to hide from this wretched customer, he was such a terrible complainer. Our corporate policy said that everyone had to use our services, and he was always complaining to anyone within earshot of how we were shafting him. I spent a zillion hours in someone's office explaining away some complaint of his. I billed my time to his jobs, but that only made him more furious, even though it was 'funny money' in his budget.

"Finally, he got permission from the CFO to contract with a service bureau for his work. My life immediately got better. I'm sorry to say that I think his did, too. According to the grapevine, the service bureau does a better job of pleasing him than I could ever do. The bureau charges him real money for giving him what he wants, but he seems willing to pay. We don't miss his business, which I think always cost us more than we could recover. We still have lots of good customers that we can satisfy—actually better now that we don't have to put up with his complaining."

The analyst's manager was not so pleased, because he could see his empire crumbling if he didn't keep every single customer. Addicted to placating, he didn't seem to recognize that it was an improvement to get rid of a customer he couldn't satisfy. As a placating addict, all he could see was a need to placate his remaining customers even more abjectly.

Of course, outsourcing can get rid of valuable customers, too—the ones who placate us by accepting inferior service at inflated prices. I personally could not be happy working in an environment whose very existence was based on the gullibility of the customers, and I don't believe any professional software engineer could be happy either.

Outsourcing does not mean you need to placate customers. Here's another story, this one from the point of view of a dissatisfied customer (not in the same company): "Quite frankly, I know nothing about computers, but I do know I was not getting good service and a fair price for my job. One day, I was flying home from Cleveland and sat next to a guy from a Big Eight accounting firm. I unloaded my troubles on him. He told me that my case was typical, and that his firm could do a lot better than any internal organization. So I moved a major new development contract into their hands.

"Well, I was wrong. These guys kept building up the cost, and stretching the schedule, and showing me little toy systems that didn't do any real work. After fourteen months, and more money than I want to talk about, I pulled the job and went back to our internal people, with my tail between my legs.

"I did learn a few things for my money, and some of them I'm sure made me a lot more tractable as a customer. I still don't think our people are perfect, but I do appreciate them a lot more."

This story illustrates another sort of freedom created by giving a customer choices. Because this customer is blaming less, the IS organization doesn't need to placate as much.

13.3.4 Internal bidding

The customer must always have alternative sources, but these may be internal to the IS organization. A number of successful Variable (Pattern 1) organizations operate on the basis of competitive bidding for jobs by software engineering teams. Customers post their requirements and various teams bid for their jobs, much as if they were external consulting firms.

Of course, internal bidding has the same drawback as outsourcing; you have to maintain your competence or the world will notice that nobody's choosing your services. To the professional, that's not a problem, but to the empire-building manager, it's a *big* problem.

For a system of internal bidding to work effectively, the IS organization must always have alternative customers, just as the customers have alternative sources. With an insufficient source of potential customers, the IS organization may be led toward placating its customers and then blaming its workers—a behavior pattern common in Routine (Pattern 2) organizations. To avoid this situation, the IS organization must be reduced to match reductions in demand, and this is not a popular practice.

13.3.5 Dispersed maintenance

Neither outsourcing nor internal bidding can help much in the maintenance situation of Figure 13-3. If a system is so big, old, and poorly documented, the customer cannot easily take the system elsewhere. For the same reasons, the sole maintenance programmer who understands the system will always have an overwhelming advantage in bidding on incremental changes.

To prevent placating in this situation, the manager must risk offending the programmer by adopting one or both of the following tactics: Rotate assignments or create maintenance teams. Both these tactics ensure that no programmer is the sole owner of any system, giving the manager several alternatives and thereby removing the need to placate.

What do you do if the programmer threatens to quit if one of these tactics is implemented? In that case, the programmer's threats should remove any doubts about what you should do next. Do you have the courage to stop placating and carry out your plan in the face of the risks?

In my experience with dozens of examples of this situation, ninety percent of the time, the programmers don't carry out the threats so long as their concerns are handled congruently and so long as you respect their contributions and calm their fears of the new assignment.

In the other ten percent, the programmer indeed leaves, but I have never seen a case in which a team cannot take over the maintenance job in four weeks or less; two weeks is more typical. As a bonus, the team almost always does a noticeably better job of satisfying the customer.

13.4 Remaining Steps

The second step in the model for dealing with addiction tells the manager to provide alternatives. Simply changing the situation that creates the placating will not be sufficient if the manager doesn't know any other way of coping. The most common temptation is to replace placating by blaming, the way heroin replaced morphine.

All forms of incongruent coping can give short-run relief, but all are followed by the long-run pain that creates addiction. Congruent actions are the only alternative to placating that can work for a manager in the long run. But congruence is not stereotypical behavior, and comes in many forms according to the dynamic balance among the self, other, and context.

The third step in the model says soften the short-term pain. This is most readily done by eliminating blaming and punishment, the subject of Chapter 14.

13.5 Helpful Hints and Suggestions

1. Very rarely, a maintenance programmer in the situation of Figure 13-3 is heard to mutter a threat as to what could be done to destroy the system if the manager stops placating. As soon as you hear such a threat, remove the programmer and prevent any possible access to the system. No exceptions! No whining about how much it will cost to put a replacement team in operation! If you need motivation, just figure the potential cost if the threat is carried out.

2. Variable (Pattern 1) organizations need not be placating. The most common effective type of Pattern 1 organization is based on a strong culture of professionalism and service. Whenever I've been able to trace the origins of these cultures, I've found one or more strong leaders who managed to propagate these values to new people in the organization. Unfortunately, many of these organizations collapsed into incongruence when the leadership changed.

3. If reduced demand forces you to trim your organization, the results of customer bidding can tell you which teams are the best candidates for dissolution. Although we know it's dangerous to select on the basis of a single factor, at least this factor is directly related to the ability to satisfy customers. If you don't like this kind of selecting, then prevent it by keeping all your teams competent so their services will always be in demand. Unfortunately, the first response of most managers to decreased demand is trimming the training budget—exactly the opposite of what they should do to maintain an attractive service.

13.6 Summary

✓ Most of the ineffective Variable (Pattern 1) cultures are placating cultures in which managers are afraid to ask questions or take positions.

✓ This Variable placating pattern is a remnant of the earliest days of computing, when expensive, inflexible machines gave technicians job security, and customers and managers were afraid of any technician who seemed to be able to make the machine obey.

✓ Placating organizations of this type produced low quality because customers were afraid make requests, for fear of offending the programmer or the entire

IS organization. The power of the programmer in this environment corrupted many programmers, and gave them a (deserved) reputation for arrogance.

✓   As soon as a few cheap alternatives arrived on the scene, customers rebelled against the arrogance of their IS organizations. But they often found their entire business balanced on the shoulders of one or a few maintenance programmers, and nobody else knew enough about a few critical systems to risk offending them.

✓   Placating occurs when self-esteem is low. Raising self-esteem will help to block placating, but in itself cannot prevent it. To prohibit placating, you must give customers alternative sources of services.

✓   Internal IS managers dread outsourcing. Contrary to their trepidations, outsourcing may be the best thing that ever happens, and customer alternatives need not be limited to outsourcing.

✓   Outsourcing does not mean you need to placate customers. When you give a customer choices, the customer has less need to blame, so the IS organization has less need to placate.

✓   A number of successful Variable (Pattern 1) organizations operate on the basis of competitive bidding for jobs by software engineering teams. Customers post their requirements and various teams bid for their jobs, much as if they were external consulting firms.

✓   To prevent placating in the locked-in maintenance situation, the manager must risk offending the programmer by adopting one or both of the following tactics: Either rotate assignments or create maintenance teams. Both these tactics ensure that no programmer is the sole owner of any system.

13.7 Practice

1.   Perceived lack of choice is always a potential source of placating with hidden blame. To convince yourself of this, ask, "How do I respond in such situations as a no-choice airline meal?"

2.   As suggested by Wayne Bailey: It's relatively easy to observe improvement in quality software and customer service, but how would you measure the status of self-worth among the managers in an organization? What could be done to directly enhance self-esteem? [5]

3.   As suggested by Phil Fuhrer: Give examples from your experience of placating that occurs between the layers of management. Do your examples represent situations unique to software engineering, or are they characteristic of hierarchical organizations?

14
Ending
the Blaming
Addiction

*The first human being who hurled
an insult instead of a stone
was the founder
of civilization.*
— Sigmund Freud

As Freud suggests, substituting insults for stones was a great beginning for civilization. When we throw stones at other people out of fear, the stone throwing causes injury, and injury results in the desire to injure, which in a circular way justifies our fear.

Blaming, like stoning, is a form of attack. We blame out of fear, and the blame creates a situation that justifies our fear—hardly the way to manage a high-precision activity. Substituting information for blame provides a substantial advance for software engineering management.

This chapter shows how blaming organizations have come into being, how they perpetuate themselves, and how software engineering managers can begin to change the addiction to blaming.

14.1 The Blaming Organization

When an addiction becomes sufficiently widespread, it becomes part of the culture. Just as a culture can be addicted to drinking coffee or chewing betel nuts, so can it be addicted to blame. Among software engineering organizations, blaming cultures are the most common type, which is why their cure is essential if software quality is to be improved.

14.1.1 The temptation to blame

Why is blaming so common in the software business? We know that blame comes from fear, but what are we afraid of?

The software business requires a high degree of perfection, and we are *afraid of making mistakes*. Because it's a way to provide corrections, blaming others can be a quick, easy way to feel better about mistakes in the short run, even though it hurts in the long run.

Placating organizations avoid blaming behavior by simply tolerating mistakes, but that leads to low-quality products. To eradicate blame in the organization at the same time they improve the software product, managers must learn congruent ways to provide necessary corrective feedback. In software engineering, as in science, refuting an erroneous idea is not a purely negative activity. Chapter 17 discusses this topic in some detail, but learning new methods of feedback is not sufficient to change the blaming organization.

14.1.2 What are your motives?

Even if managers don't blame others, many of their technical staff will. Whom do they blame? Their managers. In response, managers may resort to blaming in return. After all, they argue, isn't it our job to correct faults? Isn't it for their own good?

It's so easy to hide the fear that leads to blaming under the noble slogan "It's for your own good."[1] If you're going to eradicate blaming, the first question you must ask is, "Is it for them, or is it for me?"

Koichi Tohei, an aikido master, tells the story of a teacher who was under severe criticism from parents and other teachers for beating students. Tohei listened to the teacher's explanation of the beatings, and noticed that he was high-spirited with a quick temper. After being convinced that the man sincerely believed he was "doing it for their own good," Tohei spoke to him:

> "I see," I replied, "I am in full agreement. If you beat your students to improve them, beat them good. I will do what little I can to cooperate and be your ally."
> ... I added to my comments, however, the following remark.

"It is a fine thing that you want to improve your students because you are fond of them, and I suppose, since this is the case, you can beat them just as well when you are not angry. From now on, when you feel that a child needs a beating, check to make sure that you yourself are not angry. If you aren't then go ahead. If you strike them in anger, your own anger, mixed with the punishment, is transferred to the children and will do them no good at all. If you punish them with love in your heart and for their own good, you should be able to do it when you are calm. The students will then understand that you are punishing them with love."

He understood and from that moment never beat another student. If he were about to strike a youngster he would calm himself (and) listen to what the boy had to say, and the necessity for a beating would vanish.[2]

As we approach the twenty-first century, most software engineering managers understand that no matter how they feel, it's not acceptable to beat employees. Many, however, fail to understand that a verbal beating has precisely the same dynamics as a physical beating. Putting aside any moral issues or issues of what you would do if the employee hit you back, we still have to face the simple fact that beating people doesn't make them better programmers, testers, analysts, or whatever. What beating does is motivate them to find ways to avoid being beaten.

For instance, if programmers get beaten for faults in their programs, they will take great pains to conceal faults, or to direct the blame for the faults on someone else. Most of the continuing conflict between testing and development arises in response to a climate of blame.

14.1.3 Blaming as revenge

In Figure 13-1, we saw how large, expensive systems with long times to make changes frequently led to perfectionist cultures with incongruent coping styles. These styles were often placating in nature. What happens as times and conditions change? To answer this question, consider the following story from the ancient days of my career, in the light of modern times:

In 1957, I was working for IBM's Service Bureau Corporation (SBC) in the Southwest, helping to establish a software development organization. This was a radical idea in those days, when hardware manufacturers customarily tossed in some software development as a free bonus with hardware purchases.

One of my first and most satisfied customers was Andy, the president of XYZ Fertilizer Company. One of the reasons Andy was such a good customer was, as he said, "I know BS when I see it." But as his company grew, he began to have difficulty sifting the BS from his sales data. I vividly recall the first time we met, when he waved a thick sales report at me and said, "This doesn't smell right, and I want your computer to dig up the reason."

I wrote a program for him that analyzed the sales by marketer, product, and profit margin, among other variables. The program revealed that his "best" two marketers were pushing huge volumes of low-margin products. Although they were receiving all the sales awards, they were actually costing XYZ lots of money. Andy rectified the situation, I became his hero, and XYZ became one of SBC's biggest computer customers.

I will never forget our divisional manager, talking with Andy and me in one of XYZ's feedlots on a summer day when the temperature reached 105°. In the fashion of the day, he was placating Andy because he was the customer, and placating me because I held the mysterious key to this wondrous source of new revenue. I know he was placating because he actually yielded to our request that he remove his wool jacket, vest, and tie. When a career IBMer did that, you knew that he had submitted himself to the most abject humiliation.

Nowadays, the tables have turned. Placating has become revenge! My brilliant program of 1957 could now be written by Andy himself, using his own personal computer and spreadsheet package, for one-thousandth the cost. As a result, no IBM manager would still humiliate himself for a techie, and many have turned to blaming techies for revenge. In view of the way we treated them, I can certainly understand their feelings.

14.1.4 Methodology magic

Before the price of technology dropped by a few orders of magnitude, the wish for revenge on the techies was more often expressed as a hope, rather than in any particular actions. The most commonly expressed form of that hope was the vision of the Routine (Pattern 2) organization. That's why in the 1960s, packaged methodologies became so popular.

Without understanding this need for revenge, you couldn't comprehend why executives were willing to cough up $100,000 or more (in 1960's dollars) for a shelf full of loose-leaf notebooks. These notebooks were stuffed with idealized processes that if routinely followed, were guaranteed to produce reliable software using totally interchangeable, cheap employees.

If you can manage to find some of these notebooks today, you can learn their fate by wiping your finger through the dust they've gathered. Although these methodologies didn't work very well, and although any reasonable person could have seen that they wouldn't work very well, they continued to sell. Like all magical elixirs, they were not bought for rational reasons, but for emotional ones—in this case, the burning desire for revenge.

Although the methodologies didn't produce effective organizations, the same desire for revenge produced many organizations with the coping pattern shown in Figure 14-1, with everybody blaming the programmers. In some cases, the nerds fought back, usually by being either superreasonable or irrelevant, as shown in Figure 14-2. These two styles are the most common Pattern 2 cultures of today.

Figure 14-1. When the tables turned, many placating managers turned to avenging themselves on their techies, thereby creating blaming organizations.

Figure 14-2. Sometimes the technical professionals reacted to blaming managers by turning irrelevant or superreasonable.

14.2 Criticism As Information

Not all Routine (Pattern 2) organizations fit these incongruent patterns. Some work well in a routine fashion, managers don't blame, and the technical staff need not respond incongruently. As *Volume 1* of this series discusses, Pattern 2 can be stable and productive if the tasks are not too big or too different from past tasks, and not too technically demanding. When these conditions are not met, however, a Pattern 2 culture starts to break down.

In organizations with non-Routine cultural patterns, design, development, and maintenance of software systems can be highly creative work, requiring sensitive workers. As Federico Fellini reportedly said about people in the movie industry, "For a creative person to be criticized can be very dangerous. A creative person needs an atmosphere of approval. Like a fighter. You need to be drunk, you need to be exalted, to believe in what you're doing."

If you're a software engineering manager, what else can you do besides blame someone else when something goes wrong? Perhaps you believe that blaming is the only way to deal with situations when somebody stumbles. If so, doesn't that sound like you're a candidate for an addiction cure?

14.2.1 Pain of blame, pain of recognition

In order to avoid an addiction to blaming behavior, the first thing you're going to need is the knowledge that there is some other way to cope with your fear of mistakes. Generally, criticism is much easier to take when it's given as information, not as blame or punishment.

First, let's not deny that it can be painful to learn that you've made a mistake. Congruence doesn't mean life will be free from pain, but let's use Virginia Satir's distinction between two kinds of pain: the pain of blame and the pain of recognition. The pain of blame is the pain of feeling judged and being found inadequate. The pain of recognition is simply the cost of getting new information.

When I feel the pain of blame, I may want to relieve some of it by passing it on to someone else. "Well, perhaps I'm guilty, but you're guilty too." Even if I am right about the other person, however, when my criticism arises from my own pain of blame, most of the information is lost. As the author and martial arts expert Tom Crum observes,

> If a parent's response to a young child spilling his milk is the same as his response to the child striking matches, the child has trouble making distinctions about the true importance of each situation, even though it is obvious to the parent. It is not effective management of our employees if we use the same inflection, volume of voice, and tone of importance for the person who is two minutes late as for the person who consistently comes to work hours late and drunk.[3]

Crum's observation applies not only to the manager who is habitually shouting blame, but also to the manager who is superreasonably calm in all situations or who is placating. One of my responsibilities as manager is to be the conduit for information from the outside. By not varying my emotional expression to convey the gravity of the situation, I deprive my employees of the information they need to be effective.

When I deliver criticism, I'm delivering information not just about a person's behavior, but also about the context in which that behavior takes place, as well as about my own reaction to the behavior taking into account all three positions—the self, context, and other. That suggests a congruent way I can deliver criticism without losing its significance. I simply preface the criticism with a statement about myself and a statement about the context.

14.2.2 Example: Criticism of regression test practices

Here's what can happen when you apply this method. Tad, the manager of software maintenance in an East Coast financial services company, returned from a workshop to find that a small change to a production job had caused over 100,000 erroneous account statements to be printed. Fortunately, the statements were caught before they were mailed, but rerunning them caused a two-day delay in mailing and cost more than $10,000 to rerun.

The paper trail said that regression tests had been run. When Tad tried to find the results, he discovered that the tests had not been run. Forest, the programmer, said he had not run the tests because he had been "very careful" in making the change. Tad was furious, but decided to try applying what he'd learned about congruence. He avoided reacting immediately to his discovery, and sat down to prepare how he was going to criticize Forest's judgment. Here's what he prepared (I've marked the components of the statement in boldface following that component):

✓ I hear you say that you were very careful in making those changes, but this erroneous release cost us more than ten thousand dollars. And we were lucky, because it could have cost hundreds of thousands of dollars or more. (**Context**)

✓ I live in terror of what can happen to us and to my job when a release is not properly tested. (**Self**)

✓ So, when you report that you ran regression tests that you didn't really run, I think you don't appreciate the possible consequences to the business, to me, and to yourself, and I also lose trust in what you say about anything. (**Other**)

Forest's response was not what Tad had hoped to hear:

✓   I don't believe you when you say that a mistake like this could cost hundreds of thousands of dollars. If that were true, you wouldn't have turned down our request for regression testing tools or for a configuration management system, because they cost a lot less than that.

Tad's reaction was at first predictable, then changed:

✓   I was furious at what I heard as Forest's arrogant blaming. I wanted to punch him, or at least to escalate the blame. Knowing that I am an introvert and my on-the-spot reactions are not always wise, I managed to say only, "I'm surprised. That's not the way I looked at it. Let me think about it."

Well, when I thought about it, I realized Forest was absolutely right. From his point of view, my behavior with regard to their request for tools was incongruent with my statements about the seriousness of the problem. My first reaction was to defend myself, because I had actually submitted purchase requests to my manager for both systems, but she had turned them down. Then I realized that I had placated her, and had accepted the rejection without putting up the kind of fight that the consequences would have justified.

As a result of thinking this through, I reinstated my requests, this time fighting for them. I told Forest and the others that I understood it didn't look like I really cared about regression testing. I said that I was resubmitting the requests, and that this time I would fight for the tools until we got them. In the meantime, I asked them to support me by adhering to the standard procedures, and I would try to allow them more time for the cumbersome procedure. It's a good thing I got their cooperation, because it took a year to get the testing tool and two years to get the configuration management tool, even though I had asked for that to be first. But we did get the tools, and the entire group now uses them.

Congruence works—not always, but it works more often than any incongruent strategy. It doesn't always work as fast as you like, but in the end, it saves a lot of time. And as Tad's case shows, it usually doesn't work in quite the way you planned, so you must be prepared to respond congruently to the surprises.

When you prepare to deliver criticism in a more congruent fashion, you may discover—like Tad—some incongruence in your previous behavior. Or you may find that the context is missing, and you are merely giving your personal reaction. In that case, like Tohei's teacher, you may wisely decide not to offer the criticism at all. After all, you are managing a business, a business that has other purposes besides pleasing you.

14.3 Prohibiting Blaming

How can you transform a blaming organization? According to the model for ending addictions, you must do three things:

1.   Prohibit blaming.

2.   Provide an alternative to blaming that really works.

3.   Soften the short-term pain, if necessary, but not by blaming.

This section considers a few ways to prohibit blaming, while the next two steps will be treated in Chapters 15 and 16, respectively.

14.3.1 Openness

In practice, you cannot possibly prohibit blaming one hundred percent. People blame when their self-esteem is low, and there's no way you can ensure that self-esteem is always high for everybody in the organization. However, managers can create conditions in which blaming cannot thrive, even should it sprout.

The key to a non-blaming organization is *openness*. Like the repulsive creatures that live under rocks, blaming thrives in the dark. The first requirement for a blame-proof environment is an open-door policy all the way to the top. Openness only at the top is not sufficient, but must be part of a general openness policy. Openness is the enemy of error, and blame is the enemy of openness.

14.3.2 Preserving the open-door system

As part of the openness policy, top management must make it clear that blaming will not be tolerated, nor will threats that try to prevent the use of open-door policies, as the following example shows:

When Darlene failed to follow her supervisor's orders to falsify a testing report, Austin, her supervisor, subjected her to severe verbal abuse. Using the open-door policy, Darlene told Maralisa, Austin's boss, about the orders to falsify and the verbal abuse. The next day, Austin summoned Darlene into his office, closed the door, and screamed at her. "If you ever go over my head again," he threatened, "I'll get you fired so *#@!*% fast you'll be out the %$#*! door before I've put out my %$#**!# cigar."

Austin was in total violation of the company's open-door policy, but Darlene didn't know that. She was scared of losing her job, so she didn't dare go to Maralisa again, nor to anyone else in the company, thus effectively negating the open-door policy.

Darlene did have the courage to bring up the question with an external consultant, arguing to herself that this would not be going over Austin's head. The consultant, being very close with Maralisa, related the story in anonymous terms. Maralisa knew who it must be, but because of the private nature of the meeting between Austin and Darlene, she lacked the proof that Austin had repeated his offense in spite of her warning. Without this proof, she couldn't discharge or even reprimand Austin. The best she could do was watch him carefully for other unacceptable management behavior.

Once blaming has taken hold in an organization, it's like a disease. If the organization is already as badly infected as this story indicates, the managers must take steps to prevent situations in which blaming is possible or easy to do—that is, ban managers from technical reviews and prohibit private meetings. If there must be a private meeting, have a tape recorder present.

Perhaps these steps sound a bit severe or impractical. If the allegation against Austin were sexual abuse, would they sound too severe? From the organization's point of view, verbal abuse can be just as destructive as sexual abuse, because it's more likely to spread and become part of the culture. How well can a software organization manage itself if the project managers can browbeat workers into falsifying quality reports?

14.3.3 Making contact

Blaming is based on the exclusion of the other person from the interaction. Thus, blaming cannot survive among people who see each other fully in their humanness. Anything that gets people interacting on a person-to-person basis rather than boss-to-subordinate will tend to prevent blaming. That's why my company's seminars routinely train a mixture of people from different organizational levels to help transform blaming organizations into something more congruent.

However, blaming managers frequently refuse to attend seminars unless the seminars segregate managers from non-managers. They avoid mixing in situations that imply equality because their self-esteem is defined by being the boss, and being the boss is defined by who gets to blame whom. Indeed, some managers distinguish in their speech between their managers and their people. If managers aren't people, what are they?

14.4 Helpful Hints and Suggestions

1.   Blaming is not confined to other people. Perfectionists constantly blame themselves for not living up to their own perfection rules, so naturally they feel justified in blaming others. These rules, like all long-lasting rules, are usually well-protected by a system of other rules. If you are a perfectionist, you can see these rules in the internal talk you give yourself. For instance, you do something very well, but discount it by saying to yourself, "I did it, but not

perfectly, so it doesn't count." Here the underlying rule is, "I must approach perfection in a perfect way."

If you actually do something perfectly, you discount it by saying, "I did it perfectly, but I may not do it perfectly next time, so it doesn't count." Here the underlying rule is, "I must always be perfect."

These rules are truly humorous when seen from the outside, so if you want to reduce your blaming, set as your goal to look at yourself from the other position and to laugh at your foibles. It may be painful, but it will be the pain of recognition, not the pain of blame.

2.   If you feel you are subject to inappropriate behavior in private, do not allow yourself to be in such a private situation. If the other party insists, say politely, "I need to have a third party present because I find it hard to remember the important things you tell me." If the offending party still insists, get a tape recorder, turn it on, and say, "I'll have to have this on, or else I won't remember a thing." If you get abuse for turning on the tape recorder, you'll have it all on tape. And, if you're being unreasonable yourself, that will also be on tape, so you can listen to the tape later to check your behavior.

14.5 Summary

✓   Substituting information for blame provides a substantial advance for software engineering management, especially in those organizations addicted to blaming behavior.

✓   To eradicate blaming behavior from their organization at the same time they improve the software product, managers must learn congruent ways to provide necessary corrective feedback.

✓   Perhaps the easiest way for managers to err in response to blaming behavior is to slip into blaming in return. What blaming does is to motivate people to find ways to avoid being blamed.

✓   If programmers get blamed for faults in their programs, they try very hard to conceal faults or to direct the blame for the faults toward someone else. Most of the continuing conflict between testing and development arises as a response to a climate of blame.

✓   Managers' wish for revenge for years of abuse from their techies was often expressed as a vision of the Routine (Pattern 2) organization. That's why, in the 1960s, packaged methodologies became so popular.

✓   The same desire for revenge resulted in many organizations with a coping pattern in which everybody blamed the programmers. In some cases, they fought back, usually by being either superreasonable or irrelevant. These two styles are the most common Pattern 2 cultures of today.

✓   Not all Pattern 2 organizations fit these incongruent patterns. Some organizations work well in a routine fashion: Managers don't blame and the technical staff need not respond incongruently.

✓   In organizations other than Pattern 2 organizations, the design, development, and maintenance of software systems can be highly creative work, requiring sensitive workers. In such situations, blaming destroys any chance at achieving quality and productivity.

✓   There are two kinds of pain we may feel when we are blamed. The pain of blame is the pain of feeling judged and of being found inadequate. The pain of recognition is simply the cost of getting new information.

✓   To deliver criticism in a congruent way without losing its significance, I simply preface the criticism with a statement about myself and a statement about the context. Congruence works. It doesn't always work, but it works more often than any incongruent strategy. It doesn't always work as fast as I like, but in the end, it saves a lot of time.

✓   The key to a non-blaming organization is openness, since blame thrives in the dark. Openness is the enemy of error, and blame is the enemy of openness.

✓   Blaming is based on the exclusion of the other person from the interaction. Thus, blaming cannot survive among people who see each other fully in their humanness. Anything that gets people interacting on a person-to-person basis rather than boss-to-subordinate tends to prevent blaming behavior.

14.6 Practice

1.   One way to work on a perfection rule is to reframe the rule into a guideline.[4] Pick one of your rules that leads you to blame yourself and reframe it into a guide.

2.   Another way to work on a perfection rule is to practice making small mistakes that you know logically have no significant consequence. For instance, you might throw an aluminum can in the regular garbage rather than in the aluminum recycling bin, or vice versa. Force yourself to make one trivial mistake each day for a week, and note your reactions.

3.   As suggested by Lee Copeland: Ask someone in your organization (or family) to monitor and record your blaming behavior. After some period of time, review the record. Does it feel as if you are being blamed for being blaming? Were you aware of your actions? How can you become more aware?

4.   As suggested by Bill Pardee: Introverted managers often need to close their door to think or make telephone calls. How can an open-door policy best be reconciled with occasionally physically closed doors?

15

Engaging the Other

*My mother had a great deal of trouble
with me, but I think she enjoyed it.*
— Mark Twain

I can imagine why Mark Twain's mother enjoyed her trouble. A good test of your management style would be whether your employees would say the same thing about you: "S/he has a great deal of trouble with me, but s/he enjoys it."

The enjoyment of trouble with a person comes from engagement: truly making contact between two human beings. Unfortunately, in placating and blaming organizations, managers attempt to manage without engaging the people supposedly being managed. The particular way they avoid engaging depends upon their favored coping style.

This chapter explores ways in which managers avoid engaging people, and offers some alternatives you can use to help yourself or others combat an addiction to incongruence.

15.1 Placating

For people who placate, the lack of engagement with other people is deeply rooted and appears in many guises. If you have any doubt of what placating entails, here's Daniel Defoe's description of Friday presenting himself to Robinson Crusoe:

> At last he lays his head flat upon the ground, close to my foot, and sets my other foot upon his head, as he had done before; and after this, made all the signs to me of subjugation, servitude, and submission imaginable, to let me know how he would serve me as long as he lived.[1]

This is a revolting description of a relationship, but it's no doubt how some managers would like their employees to behave. Curiously, these managers seldom perceive themselves behaving the same way—to their customers, their own managers, and even their employees. That's not surprising, however, because placating, above all, is a technique of surviving by making yourself very small or even invisible.

15.1.1 Placating through false compromise

Much placating is hidden under the label of compromise. Here's an example from my own experience: Around 1965, I served on a committee with three other IBM software engineers to set standards for assembler code. One of the issues was line-by-line comments. Based on experiments I had done with code comprehension, I favored block comments, with no comments on individual lines of code. The other three members, however, favored commenting every single line. The argument had wasted most of a day's work, so we finally reached a compromise. We took the "average," and set a standard that three-fourths of the lines of code were to be commented $[(3 \times 100\% + 1 \times 0\%)/4 = 75\%]$.

This apparent compromise, of course, was ridiculous. If my teammates were right, the standard should have been to comment one hundred percent of the individual lines of code. If I was right, it should have been zero. Nobody supported the three-fourths figure, but thousands of IBM programmers had to follow it. From our point of view, however, we had achieved our objective: avoiding true engagement with one another over this issue.

15.1.2 Handling an out-of-control developer

Here's another common example of placating from Randy, a manager at a software products company that was an archetypal Variable (Pattern 1) organization. Randy's type of placating goes a long way toward explaining why Pattern 1 organizations are called variable. Randy explains, "I have a very dedicated and hard-working person reporting to me in the capacity of a senior-level software developer. Edgar is very bright, very capable, and quite personable. He is also extremely hard (for me) to direct.

"It seems that Edgar cannot accept simplifications, reductions, and other alternatives to his proposed designs and implementations. I am unable to convince him that we should agree on an achievable (read "limited") set of deliverables, stick to them until their conclusion, and then take stock. In every case, he decides that he knows better, and he chooses a technologically elegant (but over-ambitious) approach, and he eventually fails to meet any deadline. He feels so strongly that he is working correctly to achieve a quality result, and he does not understand why I am dissatisfied and feeling undermined."

First, let's look at the signs of placating. The first thing Randy does is build up Edgar, describing him as very dedicated, hard-working, very bright, very capable, and quite personable. Then he belittles himself—"hard (for me) to direct," as if he wouldn't want me to think that Edgar had anything to do with it. "I am unable to convince him"—as if his manager couldn't simply tell him. "He does not understand (what a victim I am)."

Notice also Randy's presumption of "I told him once, so he ought to get it." This could be superreasonable, but in this case, it's placating, as if to say, "Oh, I couldn't possibly interrupt his important work to tell him again."

From this placating stance, Randy didn't have a chance of solving the problem with Edgar. Edgar, presumably, was supposed to notice how miserable Randy was and change his behavior to make him feel better, but Randy was making himself invisible.

Sharon, Randy's manager, proposed that Randy solve the problem by building small, frequent checkpoints into his interaction with Edgar. That way, Randy would have a chance to verify the usability of Edgar's brilliant ideas before allowing him to get overcommitted. Some of Edgar's ideas might even be done in a way that was consistent with the project goals.

15.1.3 The double bind

Randy's reaction to Sharon's idea was perfectly predictable from someone addicted to placating: "But Edgar would be upset if he thought I was looking over his shoulder."

Sharon replied, "Well, then, I suppose he'll just have to be upset. If he proves that he can conform to project goals, you can gradually lengthen the checkpoint intervals." This logic, of course, did not convince Randy.

Placating omits the self. To put an end to placating, you must bring the placater's self back into the equation. Sharon did that by telling Randy that if he didn't do what she wanted, she would remove both him and Edgar from their positions. This put Randy in a double bind. If he continued to placate Edgar, he wouldn't be placating Sharon, while if he placated Sharon, he'd have to stop placating Edgar.

One way or the other, he had to put himself back into the interaction. To continue placating, he had to stop placating.

Sharon was an intuitive master at the double bind. She didn't even know the term, but I watched her handle another common placating situation in a similar way. Georgine, another one of her managers, came to her with a problem, saying, "What do you want me to do? I'll do whatever you say."

Instead of falling into the trap of allowing Georgine to play the victim, Sharon resolved the situation with another form of the double bind. She told Georgine, "I want you to discover what you want to do, and then I want you to explain it to me." To placate Sharon, Georgine had to stop placating her and do some original thinking.

In other words, when Friday puts his head under your foot, take your foot away and replace it with his own foot. That puts him feet-first back into the equation.

15.2 Blaming

Chapter 14 showed that blaming behavior can also be used to avoid engagement in a number of ways. It's hard to engage with someone when they are nothing.

15.2.1 Blaming through rules

The IBM commenting standard itself represents an example of rules used to avoid engagement. Soon after the standard was published, the assemblers were "instrumented" to count the percentage of lines commented. If the number was less than three-fourths, the program would not be assembled—a totally automated blaming tool!

When managers set an inflexible rule that three-fourths of the code must be commented, they say, in effect, "We think you're incapable of making a reasonable response to a reasonable technical requirement." This is generalized blaming, and usually is met by an incongruent, often irrelevant response. When IBM programmers realized that their under-commented programs would not assemble, they quickly adopted the practice of supplying nonsense comments on each line. For years after the comment-counting feature was euthanized, you could tell code from its era by the meaningless X's in the comment fields.

Although that was decades ago, the practice of blaming through rules continues unabated. The dynamic that locks in this practice is shown in Figure 15-1.

Here's a modern example of this immortal dynamic. At a firm specializing in Macintosh™ software development, management set a quota of number of changes per release for each module added to the release. This rigid and ridiculous rule was an attempt to gain control over changes without systemic understanding or management attention. Again, the rule was enforced by a tool, this time by instrumenting the configuration management software to count changes per module and abort the "make" operation if any module exceeded the quota. Needless to say, the programmers wasted many merry hours finding ways to beat this system, which management eventually abandoned without fanfare.

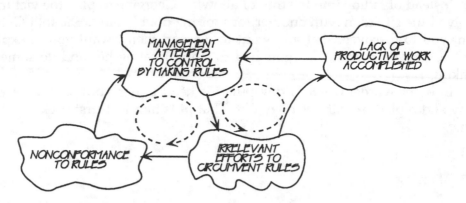

Figure 15-1.   When managers attempt to control by making blaming rules, the effort boomerangs and produces less control and even less conformance to the rules.

The congruent approach to setting standards or rules avoids this common dynamic. Figure 15-2 shows one organization's standard for adding comments to lines of code. Consider the message that this standard gives the programmers, in contrast to the message that their assembler will count their comments and punish them if there are not enough.

Clarity in Code:

Code is written once, but will probably be read many times. As you write, keep in mind the trouble that other readers may have in understanding what you create. The four main approaches to such clarity are

1.   clear coding and design

2.   overall design comments to guide the reader

3.   comments only when the code cannot be made clear by itself

4.   testing of 1-3 through reviews by others

Figure 15-2.   A congruent standard for commenting code.

A second congruent approach to this commenting standard is to follow the useful meta-standard that says,

If there is one standard, there must be at least two standards.

This gives the programmer a choice—in this case, comment all lines, or comment none and document your program's logic clearly in some other way.

15.2.2 *Blaming the lazy employee*

A common complaint of the blaming manager is that an employee is lazy, as in this example from Ervin, a team leader:

"I suppose Mayleen does all her assigned work, but never an ounce extra. And slow! But the worst thing is the way she takes assignments: totally flat, like she was saying, 'Oh, no, don't bother me with more work.' She actually asked me last time if I wouldn't give the job to someone else, because she had too much to do. I'm really getting depressed having her on my team, and I'm at my wits' end."

Once again, Ervin is making the assumption that both of them are operating in the same context. When asked to conjure up another word for "lazy," Ervin produced "uninterested." When he checked it out with Mayleen, she told him that when she came to work for the company, she had been promised a spot on a different project that really excited her. She never wanted to be assigned to this project in the first place, but the other project had been delayed, so Ervin's boss assigned her to Ervin, advising her, "Don't get too involved, so I can move you once we get started." Needless to say, this was different from Ervin's context.

Notice how in this case, Mayleen did listen to Ervin's boss when he was just making a casual, even careless, remark, "Don't get too involved ..." When it comes to language, there's no predicting what a word or phrase will or won't do, so always check the context.

To check the context, of course, you have to engage the other person. Ron, the long-time manager of a team of six people, told me that one team member, Nathan, was "goofing off." I asked him to consider whether Nathan might be having some trouble outside of work, as with a sick child. "Oh," said Ron, "do you think he has children?"

After almost two years of managing this team, Ron didn't know which of the members were married, let alone had children. It's certainly easier to blame someone when you have no more engagement than that. The prescription for such disengagement is to arrange circumstances in which people can get to know one another as something more than "human resources," "peopleware," or "biological programming tools" (BPTs).

15.2.3 The aikido way to engage blaming

For blamers, the other person is left out of the equation. Ideally, to engage blamers, you would force them to recognize your own existence. Theoretically, this would be done by moving closer to blamers until they are forced to acknowledge that you exist. However, the reaction to blamers is generally just the opposite: to put the maximum distance between themselves and you. Why should you spend any more of your life than absolutely necessary with a person who finds pleasure in being miserable and in making other people miserable?

Avoiding blamers works if you don't have to deal with them again, but this is exactly the opposite of engaging. If your work requires that you engage the blamer, you need to learn the method of the aikido masters when dealing with all forms of attack, including blame:

> When someone hits you, he is extending his ki toward you and it starts to flow when he thinks he will hit you—even before his body moves. His action is directed by his mind. You don't need to deal with his body at all if you can redirect his mind and the flow of his ki. That's the secret; lead his mind away from you and the body will follow.[2]

In aikido, you lead the mind away by physical means, though these are always as gentle as possible. The idea is not to further upset the person or draw more attention to yourself, as stiff resistance or a punch would do. In fact, skilled aikidoists often disable their attackers without even touching them, which of course is what you want to do with someone who is blaming you.

Blaming can be handled in the same way, first by yielding, but in such a way that the blame is unable to harm you. Done properly, this surprising move engages the blamer's mind, so that you can easily change its direction. For example, suppose an employee blames you for his failure to develop a specified function. "You didn't <u>tell</u> me that <u>this</u> function was part of the spec," he screams. Although you remember telling him, you don't try to deny the allegation, which only focuses his blame more firmly on you. Instead, you may say, "If you didn't know it was in the spec, I can certainly understand why you didn't develop it."

Saying this, you have agreed with his anger without accepting his blame. Next, you redirect the energy of this blame (the ki, in aikido terms) into something more productive. You have aligned with his energy, so you can push from behind rather than resisting it from the front. You might say, "What's the best way for you to be informed of functions to implement?" This makes you collaborators, rather than opponents, by turning the energy toward preventing the problem in the future, rather than belaboring the unchangeable past. Even better, you have not become a blamer yourself.

In the physical realm, the aikido approach takes years to master, but verbal assaults are much easier to handle. I can personally attest that a small amount of attention and practice can yield remarkable results in handling attacks from blamers. An excellent starting place is Crum's *The Magic of Conflict*.[3]

15.3 Superreasonable

In their actions, superreasonable managers avoid every form of engagement with other people, or even with themselves.

15.3.1 Getting small, relevant feedback

When an employee says you didn't tell him something that you are sure you did, consider the possibility that you were being superreasonable at the time. When superreasonable managers attempt to set the context for a project or organization, they believe that they do it once and for all by giving an inspiring speech, issuing a vision paper, or publishing a strategic plan. Late in a project, such a superreasonable manager will become blaming and say, "I <u>told</u> them that we were to put Function A <u>ahead</u> of Function B, and now they've done just the <u>opposite</u>! Are they <u>stupid</u> or are they <u>deaf</u>?"

What could be more superreasonable—more out of touch with real people— than the belief that everyone listens to, understands, and believes every word you say or write? Real communication is noisy. If you wish it to be effective, you must make it iterative. Small, relevant feedback is one of the keys to keeping everyone in the same context, as we'll see in Chapter 17.

15.3.2 Choosing communication channels

Managers who are superreasonable will seize any opportunity to avoid engagement. In recent years, a new method of avoiding engagement has been made possible by new technology:

> E-mail may decrease personal communication (feedback) between IS managers and their direct reports. ... some IS managers are hiding behind E-mail. Despite what some technical managers believe, research indicates that goal setting, career guidance, and feedback are learned skills that should be done face-to-face to maximize the outcomes.[4]

The E-mail recipient cannot see the sender's body, hear the tone of voice, or smell the sweat. This makes E-mail the perfect medium for the manager who wants to "communicate" with someone in the characteristic superreasonable way: without engagement.

The congruent manager has many choices of communication methods, including E-mail for those messages that are appropriate. The choice among these methods is easily made by applying the self/other/context test for congruence.

For instance, E-mail is cheaper and protects the sender, but doesn't really give the other person a fair chance when the issue may be an emotional one. A face-to-face meeting may be the best way to include the other person, but if that person works across the continent, a phone call may balance the context more reasonably in terms of time and cost.

Personality differences may provide another basis for choosing the communication channel more congruently. Introverts tend to like the way E-mail gives them time to prepare their response. Extroverts, on the other hand, may miss the quick back-and-forth interaction. An extroverted manager communicating with an introverted developer could balance the self and the other by starting the interaction with an E-mail message that outlines the issues and suggests a time and place for a face-to-face meeting. The size of the delay and the length of the meeting would be set according to the context.

15.4 Irrelevant

An irrelevant manager's coping style is out of touch with the context, and thus has a tendency to be self-correcting in an organizational environment. No organizational culture that is based on being out of touch with the context could long endure unless it is protected by a larger organization such as a government bureaucracy. In individual cases, however, these incongruent coping styles can cause much damage before being corrected, for example, by removing a high-level irrelevant executive.

15.4.1 Management availability

Busy management is bad management. To engage others, you have to be available, and availability is cited by new managers as one of the three most important characteristics in a mentor.[5] The other two characteristics are setting high standards and orchestrating developmental experiences, both of which also require a lot of engaging. Irrelevant managers keep busy doing irrelevant or unimportant things, or things they should be having others do. One vice president's secretary told me that he often sat in his office for hours arranging paper clips in the little flat drawer above the other drawers in his desk. Is that more or less irrelevant than the vice president who spent hours playing with an organization-charting application on his Macintosh?

15.4.2 Performance appraisals

Sitting in the office playing with paper clips is clearly not the road to engagement, and many organizations have introduced programs in an enlightened attempt to force managers to engage with their workers. First among these programs is the practice of *performance appraisals*, but their effect is almost invariably to foster further disengagement.

If done well, management is a tough job, which is why the pay is premium. However, there will always be those managers who want to get paid for the hard parts of management work without actually *doing* them. Offering feedback is one of those hard parts. Under a performance appraisal system, placating or irrelevant managers can think, "Well, I won't bring that up right now. I'll save it for the performance appraisal next December." Over the months, feedback accumulates to be dumped on people when it is too large and too late to do anything but create resentment and opposition. Managers appear to be doing management work, but they are simply creating trouble.

Performance appraisals can also be part of what Virginia Satir calls the Big Game, or Who Gets to Tell Whom What to Do. Blaming managers like to play the Big Game. Performance appraisals are symptoms of this kind of blaming style of management, because they let the manager play with a stacked deck. Nothing is more certain to bring out incongruence in employees. As Deming says, even the best appraisals leave

> people bitter, despondent, dejected, some even depressed, all unfit for work for weeks after receipt of [a] rating, unable to comprehend why they are inferior. It is unfair, as it ascribes to the people in a group differences that may be caused totally by the system that they work in.[6]

In a congruent organization, however, periodic performance appraisals are simply superfluous. Congruent managers continuously do whatever appraising is needed, acting while their feedback is timely, relevant, and not overwhelming.

15.5 Loving and Hating

Like irrelevant managers, loving/hating managers are out of touch with the context and thus cannot last long.

What can I say about lovers that the poets haven't already said? Should you be unfortunate enough to encounter a loving relationship, the bright side is that it probably won't last. Lovers are best left alone, to let nature take its course. The best you can do is place the lover and loved one in separate functions, so that when the fiery glow fades, an entire operation won't be annihilated.

Love doesn't last, but hate can gnaw the entrails of an organization for a very long time. The clue to handling blood feuds is to confront them with the missing context. Ask the haters, "Are you able to put this animosity aside and do this work?" If the answer is yes, establish a trial period to allow the haters to prove their assertion. If no, then break up any possible relationship involving a feud.

Hating postures exclude the context, and ordinarily do not continue for long in the real world unless supported by co-dependent behavior. If you are inclined to placate, it's easy to get hooked into these relationships and, by your own addiction, perpetuate theirs. For instance, if you must break up a feud, you may have the unpleasant task of reassigning or firing someone. Nobody likes this task, but you mustn't hesitate. And don't ever get snared in the trap of trying to make someone like someone else.

15.6 Helpful Hints and Suggestions

1. Here's a way to give feedback without words. A monthly lunch is set up with the boss, and the people responsible for the process improvement program give tickets to this lunch to those managers whose projects or functions have been most cooperative that month. This taps into the desire of many managers to climb the corporate ladder.

2. One way to engage a person who is being irrelevant is by imitating the person's behavior. If the person is jumping around, you jump around. If the person is talking rapidly, you talk just as rapidly. If the person is drumming on the table with a pen, you drum on the table with a pen. After a while, the person may notice the imitation (context), or notice that you are imitating (other), or simply stop the irrelevant behavior (self). In any case, you have made initial contact, and you can proceed from there.

3. When I'm working with a group and suddenly turn superreasonable, I'm effectively in a trance, spinning words to the distant blue sky. All it takes to pop me out of this mysterious state is the lightest touch on the back of the hand. Try it the next time that certain someone turns superreasonable on you.

4. The double bind is a good example of a technique that can be destructive if used from an incongruent position. In the story at the beginning of Chapter 13, Morie, the president, puts Charlene in this double bind:

   a. If X is your estimate, you can't be a competent estimator.
   b. If you are a competent manager, you'll be able to make schedule Z.

   If she goes along with Z, she's admitting she's an incompetent estimator. If she doesn't, she's admitting she's an incompetent manager. Children raised under this kind of lose/lose double bind have great trouble being congruent in adulthood.

15.7 Summary

✓ In placating and blaming organizations, managers attempt to manage without engaging the people supposedly being managed. The particular way they avoid engaging depends upon their favored coping style.

✓ In a placating organization, the lack of engagement is deeply rooted and appears in many guises. For instance, much placating is hidden under the label of compromise.

✓ By building small, frequent checkpoints into interactions with brilliant employees, a manager has a chance to verify the usability of brilliant ideas before getting overcommitted to something that isn't consistent with the project goals. Placating managers, however, will undermine this approach.

✓ To end placating behavior, you must bring the placater's self back into the equation. This can sometimes be done by creating a double bind: If you placate in one direction, you won't be able to placate in the other, so in either case, you'll be unable to be the perfect placater. Another form of double bind is, "If you want to placate me, you have to stop placating me!"

✓ Blaming can also be used to avoid engagement in a number of ways. One way is to create rules and even to implement them in automated tools. The generalized blaming implemented in such tools is often met with an irrelevant response.

✓ A congruent approach to setting rules and standards avoids blaming, respects the intelligence and professionalism of the staff, and gives them choices.

✓ One prescription for blaming is to arrange circumstances in which people can get to know one another as something more than human resources. Another is to take the aikido approach of never opposing blaming energy head to head, but flowing with it, then diverting it gently in a more productive direction.

✓ Superreasonable managers often attempt to set the context for a project or organization once and for all when they give an inspiring speech, issue a vision paper, or publish a strategic plan. If they wish it to be effective, they must break their communications into small, relevant feedback.

✓ E-mail is the perfect medium for the superreasonable manager who wants to communicate with someone. The congruent manager has many choices of communication methods. The choice is easily made by applying the self/

other/context test for congruence, as well as personality differences between the sender and the recipient.

✓   Coping styles that are out of touch with the context have a tendency to be self-correcting in an organizational environment. No organizational culture that is based on being out of touch with the context can long endure, unless it is protected by a larger organization.

✓   Irrelevant managers keep busy doing irrelevant or unimportant things, or things they should be having others do. For instance, when giving performance appraisals, managers appear to be doing management work, but they are simply making trouble.

✓   Lovers are best left alone, to let nature take its course. Love doesn't last, but hate can undermine an organization for a very long time. The clue to handling blood feuds is to confront the participants with the missing context without placating.

15.8 Practice

1.   Think of a more congruent way to control changes in a product release than setting a hard limit on changes for each module. Explain why this is more congruent, and why it is likely to work more effectively.

2.   Communication in software engineering organizations often takes place in an emergency situation. One way to define *emergency* is that "context dominates all," but such a definition tends to block information on the self and other. That's why superreasonable and irrelevant managers love to label situations as emergencies. How can you know quickly if it's really an emergency?

3.   Superreasonable managers often use secrecy or security as an excuse for not communicating. What should you do when you encounter this argument?

4.   Discuss how Hints 1, 2, and 3 are applications of the aikido principles.

16
Reframing
the Context

I will not listen to reason. Reason always means what someone else has to say.
— Elizabeth Gaskell

One of the manager's primary jobs is to set the context in which interactions take place and work is accomplished. Sometimes the context is set by words, as when I interrupt and shout at you in a demanding voice, "Why don't you listen to reason?" This simple sentence sets a context consisting of several elements:

- I am entitled to make demands of you.
- What I say is "reason" and what you say is something else.
- I can blame you ("Why don't you ...?").
- My role is to talk; yours is to listen.

Even in such verbal interactions, however, much of the context is set by what I do, rather than what I say:

- I am entitled to interrupt you.
- Shouting is acceptable behavior when I do it.

This chapter examines some of the ways in which problems can be solved by reframing the context through actions and words.

16.1 Reframing

The easiest way to understand *reframing* is through a series of pictures, as shown in Figures 16-1 through 16-4. In Figure 16-1 is a picture of a man. That's simple enough, until the frame is changed and you can see the same man in context. Before the man could have been doing just about anything, but Figure 16-2 shows he's a man plowing a field with two horses.

Figure 16-1.   A picture of a man.

Figure 16-2.   Changing the frame puts the man in a very different context: plowing a field.

However, framing the scene of Figure 16-2 differently results in the picture in Figure 16-3, which you can see is a picture of a house. In real-life situations, there are so many possible ways of looking at the same context that there are probably an infinite number of ways to reframe the situation. Some frames are in time, not space, as when the pessimist sees the bottle half empty and the optimist sees it half full or when the manager sees half the work still to be done, while the developer sees the work half finished.

Figure 16-3.   Framed in a different way, the picture becomes that of a house.

Other frames are in *scale*. How big is a 100,000 element database? One designer has never handled a database with more than 10,000 elements, while another has designed several systems of more than 10,000,000 elements. To the first designer, 100,000 elements seems huge; to the second, tiny. Similarly, one failure in 10,000 transactions may seem trivial in a frame of 50 transactions per day; yet in a frame of 10,000,000 transactions per day, one failure in 10,000 means 1,000 failures per day, which may well be unacceptable.

Scale can be in *time* as well as *space* or *size*. A response time of 10 milliseconds seems slow in the frame of an electronic device that operates on a nanosecond cycle time frame, but seems infinitely fast in the frame of a person looking at a screen.

Or framing can be in *type*. Change the frame of Figure 16-2 to produce Figure 16-4, and suddenly you find what you thought was the whole picture was just an incidental picture on the wall. The real picture is the cook serving that delicious dinner. Or is it? Could that be just a picture on another wall? Or a figure on a page in a book held in your hands, while you are in an even larger context that you can see all around you?

In software engineering, we are surrounded by such reframes of type. From a software engineering point of view, consider the following two pieces of code:

- code driving a screen in a flight simulator game
- code driving a screen in the controls of a real airplane

Even though the codes may be identical bit for bit, they are not the same to the software engineer. Appropriate software engineering processes to produce and verify the one are entirely different from those to produce the other. Their costs vary by several orders of magnitude, and the time to produce them could be days in one case and months in the other. Put it this way: Would you be a willing passenger in a plane whose controls were developed under the same software engineering process as the controls of a flight simulator game?

Figure 16-4.   Changing the frame once more transforms the entire context.

16.2 Discontinuity of Language

Many of the problems that arise in a software engineering organization can be attributed to different perceptions of the context. One of the most important jobs of the software engineering manager is to keep everybody in the organization working in the same frame or at least compatible frames. Are we building a simulation game or a real airplane? Or perhaps a training simulator for pilots who will fly real airplanes?

Unfortunately, management sets the context almost exclusively through the use of language, and language is a system of symbols. In physical systems, the laws of nature limit the speed with which one frame changes into another. An airplane cannot be in Albuquerque one minute and in Cleveland the next. Symbol systems, however, are far less continuous than physical systems, and an airplane symbol on a computer screen can be on a map of Albuquerque one minute and a map of Cleveland the next.

In symbol systems, any X can become any Y almost instantly. For instance, I am under great stress, attempting to ready my module for integration test by Friday. During a casual conversation, my manager says, "Not this Friday; next Friday." Instantly, the frame changes, and my stress evaporates. Even drugs (which are physical systems, after all) could not lower my stress quite this fast.

This ability to change quickly and arbitrarily is what makes computers so programmable, but also makes them so hard to control. That is also what makes people so adaptable and, at the same time, such a potentially destabilizing element in any control system. Much of management's action in setting the context must be directed toward reframing symbolic communication, to convert or harness this nonlinearity.

16.3 Presuppositions

When speaking with others, we often influence their perception of the context—and therefore their responses—through the use of presuppositions.[1] Some presuppositions are overt, as when a manager says at the beginning of a meeting, "We've never been able to solve problems like this in less than half a day." This statement sets a frame that may influence the amount of time the meeting takes, because it lowers any expectation that the participants can solve this problem in less than four hours.

Some presuppositions are overt, but not verbal. When a manager schedules a problem-solving meeting for four hours, the schedule presupposes the same degree of difficulty as in the previous example. When someone from the auditing department is invited, the invitation presupposes the problem has something to do with auditing.

The strongest presuppositions are covert, and covert presuppositions often trigger what look like incongruent, nonlinear reactions. For instance, suppose a manager asks a programmer, "What size B-tree are you going to allocate?" The programmer pouts, looks away, and turns silent, mystifying the manager.

Some of the mystery may be cleared up if we examine the presuppositions in this question:

1. There is going to be a B-tree in the program.
2. The presence or absence of a B-tree is a matter of management concern.
3. The manager is entitled to ask this programmer about technical details.

Which presupposition triggered the defensiveness? Managers who don't notice the presuppositions in their speech will continue to be mystified by such "incongruent" reactions.

This is not the same situation as the manager who intentionally asks, "What size B-tree are you going to allocate?" in order to show the programmer who's smarter and who gets to ask the questions. This case is not oblivious behavior, it's incongruent behavior. A congruent way to do the same thing might be to say, "I'm ultimately responsible for the success or failure of this project, and I'm concerned that you may not produce an effective design. That's why I've called you in to ask you some questions about the design." Now, if the programmer gets defensive, at least the issues are out on the table.

Presuppositions go a long way toward setting the environment, either positively or negatively. Contrast the following statements made by managers when discussing a problem about running an acceptance test:

✓   "If you find a solution, how will you integrate it into the next test?"

✓   "When you find a solution, how will you integrate it into the next test?"

✓   "When we find a solution, how will we integrate it into the next test?"

All three guide the programmer by presupposing there will be another test, but which manager would you rather work for?

16.4 Monsterizing versus the Helpful Model

As Chapter 11 showed, much of the most surprising nonlinear behavior arises not from what is said or done, but from what is remembered and encoded in terms of our implicit mental models we use to make meaning. Because these models set a hidden context that may differ from person to person, they often produce an interaction that surprises the participants. If you don't want to be surprised, you should become familiar with several of these models that are commonly held: the Helpful Model, the Paranoid Model, and the Stupid Model.

16.4.1 The Helpful Model

Even if you're dealing with people who are quite obviously being unhelpful, reframing the situation as if they were being helpful can improve the situation. The Helpful Model[2] says,

No matter how it looks, everyone is trying to be helpful.

For instance, in the midst of a push to prepare a release, a key tester declares, "I'm taking tomorrow off just to sleep all day." A manager who is concerned about the effect on the schedule may comment, "I'm really glad you're monitoring your own condition, because everyone will have to be in top form to get this release out on time, and I'm really concerned we won't make it."

16.4.2 The Paranoid Model

Many managers wouldn't reframe the situation this way. Suppose a manager holds to the Paranoid Model:

Things are going wrong because somebody is trying to hurt me.

This model is seldom accurate, but is most damaging when assumed to be accurate. In the "day off" situation above, a manager holding this model may shriek, "Obviously <u>you</u> don't care at all <u>what</u> happens to this release!" The worst thing about this way of reframing the situation is that it tends to become self-fulfilling. Managers who assume the world is out to get them generally become right, as shown in Figure 16-5. On a CompuServe Forum discussion, Mark Weisz described this dynamic like so: "When people are in conflict, they all too often 'monsterize' the other side, aggravating the conflict and preventing any moving forward. [This is] a terrible positive feedback loop: The more I perceive you as a monster, the more I behave like you are a monster. And, as a reaction, you tend to behave like I would expect a monster to behave. "

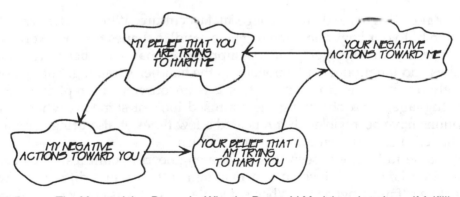

Figure 16-5.   The Monsterizing Dynamic: Why the Paranoid Model tends to be self-fulfilling.

Curiously, the Monsterizing Dynamic is the same as the Helpful Dynamic, but with negative values put on the variables, which demonstrates the power of reframing. The Monsterizing feedback loop appears in such diverse forms as studies of arms races and Peter Senge's "Beer Distribution Game,"[3] used for training managers. In both examples, the destructive loop is possible only when the participants are not allowed to communicate effectively with one another. That's the true significance of these forms for managers.

16.4.3 *The Stupid Model*

There are many alternatives to the Paranoid Model that fall short of the saintly beliefs implicit in the Helpful Model. One of the most common can be called the Stupid Model:

Never attribute to maliciousness that which can otherwise be attributed to stupidity.

Holding this model, a manager may say, "When I hear that you'd like to take the day off tomorrow, I wonder if you understand the urgency of this release?" (Notice the presupposition "you'd like to," which reframes the "I'm going to.")

In the same CompuServe Forum, Brian Richter commented that the Stupid Model has a down side, which turns out to be the same type of positive feedback loop as in the Paranoid Model and the Helpful Model: "I remember one episode of [the television series] *Quantum Leap* where he leaped into a [slow-witted] person. Everyone treated him as if he was going to mess up even the simplest tasks, and as a result of this treatment, he got so nervous he did indeed mess up the simplest tasks."

16.5 Choice of Expression

Culture makes language, then language makes culture. When you arrive at your destination but your bags don't, the baggage handler shapes the context by asking, "Did you lose your luggage?" This presupposition may have been originated by the airlines and taught quite intentionally in the handler's training, but by now it is completely unconscious. You can see that it is unconscious by replying, "No, *you* lost my luggage," and observing the confused look of someone whose cultural assumptions have been violated. If repeated a few times, it also brings you a much better chance of effective handling of your problem.

The same influence is seen in software engineering cultures. Organizations that use "bug language" develop and maintain software in a different way than those that use "fault language." When someone says, "I was late because there was a bug in my program," you could change the frame a tiny bit by replying, "Oh, when did you put the mistake into the program?" Merely changing the language may not cause people to take responsibility for their creations, but it certainly helps. Once you reach a certain threshold, social pressure starts to act on those who continue to evade responsibility by using bug language.

When someone speaks incongruently, you can move the interaction toward congruence by inserting missing self/other/context elements. Both the luggage example and the bug example insert the missing self of the speakers, which moves the interaction toward their taking responsibility.

You can use this technique in many ways. One of the most striking is to get an answer to the question "Is schedule pressure real?" Suppose your customer or manager has just said, "This is a crisis. You must do everything to make this schedule, with no excuses." Does he or she really mean this, or do you have flexibility?

One approach to achieving more congruence is to try to bring the context back to reality. You might say, "Since time is so important, here are several ways I can use money for resources to improve the schedule." One possible response is, "Well, it's not that important." In that case, you can ignore some of the schedule pressure. On the other hand, you may actually get more resources, in which case your ability to make the schedule is increased.

If it's not resources but knowledge that's the missing ingredient, you could reply, "I don't know how to meet the schedule you're proposing. If you show me how, then I'll be able to do it." This brings the speaker into the equation. You may actually get some good advice that will help you, or you might learn that nobody knows how to meet the schedule, but they were hoping that you did.

16.6 Responding to Blaming

Reframing gives you a powerful tool when you find yourself being criticized and don't know how to respond.

16.6.1 Taking the observer position

If you know how to respond resourcefully to criticism, you won't be so afraid to undertake potentially difficult interactions. Here's a tip from the neurolinguistic programming people:

> We discovered that a key distinction between people who respond well to criticism and those who feel devastated when criticized is how they see the meaning of the criticism. People who remained resourceful saw themselves as doing the behavior that was being criticized. The criticism was "out there," "at a distance." From this distance, it was easy for them to calmly make their own evaluation of the criticism, and decide what was useful in it, and what to do about it.
>
> In contrast, those who are devastated by criticism "take it right in." Many people literally imagine that the "negative meaning" of the criticism goes right into their chest, like a piercing arrow or dark beam of light.[4]

In other words, learn how to change the frame and take comments about yourself from the other observer position, not the self position.

16.6.2 *Handling temper tantrums*

It's all very nice to talk about taking the observer position, but it's not easy to do when someone is blaming you. It's even harder when someone is throwing a tantrum at the same time. With practice, it can be done.

> The most efficient way to communicate with adults who are having a verbal temper tantrum is to be still and let them exhaust themselves. Make a sound now and then to let them know that you are still there and that you are listening at least minimally, and let them wind down. THEY WILL NOT LISTEN TO YOU UNTIL THIS HAS TAKEN PLACE.[5]

In other words, take the observer position to the extreme. For me, this is difficult because I want to do something about the tantrum, so I forget that doing nothing is doing something. I find it helpful to talk to myself, "My, how interesting that a forty-two-year-old can do such an impressive imitation of a four-year-old. It's such a convincing performance that I'm almost tempted to treat him as if he were a child and I were his parent." That message usually leads me away from temptation, but I must be careful not to cross over the line and become superreasonable.

16.6.3 *Perfection belief*

Another thing that gets in the way of being able to handle blaming criticism is the perfectionist survival rule presented in Chapter 15. The rule "I must be perfect" is common enough in the general population, but among people attracted to software engineering, it's close to universal. Among the hundreds of technical people I've watched move into software engineering management (including me), perhaps five were not affected by an unreasonable need to be perfect.

Given the quality demands of the software business, a reasonable need for perfection can be a great asset. But if that need becomes excessive—if you must be perfectly perfect—it becomes a liability.

A good illustration is the following statement by Greg Louganis, winner of two gold medals in diving in the 1984 and 1988 Olympics, and about as perfect a diver as the world has ever seen. As he observed in a television interview,

> I'm a real perfectionist, but that is the irony. In order to do it perfectly, I have to let go of perfection a little. For instance, in diving, there's a "sweet spot" on the board, right at the end. I can't always hit it perfectly. Sometimes, I'm a little back from it. Sometimes, I'm a little over. But the judges can't tell that. I have to deal with whatever takeoff I have been given. I can't leave my mind on the board. I have to stay in the present. I have to be relaxed enough to clue into the memory tape of how to do it. That's why I train so hard—not just to do it right, but to do it right from all the wrong places.

If you have a perfectionist bent, pay attention to the way Louganis reframes the situation with the phrase "I have to deal with whatever takeoff I've been given." In terms of congruence, this says, "I accept that the context (the board) and the others (the judges) are what they are, not necessarily perfect the way I'd like them to be. I accept the imperfection of the world, and practice dealing with whatever imperfect situation I find myself in." In terms of management, this says, "As the one responsible for control, it's my job to deal with the imperfections in the world. If the world were perfect, I'd be unemployed."

Of course, you are part of the world, too, so it's wrong to imagine that you can be perfect. Thus, if you believe you can be perfect, you're wrong—and thus imperfect. As long as you believe you can be perfect, you can't be perfect. How's that for a reframing into a double bind!

16.6.4 *Verifying your notions*

The dramatist George Bernard Shaw once mocked the people who believed in their own perfection: "The longer I live, the more I see that I am never wrong about anything, and that all the pains I have so humbly taken to verify my notions have only wasted my time." Shaw suggests that only perfect people can operate without "verifying their notions." For the rest of us, we can avoid trouble by remaining open to new information.

The most congruent—and thus most effective—notion you can have is "Well, it looks as if I made a mistake." This opens the discussion to more information.

But perhaps you're not sure you made a mistake. (This is the kind of thought that paralyzes perfectionists.) In that case, you can say, "Well, I thought I was doing the right thing, but it looks as if I might have made a mistake. What else can you tell me about it?" As always, the most reliable way to set the context is by setting an example, in this case an example of someone who can admit the possibility of making a mistake.

16.7 Helpful Hints and Suggestions

1.   Here's a marvelous reminder from Ben Sano on the CompuServe Forum: "Only a few of the folks who manage technical personnel realize that a technical challenge is considered a reward by technical workers." This is what we call the "free game" theory of feedback. Pinball players and technical workers play for the chance to play again.

2.   People are symbol-making systems, so at any time people can quickly become totally nonlinear. People's behaviors, however, are not always as arbitrary as

they look. It's often only our poor perception. Frequently, when managers label employees' actions as arbitrary and discontinuous, it's because they haven't been watching. They usually haven't been looking at the emotional information. So in a way, it's just like any other discontinuity: If we don't understand the dynamics and don't watch the feedback, we are surprised by discontinuity.

3. Because of boomerang effects, reframing often involves actually reversing the previously assumed context. Here's an example from auto manufacturing that applies directly to the software industry:

> In fact, one way to improve productivity is not by working faster but by slowing down. On a typical final auto assembly line that produces about 60 vehicles an hour, it is not unusual for 6 to 8 of these to be diverted to a repair bay. Chevrolets are repaired in the same way Rolls Royces are built—by hand and one at a time. At a slightly slower line speed, the number of "perfect" cars coming off the line is higher and overall productivity enhanced.[6]

4. My colleague Dan Starr offers an interesting suggestion about using the Stupid Model: "So the Stupid Model is well known, and here I thought I'd invented it for myself! I've never tried to use this model to predict the future, just to keep myself out of paranoia when it seems that some schmuck is out to get me. And the Stupid Model does cover something that's not always apparent from the Helpful Model: Everyone may be trying to help, but good intentions are no substitute for competence."

16.8 Summary

✓ One of the manager's primary jobs is to set either by words or actions the context in which interactions take place and work is accomplished. In real-world situations, there are so many possible ways of looking at the same context that there are probably an infinite number of ways to reframe the situation.

✓ Frames can be in space or time. They can be changed by changing scale, again, in space or time. Frames can also be in type: Is it a thing or a model of a thing or a model of a model of a thing?

✓ Another important job of the software engineering manager is to keep everybody in the organization working in the same frame, or at least in compatible frames. This is done almost exclusively through the use of language, a system of symbols. Much of management's action in setting the context must be directed toward reframing symbolic communication, to achieve stability by converting or harnessing the nonlinearity of symbols.

✓   The context may be set through the use of presuppositions, either positively or negatively. The strongest presuppositions are covert. Managers who don't notice the presuppositions in their speech will continue to be mystified by seemingly incongruent reactions.

✓   The implicit mental models from which we make meaning set a hidden context that may differ from person to person. These models often determine the surprising character of an interaction because each person is operating in a different frame, unknown to the others.

✓   The Helpful Model says that no matter how it looks, everyone is trying to be helpful. Even if you're dealing with people who are quite obviously being unhelpful, reframing the situation as if they were being helpful can improve the situation.

✓   The Paranoid Model says things are going wrong because somebody is trying to hurt me. The worst thing about this way of reframing the situation is that it tends to become self-fulfilling, through the Monsterizing Dynamic.

✓   The Stupid Model says you should never attribute to maliciousness that which can otherwise be attributed to stupidity—a gentler reframe, but somewhat short of the Helpful Model.

✓   Culture makes language, then language makes culture, which is certainly true in software engineering cultures. Organizations that use bug language develop and maintain software in a different way than those that use fault language.

✓   When someone speaks incongruently, you can move the interaction toward congruence by inserting missing self/other/context elements.

✓   Reframing gives you a powerful tool when you find yourself being criticized and don't know how to respond. The key is to frame the situation from a distance—from the observer position. A similar technique is useful when someone is throwing a temper tantrum.

✓   Reframing is especially helpful in handling perfection beliefs, especially your own.

16.9 Practice

1. One of the frequent management questions in certain organizations is affectionately known as WISCY or "Why isn't someone coding yet?" If you ask this enough, in what way will you influence the organization's development process? What other presupposing questions are asked in your organization that tend to lock you into a certain process frame?

2. By reframing, you can emphasize the good in what someone did, even if overall it's not so great. For example, when someone interrupts, you can appreciate them for their enthusiasm. When they do nonstandard work, you can appreciate their creativity. Give several other examples of this type of part-for-whole reframing.

17
Informative Feedback

All means prove a blunt instrument if they have not behind them a living spirit.
— Albert Einstein

If a manager is to steer congruently, each interaction must balance the self, other, and context. Engaging someone can supply the missing other; reframing can furnish the missing or distorted context; but how is the self put into an incongruent relationship?

Many managers believe that praising and blaming supply the missing self. Praise tells what I like; blame, what I don't like. But both praising and blaming presuppose that I am someone who is entitled to do so, that I am the boss. But being boss is a role, not a person, so praising or blaming doesn't supply the self at all. Instead, they each supply a disguised context behind which the frightened self can hide.

Rather than praising or blaming, why not work simply on improving the flow of information? Why not take the time and trouble to establish a small increment of correct information out of each interaction?

17.1 Feedback

Many management books mention feedback as an important activity, but very few define what they're talking about. We can, however, infer various definitions of feedback. What does it mean when I give you feedback?

One of the most common meanings is "I am the boss, and I'm going to demonstrate my dominance over you by telling you what is right and wrong about you (mostly wrong)." (See Figure 17-1.) The reaction to this sort of feedback comes in several forms, generally incongruent and often silent, such as

- You may think you're the boss, but you can't even see most of what I do.
- The sooner I get out of this prison, the better.
- I guess I'd better not tell you about that <u>other</u> thing.

Figure 17-1.   "Giving you feedback" to some people means "I am dominating you."

When the giver of feedback isn't the boss, or is a placating boss, or is generally afraid to deal with people directly, the feedback may take on the meaning "I am manipulating you." (See Figure 17-2.) This kind of feedback generally has a catch that you don't recognize until hours or days later.

For instance, the boss tells you, "You're the best team player I've got." Only later do you realize that this was a prelude to assigning you the nasty jobs that nobody else is "team player" enough to accept.

When the giver of feedback is in a powerless position but isn't afraid of you, the feedback is often intended to burn (Figure 17-3). This kind of feedback is frequently delivered from a superreasonable stance, as when someone says, "Oh, yes, I remember that technique from my high school FORTRAN textbook."

Figure 17-2.   "Giving you feedback" to some people means "I am manipulating you."

Figure 17-3.   "Giving you feedback" to some people means "I am burning you."

All of these forms fit the definition of feedback, as I use the term:

- information about past behavior
- delivered in the present
- which may or may not influence future behavior[1]

They do not, however, fit my idea of congruent feedback, which is information that you may not have, that you may find useful, and that you are free to use in any way that suits you (Figure 17-4). It's this kind of feedback that offers the best chance to improve a relationship or an organization.

Figure 17-4.   "Giving you feedback" to some people means "I am giving you a chance to taste the soup, so you will have information to improve it if you wish to."

17.2 The Giver's Fact

Regardless of how congruent or incongruent the feedback, it follows a principle called the Giver's Fact:

No matter what it appears to be, feedback information is almost totally about the giver, not the receiver.

Let's look at a few examples of managers who thought they were giving information about an employee. An example of the "I am dominating you" type of feedback in Figure 17-1 is Verne, the manager who shrieks at you, "Any idiot who could make that @$&*! mistake has to be a blind jackass."

What does this feedback say about Verne? The virulent tone suggests that he feels powerless; why else would he not speak normally instead of trying to intimidate with language? The obscenity suggests he has lost contact with the context.

He certainly has lost contact with himself, for he appears nowhere in this diatribe. He thinks he is hiding himself from you, but is actually only hiding himself from himself, like an ostrich with his head in the sand.

Or take the case of Della, who cons you into taking disagreeable work by saying, "You're the best team player I've got." First of all, she doesn't think she has a team at all; otherwise she would have approached the team with the assignment and let the team figure out how to get it done. Secondly, she doesn't think much of her own leadership ability, for why else would she resort to manipulations?

Then there is the case of the manager who says, "Oh, yes, I remember that technique from my high school FORTRAN textbook." This one is so easy to see through that all I need to say is it's an amusing exercise in how the more you try to hide behind feedback, the more it reveals about yourself.

17.3 Forms of Feedback

As a manager, you'll have to give feedback, even though it is so revealing about yourself. You can give feedback in one of many forms; and with practice, you can learn to give feedback in a congruent fashion that actually contains information about something besides yourself. Here are a few tips.

17.3.1 Verbal precision

Volume 2 of this series devoted an entire chapter to precision listening.[2] You can review that same material with an eye to learning how to speak precisely and congruently. Eventually, with practice, you will be able to offer feedback that's precise and effective. For instance, consider which of these ways of communicating about a late module will be most effective in managing a project:

✓ "You don't care anything about this project."

✓ "You're always late with your part of the project."

✓ "I don't like it when you're late."

✓ "Although I appreciate your concern for quality, the schedule must be met."

✓ "I really appreciate your concern for quality, but I get in trouble when your part of the project doesn't meet the schedule."

✓ "I really appreciate that you took the time to do high-quality work. I'm having trouble, though, because I don't understand the discrepancy between my estimating model and the actual time it takes to do high-quality work. I'd like to work on this with you."

17.3.2 Trust

Not all feedback is in the words themselves. When you offer people a technical challenge, no matter what words you use, you're giving feedback. You are telling them that you trust them, and trust is the great motivator. When someone trusts you, you will do practically anything not to let the person down. On the other hand, when someone distrusts you, you've been found guilty before the act, so why bother?

17.3.3 Freedom

What if you don't have challenging assignments to offer? Because there is so much variation in programmers' abilities, it's hard to keep the high performers happy if they're treated just like the low performers. Talented programmers are likely to interpret the lack of challenge as a lack of appreciation and leave to form their own business, then sell their services back to you.

· Allowing talented people to leave can be quite a rational way to handle the variation/morale problem. One manager who needed programmers to stay and maintain existing systems, but couldn't offer a sufficient diet of new development to keep them happy, explicitly encouraged programmers to form their own businesses. Then he hired them back at a generous part-time fee to maintain existing systems. This kept them from becoming full-time employees of some other company. Another manager kept maintainers around by letting them do business on company time. Giving freedom is a way of saying, "I not only value your technical ability, but I trust your honesty and integrity."

I know that these two actions will strike some managers as placating. They would be placating if there were no true benefit for the customers and for the manager who provides this freedom. If it makes good business sense for all parties, it's not placating, but contracting.

17.3.4 What people remember

What do people remember about feedback? Irvin Yalom, the psychiatrist, once tested what his patients remembered:

> Years ago I conducted an experiment in which a patient and I each wrote our own view of each of our therapy hours. Later when we compared them, it was at times difficult to believe that we described the same hour. Even our views of

what was helpful varied. My elegant interpretations? She never even heard them! Instead, she remembered, and treasured, casual, personal, supportive comments I had made.[3]

Most of all, employees will remember the emotional tone in which your "elegant interpretations" are given. Of all the emotional messages you can offer, the most important is the time you're willing to spend listening to the person. Psychiatrists, of course, have to overcome the handicap of starting with a message that says, in effect, "I don't care enough about you to spend time listening to you unless you pay me by the hour."

Managers do not have this handicap; any time they spend with their employees is a clear message about how much those employees are valued. Managers have other handicaps, however. For instance, one of the functions of all leaders is to become a focus for hostility. But it's hard to sit and listen to someone who's lambasting you, often for things that never involved you. I find that it's easier to do this when I say early in the session, "I want to be helpful, but I'm having a hard time listening to your unhappiness about these things, partly because I'm really not sure what you'd like me to do about them."

Another approach that helps is empathic listening, or listening from "inside another person, observing from his/her point of view."[4] Much has been written about empathic listening, but when I interviewed eleven software engineering managers in one company, only four could give a reasonable definition of *empathy*, such as "a feeling for or a capacity for sharing in the interests of another."

One way of achieving more empathic listening is by knowing and using the other person's Myers-Briggs type (as well as your own type). Type understanding can facilitate effective communication in several ways:

- By talking the other's type language, you can build rapport more quickly.
- By listening in the other's type terms, you can quickly assess what is bothering the speaker.
- Knowing the other's type helps set goals that will be satisfactory to both of you.
- Knowing the other's type helps create interventions that will work for this person.

17.3.5 Modeling desired behavior

People are great imitators, and imitation is the sincerest form of flattery. One of the strongest ways to praise people is to imitate their behavior. Anything you do that they also do will be seen as praise for what they are doing. For instance, if you proudly show your status by bragging that you don't bother to answer your phone messages, you will be praising those employees who are similarly lax.

The power of setting an example is humorously and beautifully expressed in Wain's Fifth Conclusion:

"Nothing motivates a man more than to see his boss put in an honest day's work."[5]

St. Francis of Assisi said, "It's no use walking anywhere to preach unless our walking is our preaching." In my view, our walking cannot help but be our preaching.

17.4 Softening the Pain

Some managers cringe at the idea of having power over people's lives. They feel that the power to fire someone is so intimidating that they instead keep non-performers but intentionally or unintentionally make them miserable. This strange behavior is based on two false views: the belief in the absolute nature of hierarchy, and the belief in there being no alternatives to this kind of organization. If you fire people, they can go somewhere else. You are not God, and knowing that makes life a lot easier for you and the people around you.

I find it puzzling that simple, informative feedback should also be a source of pain, but it seems to be. When it comes to doling out rations of appreciation, some managers act like the Norwegian husband whose wife, on their tenth anniversary, asked if he loved her. He looked at her with a stern yet puzzled expression and said, "I told you I loved you when I married you, and if I change my mind, I'll let you know."

When I talk to managers about appreciating behavior they wish to reinforce, these strong, self-reliant men and women seem to turn into mush. The one ability they retain is the ability to produce rationalizations, such as

✓   "They should know if they're doing well."

✓   "They're paid to do a good job. That's appreciation enough."

✓   "I'll tell them at appraisal time (ten months from now)."

Where does their fear come from?

17.4.1 Shame

One source of this fear is shame. As Tagore, the Nobel-prize winning Indian poet, said, "Praise shames me, because I secretly crave it." Managers who are ashamed to want appreciation for themselves are unlikely to offer it to their own employees. It would help for them to know this big secret:

All people like to have their work appreciated.

17.4.2 Fear of the hook

One of the reasons the universal craving for appreciation is a big secret is that people do seem reluctant to accept appreciative comments. A plausible explanation is that they view the appreciation as the bait that conceals the hook, as in "You're the best team player ... "

17.4.3 Technical envy

Another possible explanation is technical envy. An effective manager must be able to enjoy empowering others to experience the joy of technical work. But, says colleague Mark Weisz, it's not always easy for some managers with technical backgrounds to experience this enjoyment:

> These managers envy their workers' success, their joy, their camaraderie. If the manager has it bad, he may act so as to prevent that success and joy from occurring again by subtly (and quite unconsciously) undermining the goals he is supposed to achieve with the team of workers.
>
> Some managers might be threatened by the success of those they manage; that is, they may feel personally diminished if the credit for a good project outcome falls on their team members rather than on themselves. Some organizational cultures reinforce this attitude.
>
> Since these things are largely outside the awareness of the manager involved (i.e. "unconscious"), there is little point in bluntly calling his attention to them. To do so will make the manager defensive—his typical response will be denial, indignation at the very suggestion, and anger.

Envy is the enemy of praise. If you find it difficult to praise someone's fine work, take a look inside yourself for a whisper of envy.

17.4.4 Lack of practice

Even after all these obstacles are put aside, many managers feel awkward offering appreciative feedback because they simply don't have any experience either giving or receiving such feedback. So practice every night in bed, reviewing the good things you did during the day and appreciating yourself for them. There's no hook, there's no shame, and if it bores you, at least it will put you to sleep.

17.5 Helpful Hints and Suggestions

1.   One reason blame is ineffective is that familiarity breeds contempt, and we are all very familiar with criticism. Crum cites a study that showed a normal two-

year-old child in one day was told what not to do 432 times, as opposed to 32 positive acknowledgments.[6] He estimates that the national average of parent-to-child criticisms is twelve criticisms to one compliment, while in secondary school the ratio is eighteen to one from teacher to student.

By my calculations, by the time most people have reached the age of thirty, they have received several million criticisms, compared to a few hundred thousand positive strokes. For the manager, this probably means that an employee probably won't benefit much from another tongue lashing, but that some approving remark might be heard as exceptional. Since excessive criticism tends to lower self-esteem, perhaps blaming is not the ideal way to deal with an incongruent employee.

2.   The animal trainers Jack and Wendy Volhard observe that an animal will perform a trained task only a certain number of times without reinforcement before failing in the task.[7] If this applies to humans as well, someone's failure could puzzle you because you don't know how many repetitions have already been done without reinforcement. By positively reinforcing employees' work every time, you can remove a dependency on this unknown variable.

17.6 Summary

✓   If a manager is to manage congruently, each interaction must balance the self, other, and context. The best way to do this is to concentrate on improving the flow of information, making the effort to create a small increment of correct information out of each interaction.

✓   Both praising and blaming presuppose that I am someone entitled to do so, that I am the boss. They supply a disguised context behind which a frightened self can hide.

✓   *Feedback*, as used in management texts, has several different definitions. One of the most common is "I am the boss, and I'm going to demonstrate my dominance over you by telling you what is right and wrong about you (mostly wrong)." When the giver is afraid to deal with people directly, the feedback may take on the meaning "I am manipulating you." Sometimes, the feedback is clearly intended to burn the receiver.

✓   All of these forms fit the definition of feedback as information about past behavior, delivered in the present, which may or may not influence future behavior. Congruent feedback, however, is information that you may not have, that you may find useful, and that you are free to use in any way that fits for you. Congruent feedback offers the best chance to improve a relationship or an organization.

✓   Feedback always follows the Giver's Fact: No matter what it appears to be, feedback information is almost totally about the giver, not the receiver. It takes skill and hard work to provide feedback that actually contains other information.

✓   Feedback comes in many forms: offering verbal statements, showing trust, giving a challenge, allowing freedom, showing feelings, listening empathically, and especially modeling desired behavior.

✓   Simple, informative feedback can sometimes be a source of pain, which many managers fear to give. Often, the managers themselves have had painful experiences with feedback. They are ashamed to want it, are afraid of a hook concealed within it, envy the people to whom they are giving it, or are just unskilled from lack of practice.

17.7 Practice

1.   See if you can go an entire day giving feedback without blaming. Allow yourself a few mistakes.

2.   See if you can go an entire day receiving feedback without flinching, but taking only what useful information you find in it. Allow yourself a few mistakes. On the next day, repeat the exercise, but actually ask for the feedback.

3.   Suggested by Lee Copeland: On the day after doing the previous practice, reexamine the feedback you discarded. Did you throw out useful information? Why?

4.   What does the statement "Oh, yes, I remember that technique from my high school FORTRAN textbook" say about the manager who makes it about the work of one of the programmers?

Part IV
Managing the Team Context

Many times a day I realize how much my own outer and inner life is built upon the labors of my fellow-men, both living and dead, and how earnestly I must exert myself in order to give in return as much as I have received. My peace of mind is often troubled by the depressing sense that I have borrowed too heavily from the work of other men.

— Albert Einstein

This is a test. Does this quotation fit your image of Albert Einstein, the archetypal individual genius? Can you believe that Einstein actually felt so indebted to the labors of others?

If you truly understand the essence of human genius, Einstein's quote will be no surprise. Genius is a group activity, but our cultural mythology doesn't support this understanding. We prefer Lone Ranger stories, but the essence of human genius is our ability to work adaptively in concert with others. Through teamwork, we are able to produce things: the theory of relativity, the hydrogen bomb, Chicago, babies, General Electric, or any one of a million software systems. Even the Lone Ranger didn't work alone. How many times did Tonto or some other good person save his hide?

Many living creatures—ants, bees, and wolves, for example—can work cooperatively, but their cooperation consists of programmed behavior for a relatively fixed set of tasks. People, on the other hand, seem to recognize no limits—good or evil—to what they can produce when they decide to work together.

When they work together, the role of manager emerges. Without cooperative undertakings, managers would have nothing to do. Thus, one of the unique tasks of managers is creating and nurturing adaptive teams. Without such teams, no software engineering organization can create a Steering (Pattern 3) culture, or go beyond to Anticipating (Pattern 4). That's why I have been collecting observations on software teams for many years. Some day, I hope to assemble these observations into a book for team members, but the following chapters will confine themselves to describing the manager's role with respect to teams.

18
Why Teams?

A group of people executing a design are closely analogous to an orchestra and decidedly not to a team. A team has either a driver with a whip, or another team opposing it. In an orchestra, each player— (workman)—is interpreting—(working to)—the same score—(design)—and is called on to play the instrument—(apply the technique) —in which he is expert, at the stage in the performance where it is needed.[1]
— David Pye

Most everyone resonates with Pye's romantic description of teamwork. Surely, no one could be against teamwork. Then why are so many managers frightened by evidence of teamwork? And why is teamwork any more important in software engineering than in other professions?

This chapter develops principles underlying the importance of teamwork in software engineering and elaborates several forms of a team that can be useful to the manager, including

- fault location teams
- fault resolution teams
- technical review teams
- development project teams
- independent software quality assurance teams
- software engineering assessment teams
- Software Engineering Process Groups (SEPGs)

The discussion will show how each team fits or fails to fit with various temperaments and software engineering cultural patterns.

18.1 Teams Move Toward Perfection

All temperaments find teamwork satisfying, but each for a different reason. The NT
Visionaries, for instance, find great satisfaction in the quality that a team can produce.

   One of the easiest places to see the impact of teamwork on quality is the fault
location team. These teams are trained to work together on fault location and to
prevent the problem of failure reports circulating endlessly and not reaching the
person who can solve them.[2] These circulation problems are characteristic of Variable (Pattern 1) organizations, and in such organizations, managers can often have
an immediate impact by creating more effective fault location teams.

18.1.1 Multiple eyes

To create an effective fault location team, you first need to select a diverse set of
members. Diversity is the key to effective fault location teams—diversity of experience, of organizational connections, and especially of thought patterns. If your
thought pattern differs from mine, most of the errors I miss will not be the same as
the errors you miss. Figure 18-1 thus explains why fault location teams are easy to
form and easy to get quickly to a productive state: The errors missed by both of us
will be much fewer than missed by either one. Just getting us together and looking
at the same failure information will provide immediate payoff, so long as we don't
interfere too much with one another.

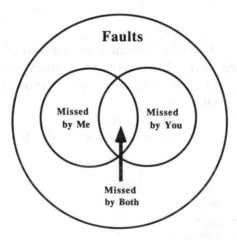

Figure 18-1.   Why teams can do a better job of locating faults: When there are multiple pairs of
                      eyes, there are many more chances to see a fault.

18.1.2 Tours of duty

After selecting a diverse team, the manager's next job is to get all the members together in a room and locate the fault or faults in a single session. The single session limit is essential, because it concentrates thought and eliminates administrative burdens. SJ Organizers especially like the efficiency of this practice. Several of my clients use a system in which each morning a different team takes a tour of duty. When a system trouble incident (STI) has been handed off more than three times, or when it has been in the system for more than three days, the manager puts the STI on the agenda for that morning's team.

Creating fault location teams is an effective management intervention in crisis situations, which SP Troubleshooters really enjoy. Teams can be assembled quickly and immediately begin to handle STIs faster than other approaches. By putting people in the same room to work on problems, you raise their level of excitement and hope, and, as a bonus, these emotions are communicated throughout the organization, which the NF Catalysts love. That's why they're also called Teambuilders.

The advantages of fault location teams for the Teambuilders don't end there. Because the teams work together openly, the members quickly share techniques for locating errors, and their efficiency grows. This growth, of course, is deeply satisfying to the NF Catalysts. For instance, I watched as one team learned that after locating a fault, they needed to spend a few minutes searching for other occurrences of the same fault in code that was written by the same programmer, or that used the same confusing data structure. This and similar techniques actually found faults before they generated STIs, which pleased all the temperaments and the manager as well.

18.1.3 Parallelism and "comperation"

Sometimes, it's critical to reduce the elapsed time to locate the fault behind certain failures. For instance, a single fault can block progress in several areas. In such cases, the manager can create parallel teams working to locate the same fault. A mild, friendly competition to see who locates the problem first can prove motivating, as long as it doesn't get out of hand. I call this way of working "comperation," for "competitive cooperation."

It's quite easy to predict the reactions of each temperament to the suggestion of "comperation." Teambuilders (NF Catalysts) may resist because they fear that the "losing" teams may be embarrassed. SJ Organizers are concerned with the inefficiency of two or more teams working on the same problem. NT Visionaries sometimes feel that the "best" team ought to be left to do the job alone. SP Troubleshooters, however, seem to relish the idea of making a game out of work.

Managers use "comperation" to tackle the toughest STIs without slowing down everything else. One client uses a super-team composed of one member from each morning team. The super-team meets once a week to tackle any serious STIs that had survived more than a week. Once the problem is solved, super-team members bring solved problems back to their daily meetings, so that everyone shares their knowledge and methods.

18.1.4 Fault resolution teams

The idea of fault location teams can be extended into fault resolution teams. Figure 18-2 shows why teams are potentially better than individuals at repairing errors. My vision of possible repairs is sure to be different from yours, so by combining visions we get to choose from a larger set. Some of the time you'll have a better idea than I do, and some of the time my idea will be better. As long as we can develop a spirit of "comperation," the average repair will be better.

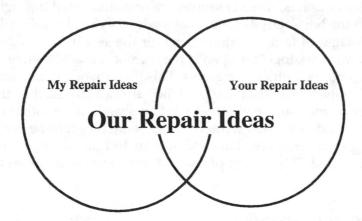

Figure 18-2.   Why teams can do a better job of repairing errors: When there are multiple ways of thinking, there are many more repair ideas from which to choose.

18.2 Review Teams

One part of the fault resolution process is choosing a resolution. Another part is conducting technical reviews of each proposed resolution to prevent surprising side effects.

18.2.1 Fault prevention

In fault resolution, the greatest losses may come from side effects or faults introduced by resolving other faults. Teams must be trained to work on preventing side effects in fault correction. A properly structured team is better at anticipating side effects than any individual can be, because of the dynamics illustrated in Figures 18-1 and 18-2.

SJ Organizers like the efficiency of technical reviews. One report on the use of the inspection form of technical review in large software projects (of at least 2.5 million lines of high-level code) found that

> You can find approximately one defect for every man-hour invested. Each hour spent on inspections avoids an average of 33 hours of subsequent maintenance. ... Inspections can be up to 20 times more efficient than testing.[3]

18.2.2 Process improvement

Reviews work by directly finding faults. Tests work by forcing failures, which then must be traced to the faults behind them. Both tests and reviews work on product improvement, but reviews also work on process improvement. Indeed, technical reviews are usually the first and easiest method of process improvement to introduce into Variable (Pattern 1) and Routine (Pattern 2) organizations.

NF Catalysts like the social aspect of technical reviews, although they may become unnecessarily protective of the people whose product is being reviewed. They particularly like the way reviewers can learn without having to admit to ignorance. NT Visionaries just like the new ideas they get for themselves.

Learning always takes place in the review itself. In addition, a manager can harness the power of the review to improve the current process outside of the review by having someone classify coding issues and publishing the statistics. This enables individual developers to improve their own work, and those who train others to improve their training.

The manager can also use the power of the review to improve other processes by classifying faults as to their stage of origin (Figure 18-3). Thus, issues from a code review can show that improvement is needed, say, in design or requirements. In Pattern 1 and 2 organizations, developers may not be eager to have the manager dictate what is done with such information. The wise manager will simply allow the classification to be made public and gently encourage actions motivated by the professionalism of the developers.

Statistics:

Type	Code	Design	Definition
Errors			
Performance Flaws			
Style Problems			
Testability Flaws			
Total Defects			

Figure 18-3.   A simple form such as this can be used to record types of issues raised in a review, and to classify them according to the stage in which they originated.

Once the benefits of reviews are viewed in this way, their timing becomes all important. Having late reviews means that you have a chance to catch all faults up to that time and catch more faults than earlier reviews. On the other hand, late reviews make it harder to pinpoint the origin of the faults. Early reviews improve this identification, which is the true payoff for reviews. Thus, the manager can influence both product and process quality by scheduling the reviews as early as possible.

In fact, some reviews lead to a recommendation to throw away the product and rebuild it from scratch. Such reviews also tend to yield valuable information about the process. Although these are potentially the most beneficial reviews, many managers are too fearful of the consequences of starting over to act congruently. They override the review recommendation and command that work continue on the unhealthy product. This placating decision almost invariably leads to a poor-quality product, if it leads to a product at all. It also leads to prolonged agony for everyone involved.

Some managers also feel they must justify their decision to proceed with an obviously sick product by blaming the review team. This is a major mistake. The reviewers are the messengers, not the source of the message. The manager's job is to see that the message is heard and that the messengers aren't killed.

18.2.3 Reducing variability

The most striking effect of technical reviews (when used in combination with well-designed machine testing) is the way they reduce variability. Here's a case in point.

In one Variable (Pattern 1) hardware organization, the operating systems developers would frequently implement changes that would save time or money, yet they would fail to see the wider systems effects that would lose more time or money in the long run. The development manager instituted a procedure that tied any use of the configuration management system to a prerequisite for reviews. A cross-functional review team would have to approve any change before it could become part of the system. As a result, quick fixes with unplanned systems effects were always detected, and subject to intelligent consideration of their true value.

More conventionally, reviews and machine tests are used to improve quality and consequently reduce subsequent testing time (Figure 18-4).

More important for manageability, reviews also reduce variability in quality and subsequent testing time. Figure 18-5 is based on a sample of 147 software modules kept by one client's manager who introduced code reviews to his Variable (Pattern 1) organization. The first row tabulates 39 modules that were built before reviews were introduced, and thus were not reviewed at all. The remaining 108 modules were divided into three groups of 36 modules according to when the reviews were conducted—early, middle, or late in the review learning cycle. One obvious effect is the improvement in the average quality of the reviews themselves.

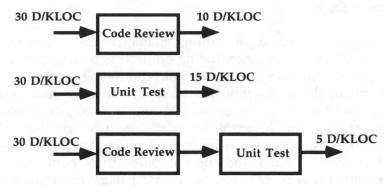

Figure 18-4.   Reviews are a form of testing. Reviews and other tests used in tandem can produce low-defect systems, while also reducing machine test time at the end of a project. The figure shows how various combinations of tests reduce the defects per thousand lines of code (D/KLOC).

Review Time	Review Quality (% faults found)	Test Time (Hrs) /(Variance)	Faults→Test /(Variance)
None	0	18/(7)	12/(7)
Early	32	14/(4)	9/(5)
Middle	58	11/(2)	5/(4)
Late	73	9/(2)	3/(2)

Figure 18-5.   Some statistics on a set of software modules that were subjected to reviews of various quality before being delivered to system test.

The first group of reviews found an average of 32 percent of all coding faults eventually found, while the late group found 73 percent.

A second effect is the reduction of average test time per module from 18 hours to 9 hours, while at the same time the number of faults per module delivered to system test dropped from 12 to 3.

A more subtle effect is the way variability goes down as the quality of a code review improves. Reduced variability in test time (from a standard deviation of 7 to 2) means that the testing phase of the project is much more manageable. Less variation in the number of faults shipped to system test mean more predictable system test time, which again means better manageability.

In the light of such results, we can see why software engineering mavens recommend the introduction of technical review teams as one of the most effective steps a manager can take to move an organization from Patterns 1 and 2 to Pattern 3 (Steering) and possibly beyond.[4]

18.3 Other Teams

In Steering (Pattern 3) organizations, managers rise above the level of product management and begin concentrating on process management. Thus, a great deal of management time is spent creating and controlling teams. The types of teams are limited only by the imagination of the manager and the work force.

The obvious and most-mentioned example is the project team, ordinarily for a development project. This emphasis existed even before Boehm demonstrated that team effectiveness was a larger influence on project cost than any technical factor.[5] In 1981, Mantei[6] summarized and compared three competing team models for development: my concept of egoless teams;[7] Baker's chief programmer teams;[8] and Metzger's controlled decentralized teams,[9] which are more or less an attempt to combine the best features of the other two.

These three models were introduced in the literature from 1971 to 1973, thus illustrating that a generation ago the debates among the software engineering philosophers concerned the ideal team form, not whether teams were the ideal development unit. Over the years, the idea of the project team has continued to develop in a number of directions.[10] At the same time, the maintenance team has been largely ignored in the literature, perhaps as part of the overall bias toward development. Chapter 19 will consider this sadly neglected topic.

Another sort of team is the independent software quality assurance team. This type of team creates an interesting tradeoff between teamwork and independence. My colleague Mark Manduke points out

> Independence lets Software Quality Assurance (SQA) raise the issue of lack of realism in development plans and schedules so that enlightened management can balance the quality-cost-schedule equation to the optimal understanding and satisfaction of the company and customer.[11]

How can SQA be both independent and part of the project team at the same time? What the manager must do is to reframe the definition of teamwork, so that being a team player means performing your assigned role, not submitting to pressure to think like every other member of the team wants you to think.[12]

Similar to the quality assurance team is the software engineering assessment team, as described by Humphrey.[13] The job of the assessment team, he notes, "is not an audit but a review of a software organization to advise its management and professionals on how they can improve their operation."

While the assessment team looks at the organization, other teams may be assembled to review specific projects from an architectural point of view. In large projects, of course, the project and the organization may be one and the same.

Humphrey also describes the Software Engineering Process Group (SEPG), which may derive from the assessment team.[14] The SEPG "is the focal point for the total effort" of ongoing software process improvement. One group suggested to me that a better name would be SEPT for Software Engineering Process Team. That was the name they used, but they also had seven members, all born in September!

18.4 Helpful Hints and Suggestions

1. What about the argument that teamwork violates the natural force of aggressiveness? Tournier, for one, argues that violence or aggressiveness is indeed a fundamental force within human beings, and thus cannot be eliminated.[15] He goes on to say, however, that aggressiveness can be invested in different objects.

    In other words, competitiveness is just one form of aggressiveness, and itself can be directed in other ways, such as against various people outside the team (the "common enemy"), or as a team against "nature" (such as beating common goals). So there is nothing contradictory between the ideas of competition and teamwork. Indeed, in a healthy team, the members compete to see who can be the best team player.[16]

2. Virginia Satir's transformation of rules into guidelines can be modified to remove one more source of compulsion. "I must always ..." can be transformed into "I can sometimes ...," but then be further transformed into "The team and I can sometimes ..." Even when the "must always" seems to remain, the transformation to "The team and I must always " reduces pressure to perform and may restore performance to a more effective level.[17] This regulation of stress is one of the most important functions of teams. I don't have to do it all, so if I trust my teammates and tap their diverse potentials, then it becomes easier for me to do a terrific job.

3. Blaming cultures neither accept nor understand teams. When teams are proposed, managers ask, "Who will be responsible?" This is a code phrase for "Who will be blamed when the teams fail?"

    One organization—for the first time in living memory—delivered a project ahead of schedule, under budget, and to the complete satisfaction of the customer. Everyone attributed this success to their use of a team, but the manager immediately dissolved the team, saying, "I couldn't manage them." What he meant was that the team members didn't fail, so he couldn't blame anyone, which was his principal management tactic. Because they were a team, they wouldn't allow him to practice his addiction.

    I tried to get him to change his mind by asking, "Would you rather succeed and not know who was responsible, or fail but know someone to blame?" I thought it was a rhetorical question, but he answered, "I'd prefer failure," without the slightest hesitation.

18.5 Summary

✓ All temperaments find teamwork satisfying, but each for a different reason. The NT Visionaries, for instance, find great satisfaction in the quality that a team can produce. The SJ Organizers especially like the efficiency of well-functioning teams, while the SP Troubleshooters really enjoy the team as a crisis management tool.

✓ The NF Catalysts particularly like teams. They appreciate the communication, excitement, and hope generated by teamwork, and they especially like the way the team fosters the growth of its members.

✓ Fault location teams are easy to form and easy to get quickly to a productive state because the errors missed by two people will be much fewer than the errors missed by either one.

✓ "Comperation," my term for competitive cooperation, is a normal team mode. One example is a mild, friendly competition to see who can locate a problem first. Super-teams, composed of representatives from different teams, can be another form of "comperation." The super-team meets to tackle the most serious problems, and super-team members bring solved problems back to their daily meetings, so that everyone shares their solution methods.

✓ Teams also excel at problems when the combined set of solution ideas is bigger than any one member could provide. Technical reviews of proposed fault resolutions prevent surprising side effects. A properly structured team is better at anticipating side effects than any individual can be because of this combination of ideas.

✓ Both tests and reviews work on product improvement, but reviews also work on process improvement. Technical reviews are usually the first and easiest method of process improvement to introduce into Pattern 1 and Pattern 2 organizations.

✓ The manager can influence both product and process quality by scheduling the reviews as early as possible. Although some reviews may lead to discarding the product, they yield valuable information about the process.

✓ The most striking effect of technical reviews when used in combination with well-designed on-line testing is their reduction of variability. More conventionally, reviews and machine tests are used to improve quality and consequently reduce subsequent testing time.

✓   Even more important for managers, reviews reduce variability in quality and subsequent testing time. Less variation in the number of faults shipped to system test mean more predictable system test time, which again means better manageability.

✓   In Steering (Pattern 3) organizations, managers begin concentrating on process management, and spend a great deal of time creating and controlling teams. The types of teams are limited only by the imagination of the manager and the work force.

18.6 Practice

1.   Figure 18-6 shows a graph of several statistics taken from the technical reviews of five different programs. What hypotheses about these programs might you as manager draw from the variance among these statistics?

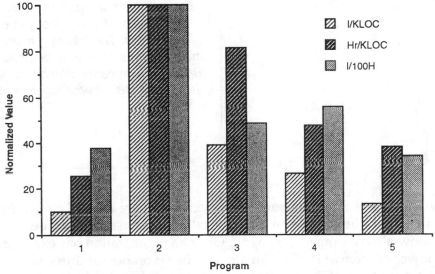

Figure 18-6.   A histogram of some statistics taken from the technical reviews of five different programs, showing issues raised per thousand lines of code (I/KLOC), hours to review a thousand lines of code (Hr/KLOC), and issues found per 100 hours of reviewing (I/100H).

2.   Would you rather succeed and not know who was responsible, or fail but know someone to blame? If you don't know who was responsible, can you succeed again?

19

Growing Teams

> *We realized that, while understanding is an essential part of organized activity, it just is not possible for everybody to understand everything. The following is essential: We must trust one another to be accountable for our own assignments. When that kind of trust is present, it is a beautifully liberating thing.*[1]
> — M. DePree

Review teams and fault location/resolution teams are a good choice for Variable (Pattern 1) and Routine (Pattern 2) organizations because they can be started quickly and show almost immediate payoff. Once an organization has experienced some of the power of teamwork, the climate may be favorable for introducing more permanent teams to deal with software maintenance and development, especially reusable development teams and reusable maintenance teams.

19.1 The Reusable Work Unit

The idea of *reusability* is not new for the manager with technical experience in software. When code used in one place can be reused in another, the savings can be enormous, as can the increase in reliability and decrease in variability. Once we have fabricated a collection of useful, reliable, and reusable modules, we are prepared to lower the cost, raise the quality, and improve the predictability of software development.

One of the arguments against reusable software is that it doesn't come free. We cannot reuse just any old software that's been slapped together; we must make an additional investment to render it truly reusable. The higher that investment, the more times we must reuse the module to recoup the investment.

A similar argument is often made against using teams for software development and maintenance. Teams do require a startup cost, and in many projects this startup is so long we never recover the cost during the life of the project. This argument, however, is not against the use of teams, but in favor of better management of team formation.

Even if management were poor, the cost of team startup could be recovered by reusing the teams over a series of projects. Unfortunately, only the better software organizations seem to reuse their teams. Given that breaking up successful teams is economic nonsense, why is it so common? Long before the days of software, people understood that the practice of dissolving well-functioning teams ultimately derives from insecure management:

> What is feared of integration within a small group is that it may organize itself in opposition to the larger whole—and this it certainly will do if its existence be threatened; but equally, a protected group will endeavor to satisfy its wider interests by collaborating with the organization of which it is a logical part. In this way, its loyalty will extend to the firm as a whole.[2]

Isn't it time that your software organization woke up? Just as reusable components are the basic units in hardware and software development, the software team is the basic design unit for software engineering processes. The job of the manager is to create, nurture, and maintain the teams that can be configured and reconfigured into reliable, predictable projects. Without such teams, no software organization can ever emerge from a Variable (Pattern 1) or Routine (Pattern 2) culture.

19.2 The Maintenance Team

One of the strongest arguments for the reusable team is that they already exist throughout the organization in the form of maintenance teams. Unfortunately, many managers don't notice maintenance teams that are performing well, and these are precisely the teams that are most reusable.

In Pattern 1 and Pattern 2 maintenance environments, I often find maintenance teams in places the managers claim they don't exist. Teams just seem to form spontaneously, even though the managers have assigned responsibility for each living system to one person.

Of course, the team doesn't really happen "spontaneously." Maintenance engineers gravitate to teams because they reduce the high risk of mistakes in maintaining living systems. In *Volume 2* of this series, I call this phenomenon the Universal Pattern of Huge Losses: A quick "trivial" change is made to an operational system without any of the usual software engineering safeguards. The change is put directly into the normal operations. A small failure is multiplied by many uses, producing a large consequence.[3] At the very least, engineers seek each other's help in reviewing proposed changes; at the most, they operate as a fully integrated team. Their managers, often former developers with no maintenance experience, simply don't understand or recognize what they're doing.

The danger in such seemingly hidden teams is that managers don't give credit to the teamwork and may unknowingly destroy well-functioning team arrangements. In Steering (Pattern 3) organizations, managers form such teams explicitly not just to prevent huge losses, but to obtain continuity through multi-person coverage of each system. Using maintenance teams, the organization ensures that critical systems are less vulnerable to a person leaving.

Because of this multi-person coverage, maintenance teams also remove the maintenance career trap (Figure 19-1), which goes like this: The longer you maintain a single system, the more you know about that system and the less you know about other systems. The longer this goes on, the more your manager fears moving you to a new assignment. This combination creates two self-reinforcing feedback loops which bind you to one system, for better or for worse.

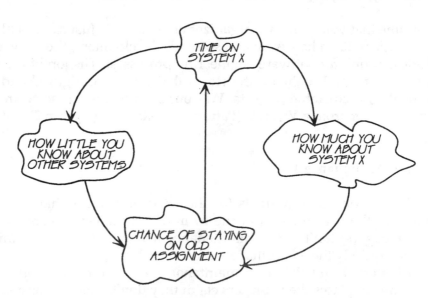

Figure 19-1.   The maintenance career trap means that the longer you spend maintaining a critical system, the less chance you have of getting a new assignment.

Eventually, the cycle breaks when any of these occur:

- The system you maintain becomes obsolete, making you obsolete at the same time, so that you get downsized.
- You realize you are stuck and the only way to escape is by finding a job in another firm.
- You get a competent manager who makes the decision to further your career development, and takes the necessary actions to back it up.

The paradox is that poor management creates the situation in which the organization is most likely to suddenly lose those engineers who maintain the most critical systems. The manager who creates and nurtures maintenance teams, however, avoids the trap and minimizes such nasty surprises.

19.3 Examples of Team Performance

My colleague Randall Jensen wrote to me about two studies he made fifteen years apart that illustrate how important teamwork is in software development, and how teamwork can be built in different ways. But building such development teams always needs leadership from management. Here's what Jensen reported:

> Study 1. Five concurrent tasks were required to build a 30K-line military-standard real-time system executive. The system was built by a group of 10 programmers with 1 project leader. The average productivity of the team members prior to the project was about 75 lines per person-month. The leader divided the programmers into 5 two-person teams, each with figuratively 1 pencil. The concept followed was that the teams developed every line of code and documentation with their partner. The result was a system produced at the rate of 175 lines per person-month with less than 1 percent of the errors the individuals previously produced.

> Study 2. Given a 90K real-time process control system to be written in Ada under military guidelines. The development team was 20 persons including the project leader. The project was the team's first Ada project. The leader organized the group as a cross-functional team working in a physically isolated area. The result was a product delivered at the rate of 218 lines per person-month, contrasted with an organizational norm of 90, even though this was the first use of Ada by the team, and the first for a real-time system anywhere in the organization. The error density was again near 1 percent of the traditional figure for the team members.[4]

The key descriptors Jensen assigned to these projects are "motivated," "teamwork," and "effective people-oriented management." He then offered me a mild rebuke for not mentioning motivation and teamwork in the index of *Volume 1* of this series. I hope that by now it's clear that intelligent discussion of real motivation and teamwork must necessarily follow a discussion of congruence.

In *Volume 1*, I mention what ineffective managers often call motivation and teamwork. To them,

- *teamwork* equals "everybody doing what I say, without question"
- *motivation* equals "pressuring everybody to work hard under poor conditions"

In other words, to such managers, "teamwork" means "management by telling," and "motivation" means "management by yelling."

19.4 Management by Team Process Improvement

Chapter 9 contrasted two management styles for improving performance: Selection (or "Management by Culling") and Systematic Improvement (or "Management by Enrichment"). The individual enrichment process can be extended to management by team process improvement. This approach is based on multi-dimensional co-creative thinking:

1. Establish teams and train them in techniques for drawing the best from each member.

2. Analyze the performance of the best teams and individuals to determine why they are doing so well.

3. Develop systems of training and technical reviews for passing on these best processes.

To justify the selection approach he was using, one manager cited studies of mine and others that had measured twenty-to-one differences among individuals.[5] What this manager didn't note was that individuals in teams show two-hundred-to-one differences over individuals operating alone. He also failed to note that the twenty-to-one difference among programmers is among programmers working in the same organization—an organization in which selection has been operating for some time. What this suggests is that the managers are selecting, but not for programming performance. If they had been, the ratio should eventually be smaller than twenty to one.

Figure 19-2 compares team process improvement with the other two management approaches for improving an organization, as well as with an unmanaged improvement process—the organization left to improve on its own, as is typical

Method / Characteristic	Unmanaged	Selection	Individual Process Improvement	Team Process Improvement
Improvement Based on	individual	individual	individual	team and individual
Measure	none	one-dimensional individual performance	n-dimensional individual performance	n-dimensional individual & team performances
Primary Improvement Process	happenstance	get rid of "worst" individual	learn from each "best" individual	each individual & team learns from the "best"
Secondary Improvement Process	individual initiative	individual learning	self-selection	team help, self-selection
Relative Rate of Improvement	1	1.2	5	20
Variability of Performance	very high	high	low	very low
Morale	variable	low	high	very high

Figure 19-2.   Comparative characteristics of four management styles of improving an organization.

in Variable (Pattern 1) organizations. Comparing the columns in this chart should show you why in all Steering (Pattern 3) organizations, the team is the fundamental unit of production.

19.5 Helpful Hints and Suggestions

1. Many thoughtful writers on software engineering recognize the critical role of the software team, although most concentrate on the new development team. As a prelude to moving your own organization toward team process improvement, you should avail yourself of their wisdom.[6]

2. A number of observers indicate that in technical work, only a small percentage of engineers' time is actually spent solving technical problems. This means that managers have a great deal of leverage. For instance, if engineers are now spending ten percent of their time on the problem (a generous estimate, by many accounts), then ninety-percent of their time is spent on other things. If the managers can reduce this ninety-percent overhead to eighty percent, the amount of time devoted to problem solving doubles.

3.   Many managers attempt to increase productivity by working opposite to the
      direction that point 2 above suggests. They double their engineering staff,
      which increases the overhead perhaps from ninety percent to ninety-five per-
      cent. This reduces productive time to five percent, which means that twice as
      many engineers now produce no more than the original crew, and everyone is
      less happy.
         When you make teams the primary unit of production, you don't hand five
      tasks to five individuals, but assign one larger task to a team. Even if the team
      were intrinsically no more productive than the individuals in it, the overhead
      load would be reduced, and the contributions of the individuals would be
      highly leveraged.

4.   As suggested by Gus Zimmerman: The idea of a reusable work unit can be
      extended into the process also. Developing a PPPP (Public Project Progress
      Poster) style plan to define a problem for one project gives you a great starting
      place for your next project.[7] Having a reusable process makes the concept of a
      trained and experienced reusable team even more attractive.

19.6 Summary

✓   Once an organization experiences some of the power of teamwork, the climate
    may be favorable for introducing more permanent teams to deal with software
    maintenance and development.

✓   Teams require a startup cost, and in many projects this startup is so long that
    the cost is never recovered during the life of the project. This argument favors
    better management of team formation.

✓   Even if management were poor, the cost of team startup could be recovered by
    reusing the teams over a series of projects. Unfortunately, only the better soft-
    ware organizations seem to reuse their teams. Insecure managers tend to dis-
    solve well-functioning teams.

✓   Reusable components are the basic units in hardware and software develop-
    ment, and the software team is the basic design unit for software engineering
    processes. The manager's job is to create, nurture, and maintain the teams that
    can be configured and reconfigured into reliable, predictable projects.

✓   Many managers don't notice maintenance teams that are performing well, and
    these are precisely the teams that are most reusable. Maintenance program-
    mers gravitate to teams because they reduce the high risk of mistakes in main-
    taining living systems. Maintenance teams also remove the maintenance

career trap, a situation created by poor management such that the programmers who maintain the most critical systems are most likely to leave.

✓   What ineffective managers often call motivation and teamwork is not the same as the real meaning of those terms. To them, *teamwork* equals "everybody doing what I say, without question," and *motivation* equals "pressuring everybody to work hard under poor conditions."

✓   Management by Systematic Improvement can be extended to Management by Team Process Improvement. This approach establishes teams and trains them in techniques for using the best from each member, analyzes the performance of the best teams and individuals to determine why they are doing so well, and develops systems of training and technical reviews for passing on these best processes.

19.7 Practice

1.   In a Variable (Pattern 1) organization, there may be many layers of management, because the span of control is small in an attempt to control variability. Each person must be managed over the shoulder, especially at the bottom level. The typical person with the title "manager" is a technical leader with a team of two or three or four members. Variability is reduced by this manager taking away the parts of the technical work that prove difficult for some team member. Show the dynamic of this practice and why it works to reduce variability, but also overloads the manager and doesn't develop people on the so-called team.

2.   As contributed by Phil Fuhrer: Answers to the following questions are good indicators of the health of an organization and its congruence:

    a.   Do you want your manager on your team?

    b.   Does management contribute to team success in your organization?

    How would the people in your organization answer these questions? Could you ask them?

3.   Again, suggested by Phil Fuhrer: Discuss the reasons for and against the following statement: "Strong team behavior is the acid test of congruency in an organization."

20
Managing in a Team Environment

A team effort is a lot of people doing what I say.
— Michael Winner

Many managers seem to think they are directors like the British film director quoted above, and they share the view that team effort means everyone will be subservient to their high-and-mightiness. At one company, the managers showed their team spirit by having parking places closer to the door than the parking spaces for people in wheelchairs! For managers with such attitudes, this chapter will not help.

Other managers, however, realize that teamwork means more than following orders from the Emperor, yet they unconsciously undermine their own efforts to reap the benefits of effective teams. This chapter points out some of those unconscious behaviors and suggest some conscious behaviors that should enhance team performance.

20.1 The Manager's Role in a Team-Based Organization

Perhaps the most common confusion about the manager's role in a team-based organization is between the manager and the team leader. The team leader (or, if a self-managed team, the entire team) is responsible for the technical task of the team.[1] The manager, on the other hand, is responsible for the nontechnical direction of two or more teams. Seen from inside the team, the manager's role is to unburden the team leader by handling certain nontechnical tasks. Seen from the manager on the outside, the manager's role is to control the team in terms of the higher goals of the organization.

20.1.1 Delegation

The manager initiates work units by delegating standard task units to teams.[2] These standard task units are specified in terms of the prerequisites that must be in place for the task to be completed, such as requirements, human resources, tools, products of earlier tasks, working space, funds, and training.

20.1.2 Control

Each task unit must also specify the process (usually a review of some kind) by which the product of the task will be measured. The manager's job is to work with the team to establish control points based on these measurements and to monitor these check points externally. The manager steps inside the team only when some checkpoint is not reached, or when a team breaks down.

20.1.3 Coordination with the rest of the organization

The manager is the primary coordinator of issues between teams, which doesn't mean that the manager must directly supervise all communication between teams. The manager's most important functions are to ensure that commitments between teams consider the larger context, that the decision processes are appropriate, and that the decisions are explicitly documented.

Coordinating between teams is part of a more general role of acting as the team's buffer to the outside world. As part of this role, the manager handles company policies, budgets, and personnel administration.

20.2 Delegating Work

According to Katzenbach and Smith, the most important way to build teams is to delegate challenging work:

Teams do not become teams just because we call them teams or send them to team-building workshops. In fact, many frustrations with broad-gauged movements toward team-based organizations spring from just such imbalances. Real teams form best when management makes clear performance demands.[3]

Challenge is an emotional reaction, influenced as much by the way the task is assigned as by the task itself. *Volume 2* lays out the physical structure of a standard task unit, but gives no guidance on the question of the emotional structure. For success with teams of mixed temperaments, tasks must be delegated in a way that is challenging, clear, and supportive.

20.2.1 Challenging

The SP Troubleshooters are the ones most challenged by the task itself, while the NT Visionaries are most concerned with communicating the challenge to the rest of the team. Here are some of the things NTs and SPs want from their managers in order to be challenged:

✓ "Don't ever give us an insultingly easy task. It must be difficult, but not impossibly difficult and especially not made extra difficult by rigid constraints that have nothing to do with the task itself."

✓ "Assign tasks that are defined in terms of results, not the methods for achieving those results." (The definition should be a vision of the problem to be solved, a definition that the team members can interpret in a way that is meaningful to them, and will satisfy them when they achieve it.)

✓ "We don't mind complexity, but resent complexity created by changing the rules in the middle of the game. If those rule changes can be related to the vision of the problem to be solved, we don't object. Challenge us with unfamiliarity, but make allowance for our learning. "

✓ "External control checks are acceptable. We especially welcome quality checks and will tolerate time checks; we don't appreciate budget checks unless made part of the challenge."

✓ "Allow us to be creative and enjoy ourselves."

20.2.2 Clear

For the SJ Organizers, challenge is all well and good, but it is essential that the challenge be expressed clearly, right from the beginning. They may express their needs to their managers in the following way:

✓   "Be up front, giving precise and clear instructions that are complete in all details."

✓   "Put everything in writing. Explore all possibilities, but simplify what you present."

✓   "Be available to answer questions, because the first two needs are rarely met."

20.2.3 Supportive

The NF Teambuilders (Catalysts) want challenge and clarity, too, but mostly because the others want them. They are less interested in the task than in the environment in which the task is to be done. Here's what NFs desire from the manager who delegates a task to them:

✓   "The most important thing you can do is hope for our success and structure the task so that success is possible, perhaps in small increments as the task proceeds."

✓   "Balance the workload, so that our team has a fair share with others. Give us something that fits in a balanced way with the skills we have on our team. Don't ask us to do things we are unable to do, and especially don't ask us to do things we aren't willing to do."

✓   "Trust the team to do the job, but deliver the resources you promise."

✓   "Give us feedback in whatever flavor, but be generous in interpreting what you see."

✓   "Protect the team from outside demands, and provide guidance in steering through the organizational waters."

20.2.4 Mistakes in delegating

Many new managers have told me that what surprised them the most in their new role was the amount of work it takes to get someone else to do work. It's hard enough to satisfy the diverse demands of the different temperaments, but as a manager you also have to behave in ways that satisfy some universal human needs:

✓   "No matter how clear you've tried to be, you will be misunderstood. You must be available to answer questions and never lose patience, no matter how dumb the questions seem to be."

✓ "You have to be prepared to enter into other people's favored communication modalities, as when they draw you a picture of what they think you said, or say in words what you drew for them in a picture."

✓ "No matter how much work you've done, you'll make some mistakes. Admit your own your mistakes and accept their corrections."

✓ "You must listen to complaints without being defensive or taking them personally. People will be frustrated, overworked, befuddled about what you want, anxious about meeting the schedule, protective of each other, and feeling angry because they believe you aren't listening to them. When they've finished complaining, you'll have to nudge them into problem-solving mode, and be prepared to make compromises."

If you do all these things, you may begin enjoying modest success in delegating to others and watching them actually doing the task you assigned. But you won't be able to rest long because as soon as they start working, they may slip off track, and you may be called upon to do a little steering.

20.3 Controlling

Managers make two kinds of mistakes concerning the amount of control they exert over internal team affairs: too much or too little. Variable (Pattern 1) managers tend to intervene too little, placating the team. Routine (Pattern 2) managers tend to overcorrect by intervening too much and blaming the team, often in the form of claiming to be better able to do the job themselves:

> The viewpoint of business executives who usurp the function of lesser managers only to discover that in the real world no improvement results has been well summarized by the baseball manager who yanked his centerfielder after he dropped three straight fly balls. Having decided personally to take the place of the errant fielder, the manager suffered the ignominy of himself dropping what proved to be the game-winning pop fly. Returning to the dugout and the penetrating stares of his players, the dismayed manager explained, "He has that position so fouled up that now no one can play it."[4]

Both placating and blaming usually stem from feelings of personal inadequacy—that is, from the manager's internal needs rather than the team's.

20.3.1 How to tell if the team needs an intervention

For effective steering (as in a Pattern 3 organization), managers' interventions or noninterventions into team affairs must be done on the basis of what the team is doing, not what the manager is feeling. Ironically, you as the manager can tell a great deal about whether or not the team members are working well as a team by observing their emotional state. Here are examples of what you can observe in a well-functioning team, followed by parenthesized examples of what you may hear to indicate a malfunctioning team:

1. Well-functioning teams make sure that everybody participates in decisions. (Versus a malfunctioning team: "Nobody asked me if I wanted to work overtime to get the release finished.")

2. Members stay in touch with one another, so they have the information needed to make their decisions. Even if there are no specific decisions to make, the contact must be maintained. As noted in the book *A Pattern Language,* "No social group—whether a family, a work group, or a school group—can survive without constant informal contact among its members."[5] (Versus a malfunctioning team: "I never heard that the interface was changed." "I haven't seen Phil for a couple of weeks.")

3. All team members feel that they each have a chance to contribute. (Versus a malfunctioning team: "They never listen to my ideas.")

4. Team members are united. (Versus a malfunctioning team: "It's not my fault that Wally didn't follow the recommended process.")

5. Closely related to the necessity for unity is the team's feeling good about "what we did." (Any statements opposing "me" or "they" to "we" are indicative of less than optimal team functioning. For example, "Their work isn't up to the standard of my work.")

6. The team has fun. This one seems exceptionally difficult for certain managers to accept. Apparently, they believe that "fun" and "work" are opposites and that you shouldn't be paid for having fun. Not all fun teams are productive, but all productive teams enjoy themselves. (Some of the team members may share the fun/work dichotomy, so you have to be careful how you interpret complaints about how hard the work is. "We're killing ourselves" could be a complaint about not having fun, or it could be bragging about how proud they are of how well they're doing.)

7. Team members rely on each others' individual strengths, and all do what they can that's best for the team. (Versus a malfunctioning team: "I did that myself because Wanda wasn't likely to get it right, even though it was assigned to her." "I'm a database expert, and I'm certainly not going to spend my time preparing test cases for Jack's module.")

8. When members speak, they take care to be sure that everyone understands. (Versus a malfunctioning team: "I haven't got time to explain that to Sarah.")

9. Team members each feel strong and useful, but not out of proportion to their competence as a team. (Versus a malfunctioning team: "Well, my part isn't having performance problems." "Go on without me; I just can't keep up with Alex and Demma.")

10. Members show how they are truly feeling. (Versus a malfunctioning team: "I'm not going to let Harry know how angry I am he did that.")

20.3.2 *Intervening for the team's benefit*

Of course, you don't use a single incident to trigger an intervention. Instead, you use it to trigger a state of alertness for other signs. If other incidents reinforce your interpretation, you can reframe them into opportunities for team building and team problem solving. For instance, suppose the last piece of evidence of team trouble is when Marilynne tells you, "I'm not going to let Harry know how angry I am he did that." You could get yourself in the middle by talking to Harry yourself, or you could try to convince Marilynne to talk to Harry.

But here's an approach more congruent with your desire to build the team. You say to Marilynne, "When I hear you say that you're angry with Harry and you aren't going to let him know, I get worried about the way your team is functioning. I think an effective team needs to be able to deal with its members' feelings, no matter how strong or negative they may be. I'm going to call a team meeting, raise this issue, and sit back and watch you resolve it."

Marilynne may protest, but probably without great conviction, for why do you think she brought this up with you in the first place? Of course, she may have thought you were going to tell Harry for her, but this way you demonstrate to her that you expect the team to solve problems like this for itself—perhaps with a bit of help from you, early on.

20.3.3 *Envy of the well-functioning team*

Seeing the list of attributes of a well-functioning team, we can understand how easy it is for managers to envy their best teams. The cure for that envy is to reframe it. At the first pangs of envy, you would do well to reframe your model as described by my CompuServe colleague Mark Weisz:

> Any manager's job can be terribly lonely at times, but hopefully it isn't all that grim. The greatest joys I experienced as a manager (and there were many) were when I brought people together to work successfully as a team. There is some-

thing especially gratifying in creating a sound work team and, until the next crisis at least, you can relax a bit and watch it hum like a finely tuned engine. There's no better feeling. When the next crisis comes, as it inevitably will, you've built in a reserve of resilience to handle it successfully. That team is your insurance policy. Management is a noble profession. Like any job, it has its frustrations and pain, but also the capacity for great achievement. If you can cultivate a sense of humor (and perhaps Stoicism) to get you through the tough times, you'll probably find you have a lot more good ones.[6]

20.3.4 *Rewards that don't reward*

Managers who are uncertain about how to interact with a team often try to win their friendship by giving them rewards. This is not as foolproof a strategy as you might suppose. Brooke, a member of a client team, told me how their manager had "rewarded" them for heroic work to salvage a dying project:

"We had worked extensive unpaid overtime for about two months to get the release out the door. The day after the release, we each found on our desk a one-dollar gift certificate from the local coffee shop. There wasn't even a note with it, but someone asked and he explained it was his way of thanking us. Several of us were so enraged we returned them in his mail slot. The calmer ones just ignored it. I personally would have preferred he spend the dollar on a card, which he could have signed with his own name and handed to me personally. If he wasn't capable of that much human interaction, I would have preferred he take his dollar and ..." (I have deleted what Brooke said she wanted him to do with the dollar.)

20.3.5 *Rewarding congruently*

If you fear that you, too, may be as socially inept as Brooke's manager, here's a suggestion from Georgia, one of my students, about how she handled this managerial situation congruently:

"When I got back from class, I called the team together and said, 'In addition to all the other things you've accomplished, you've really saved my skin. I truly want to find some way to show my appreciation to the whole team, but I'm not very sensitive about these things. I'm afraid that I won't know how to express myself in a way that you felt was really appropriate. Would you help me find some way?' Then I trusted them."

Georgia was amazed at what this congruent expression of her position could accomplish. You will be, too.

What about punishing them? Can this be done congruently, too? Frankly, I don't think there's any way to punish congruently, and that's because it's not your job to punish people. If you have delegated a properly formed task in an appropriate way, and if you have exercised appropriate control, and still the team fails, the members will know without doubt that they have failed, and that will be more than enough punishment. They will also know—and so will you—that in this failure you are part of the team, so who are you to punish them?

Instead of punishing, try to adopt the description I cited in Chapter 6:

> The middle manager's job is to "grow people"—not to build a file of lifeless documents, or to spend half of each day in boring meetings. His role means walking around with an open mind toward listening and helping, and taking time to talk things over. It means being concerned about individual welfare and fostering the full potential of each person.[7]

One congruent way to do this is to sit down with them and say, "I feel bad because we blew this one. Obviously, there's something I didn't know about how to accomplish this job, and I want to learn what it is so I can do better next time. Can you help me with this, and is there anything you want to learn that I may be able to help with?"

20.3.6 Are you the problem?

When you are unable to get teamwork, it's often because of something you are doing. It may be something you are doing consciously, but that has a boomerang effect. Performance appraisals—intended to help each member of the team learn— often have this effect. By evaluating the individual members of the team, no matter how well you do it, you are sending a message that you're not able to trust their own evaluation of each other.

If you feel you have to give performance appraisals, a more effective way is to appraise the team performance and ask the team to appraise the performance of each member. The external performance rating for an individual is obtained by multiplying the team's overall rating by the individual's rating as given by the team. This approach says you trust the team to do what's best for meeting the goals you give it, and that they all get credit equally from you for meeting those goals as a team.

Most people are aware of the divisive nature of conventional performance appraisals. You may, however, be giving signals in other situations that are quite beyond your awareness, as in the following story:

Cora, the senior vice president of Information Services, had two VPs working under her who were supposed to team up to create a strategic plan. Tom and Len argued for eight months over approach T versus approach L.

Cora was, in fact, unconsciously contributing to the endless discussion because she was giving signals that indicated the winner would be next in line for her job. Thus, the matter was not settling T versus L, but Tom versus Len.

Once Cora discovered what was going on, she told Tom and Len one morning at 8:30, "You two go in the conference room and don't come out until you've settled this. If you don't come out by noon, you're both fired."

The matter was settled by 9:15. I don't recall if T or L won. But of course, it didn't matter since Tom and Len were working as a team.

20.3.7 Using the MOI model for interventions

When choosing interventions, a good guide is the MOI model.[8] This model says that when a team or individual isn't functioning well, there may be a missing ingredient. It could be motivation, organization, or information. Your job is to find out which and intervene accordingly.

The MOI model will help you avoid egregious mistakes like this one: A company had embarked on an ambitious campaign to improve quality. As part of that campaign, they formed an all-volunteer group of twenty-five software engineering advisors. The members of this group were to receive some training, then act as coaches to other members of the organization. In order to be selected, they had to put themselves through a time-consuming and rigorous process involving interviews, essays, and five recommendations. They also had to agree that all work would be over and above their normal workload, so that any classes or coaching time would have to be made up by working unpaid overtime.

The selection had been highly competitive, so the software engineering manager decided to reward those chosen. He hired a famous and expensive motivational speaker to give them a one-hour pep talk—exactly what they didn't need. After all they had gone through and committed to, they were insulted that the boss thought they needed a motivational push. What they wanted was some organization to their work and information to equip them to coach others. The meeting, which was certainly well-intentioned, wasted a lot of money, but more important it undermined the relationship between the volunteer team and the boss.

20.4 Communicating with the Outside

All new managers have to wrestle with their role as interface between the team and the rest of the organization.[9] One role is serving as conduit for messages and directives from upper management; another is as a conduit for messages traveling in the other direction.

If the new manager gets any formal training at all, it generally deals only with the company's policies and procedures concerning administration and personnel. This training suggests that the company, at least, views the manager's most important role as inward communication.

On the other hand, if the new manager has been moved from the ranks of the workers, it's easy to slip into the outward communication role.

Mark Weisz had this to say about a third possible role of the manager with respect to the exterior of the team:

> Now that I have someone working for me it's really made me "protective." For example, I try to grab all the interrupts for myself so at least someone is making steady progress. Protecting your work group is absolutely necessary—that's a good instinct to have. Back in grad school, they called it "boundary management," but in less stuffy language it's "air cover" or "The Mother Duck Syndrome." "Grabbing all the interrupts" sort of sounds like hardware, like an interrupt controller. Would that sound good on a resumé? "Hi, I'm a professional interrupt controller."[10]

In other words, not only do you send communications outward, but you act to filter as much inward data as possible. Your job is to screen data that pester the team and to allow data that genuinely help the team. A good example of using the Mother Duck role effectively is in negotiations between software developers and marketers. The typical age of the marketer may be ten years greater than that of the developer. Thus, you often have children negotiating with adults, who also happen to be professional negotiators. This bias often pushes the negotiation one way, leading to the common symptom of "schedule macho."

Managers who want to protect their teams would do well to forget about C coding and develop their negotiation skills and congruence, as suggested by this story told by my reviewer Mark Manduke when he had read a draft of this section:

> I was software manager for a team of seven programmers. Several members of my team were foreign-born, young, and easily intimidated by the burly marketers and senior management, who would interrupt them to get agreement on "just one more bell and whistle for my special customer." We were having significant problems meeting our schedules, which also seemed to make the marketing and management folks grin as they tortured us with deadlines and watched us put in exorbitant overtime.
>
> One day, I called a meeting for the team and explained, "From now on, we will reach a team consensus on our schedules for assigned software tasks. They will be reasonable and reflect what we believe we can do in a forty-hour week. I will negotiate those schedules with Marketing and Engineering management. Once we are all comfortable with a development and delivery schedule, any private attempts to change or add requirements will be politely referred to me. If we can't meet our own estimates, then we will work for any necessary overtime to compensate. But one of my duties to you, the team, will be to act as the single negotiator for any changes. If we all stick together and speak as with one voice, we will have unchallengeable power. They can't fire all of us."
>
> The result was amazing. This team became the hardest working and most fiercely loyal software compatriots I have ever had the pleasure of working with.

That's the kind of congruence you need to be a successful manager of software teams.

20.5 Helpful Hints and Suggestions

1. If you become too effective as a Mother Duck, team members may come to believe that you are hiding things from them. You will also prevent them from having the information and experience they need to make their own career decisions, such as whether they would like to try their hand at management.

2. My colleague Phil Fuhrer suggests a relationship between failure to support teams and a common survival rule: "For many managers the rule 'I must always be in control of my staff or at least look that way' is a major source of incongruence. I think this might come from early childhood when Mom or Dad controls the family or the teacher controls the class. I also think this rule is re-enforced by upper management wanting to feel that middle management is in control. I think this control rule is the chief reason that teams are not really supported."

3. Another colleague Dan Starr notes that in his experience, customer relations are an important part of setting up a successful team: "Another thing that teams need is a good definition of the real client and problem to be solved, for a team builds enthusiasm and commitment as it grows. This is especially true in an organization where teamwork is not the norm. The team will come to perceive itself as something different and a little special, and it hurts big time if all that energy and work are wasted because you got the problem definition wrong."

20.6 Summary

✓ Many managers undermine team spirit by their high-and-mighty attitudes. Other managers unconsciously undermine their own efforts to reap the benefits of effective teams. The first group is hopeless, but the second can be helped by learning to become more congruent.

✓ Perhaps the most frequent confusion about the manager's role in a team-based organization is between the manager and the team leader. The team leader is responsible for the technical tasks of the team. The manager is responsible for the nontechnical direction of two or more teams.

✓ Seen from inside the team, the manager's role is to unburden the team leader by handling certain nontechnical tasks. Seen by the manager on the outside, the manager's role is to control the teams in terms of the organization's higher goals.

✓   The most important way to build teams is to delegate challenging work. Challenge is an emotional reaction, influenced as much by the way the task is assigned as by the task itself. Each temperament, for instance, is challenged in a different way, so an effective leader has to reframe a challenge for each temperament.

✓   Delegating is not as easy as it seems to non-managers, for several reasons. It's easy to be misunderstood, to use the wrong communication medium, to make mistakes, and to get defensive when things don't work out and people complain about what you did.

✓   Managers make two mistakes concerning the amount of control they exert over internal team affairs: too much or too little. Variable (Pattern 1) managers tend to intervene too little, placating the team. Routine (Pattern 2) managers tend to overcorrect by intervening too much, blaming the team, often in the form of claiming to be better able to do the job themselves. Both placating and blaming usually stem from the manager's internal needs rather than the team's.

✓   Well-functioning teams can be recognized by the behavior of their members. They make sure that everybody participates in decisions. They stay in touch with one another, and everyone feels the chance to contribute. They are united, and speak in terms of "we." They have fun. They rely on each others' individual strengths, and all do what they can that's best for the team. When they speak, they take care to be sure that everyone understands. They each feel strong and useful, but not out of proportion to their competence as a team. Finally, it's easy to monitor them, because they show how they are truly feeling.

✓   You manage a team gently, using single incidents only to trigger a state of alertness for other signs of problems. When you do make interventions, you use them as opportunities for team building and team problem solving.

✓   It's easy for a manager to envy a well-functioning team. The cure is to emphasize the joys of successful management and the part that it plays in the team's success.

✓   Attempts to reward a team can often backfire. Work with the team to find out what would truly reward them. Use the MOI model to determine what kind of intervention a team needs at any moment.

✓   It's not the manager's job to punish people. It is the manager's job to arrange opportunities for people to learn. To do that, the manager may have to play Mother Duck, protecting the team from inappropriate influences from outside.

✓ Performance appraisals can destroy team spirit. Avoid them if you can. If you can't, a more effective way is to ask the team to appraise the performance of each member. An external performance rating is obtained by multiplying the team's overall rating by the individual's rating as given by the team.

20.7 Practice

1. Probably the worst intervention a manager can make in a team is giving performance appraisals to the individual members. Explain this statement, using diagrams of effects to support your argument for or against. (Consult Appendix A for details on drawing these diagrams.)

2. What are your three top candidates for the worst intervention a manager can make in a team? Explain each.

3. As suggested by Bill Pardee: Since so many people abuse the term *team* by using it to describe any group that the speaker wishes had a common goal, compose a short explicit description of what would constitute a *congruent team* in your organization.

4. Bill Pardee asks, "If we think teams constitute the indivisible atom of effective software development (and I do), wouldn't it help to reduce the baggage associated with the classical term, in which so many people call any group a team?" Katzenbach and Smith[11] use the term "real team" to make this distinction. Can you propose a better term to describe such teams?

5. In Mark Manduke's negotiations for his "fiercely loyal software team," identify how he balanced the self, other, and context. Can you apply this approach to a team you're involved with?

6. As suggested by reviewer Peter de Jager: When you delegate tasks, do you delegate problems or solutions? Which do you think is a better way to get effective performance from a team?

21

Starting
and Ending
Teams

Nobody knows himself until he has come
face to face with calamity; it is only in crises
that we learn our true identity; and many a
man has gone through life thinking he was
strong, when he was only safe.
— Sidney Harris

The manager's job with respect to a team is to start it when a team is needed, leave it alone when it's working effectively, and stop it when it's not.

21.1 Forming Teams During a Crisis

One payoff for investing in team development comes when the manager faces a crisis. Unfortunately, many organizations wait until they're experiencing a crisis before they decide to form teams as a way of dealing with it. For a variety of reasons, this is not the best time to form a team, but you don't always have a choice.

Software crises commonly take the form of a deluge of failures, so the team that you most commonly want to form is a fault-handling team. Let's see what some of the difficulties are, and how a manager can address them.

21.1.1 *Depression*

If the organization's environment is severely depressed, you may need a skilled facilitator in the first meetings of a new team. The facilitator can teach a few problem-solving techniques and, more importantly, keep the meetings from degenerating into funerals. Ideally, you would start a new team with a strong team-building experience, but in a crisis, the experience of working successfully together to locate problems under the lead of a facilitator may have to suffice.

21.1.2 *Exclusion*

Keep in mind that the key principle in forming teams is

Everyone on the team has <u>some</u> unique contribution.

If I have no contribution that you couldn't make equally well, the team advantages pictured in Figures 18-1 and 18-2 do not apply. Figure 21-1 shows this situation: You can find all the faults that I can find, and more; and your design vision includes mine and surpasses it. In this situation, my self-esteem will plummet, and your irritation will explode.

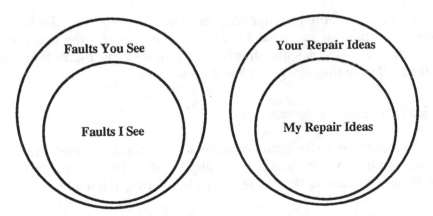

Figure 21-1.   If your abilities completely overshadow mine, there is no purpose for me to be on the team, because I see nothing that you can't see.

When not under crisis pressure, team members have time to discover and nurture the more subtle contributions of each team member. In crisis, such discovery time is a luxury, so you need to be much more careful in choosing the initial makeup of the team. Then you need to take every opportunity to make the team members aware of each person's contribution.

The composition of a team formed in crisis tends to be focused on the ability to deal with the immediate crisis problems. Thus, such a team may fall apart when asked to transform itself from crisis mode to something more normal. That's why a better starting point for long-lived teams is a team that has formed organically in maintenance or development. For development teams, the trick is not to dissolve them just because their project was completed successfully.

21.1.3 Existing teams

Existing teams in the organization can also be an impediment to change, particularly to these special problem-solving teams. In the depth of chaos, about the only team activity some people exhibit is huddling together like musk oxen facing the wolves. They may see attempts to create special problem-solving teams as a way of breaking up their ring of solidarity, or of placing blame on their team for not doing a better job.

One way to overcome this problem is to have each team elect one member to investigate the new process and report back to the team. In this way, the people on special assignment remain part of the herd, rather than becoming one of the wolves.

21.2 Letting the Team Solve Problems

Would you like to be more effective with less work? A well-functioning team is the busy manager's biggest potential asset if the manager lets the team do its work. The following six examples are simply illustrative of the many that are handled well by teams if only they are given the chance.

21.2.1 Placating upper management

Remember in Chapter 13 the situation in which Charlene placated Morie, the president, by agreeing to an unrealistic schedule. My own preference for handling this situation is for Charlene to tell Morie the truth, offering at least two choices, such as

- meeting the schedule by dropping some functionality
- keeping the functionality and slipping the schedule

I don't have much trouble doing this, and I've found that presidents are happy to hear the truth, even though they may not be happy about what that truth is. Few people become company presidents by hiding their head in the sand.

But I am usually in the role of a highly paid outside consultant and thus much more likely to be listened to than the average inside manager like Charlene. I'm also not terribly afraid of offending the rare president who really doesn't want to face the truth.

The manager who is afraid to face the president with the technical truth has an easy out, but only in a team-based culture. Because this is a technical issue, it's really the team's business to present the facts to the president, and Charlene need not be involved. A real team is much stronger than your typical manager, and not as likely to be intimidated by upper management. In addition, their technical opinion carries a lot more weight when the president sees that this is not just one person's off-the-top-of-the-head idea.

Of course, this approach wouldn't work well in the hard-core blaming organization, but, then, such an organization won't have real teams anyway.

21.2.2 *Panic when late*

Brian Richter, another of my CompuServe colleagues, suggests a common software problem that is well-addressed by leaving things to teams: "The project is late, and all hell breaks loose as everyone tries to cut corners to get it done as soon as possible."[1]

In the same way that they aren't as likely to yield to top-down pressure, real teams are less likely to panic when the project is late. Incongruent managers, who don't like to see other people remaining calm when they themselves are panicking, often try to spread their panic to others. An experienced team, however, simply absorbs the manager's incongruence and usually has a calming effect.

21.2.3 *Excessive demonstrations*

Another colleague Arthur George raises the following problem: "We do a hellaciously distracting number of demonstrations of the project concept [like] dog-and-pony shows. I know that the demos are for communicating with the brass and/or the people who supply our funding. But our demonstrations must be presentation quality, which takes up too much of a workday. At the end of the day, the people on the project who participate in the demos have spent little time doing project work proper. Lost time, of course, translates into schedule slippage."[2]

In some projects, such demonstrations of project concept are so disruptive because the managers panic and intervene in the team's resource allocation. A better strategy is to leave the management of the demonstrations up to the team, just like all their other work. One piece of unmanaged work injected from the outside can disrupt any amount of planned work.

I've seen teams handle this situation by setting up a demonstration specialist, usually a personable junior member of the team. The specialist doesn't have to have a deep knowledge of the product, but setting up all the demonstrations quickly leads to finding out what it takes to please customers and upper management.

21.2.4 Setting technical priorities poorly

My colleague Ed Hand raises a similar problem of interference in the team from the outside: "In my previous job, we kept a list of Current Problems. It was ALWAYS the list of super-critical HAS TO BE FIXED NOW! problems. We had a couple of people in the group who would occasionally recognize a small bump in the road for the future disaster it could become, and they would try to bring it to management's attention. The trouble was that management was always so caught up in the current crisis they always dismissed the ones on the way. The track records of the couple of people who could pick the 'winners' carried little weight."[3]

A team environment drains away the problem of such super-critical issues. The team can accept the management's judgment of what is super-critical, but management doesn't know who on the team is handling them—that would be considered micro-management. Thus, the team can assign someone to a "bump in the road" without management's attention being raised.

Another approach is to throw the power of the team's consensus into the argument with the management of what is really important. Few well-functioning teams adopt this approach, however, for they know the futility and waste of arguing technical points with management.

21.2.5 The bright but sidetracked employee

Elsie, a manager with a software vendor, brought up this common problem of irrelevance: "What do I do about Wendel, an employee who is extremely bright but who is always interested in thinking about side issues? He can't seem to concentrate on the real problem of building the product we're supposed to be building."

Managers always seem to have trouble with such irrelevant behavior, but teams seldom do. After a few instances, the team confronts the offender and lets him know what is acceptable and what is not. Sometimes he decides to yield to the formidable peer pressure, but sometimes—as happened in Wendel's case—he runs whining to the manager about how the team is treating him.

All the manager has to do is say, "This is an issue between you and the rest of the team. It doesn't involve me. If you can't resolve it, however, I'll remove you from the team and consider where you can be useful." Elsie, however, had been trying to coach Wendel on how to be a better team player. This is a futile job if done by the manager, but relatively successful if done by the team. As soon as Elsie stopped, Wendel went back to the team, and they worked it out. Certainly Elsie didn't hear any more about it.

Another variant is that the team comes to the manager whining about Wendel. Elsie's behavior should be precisely the same. Turn the problem back to the team, saying, "This is an issue between all of you and Wendel. It doesn't involve me. If you can't resolve it, however, I'll remove Wendel from the team and consider where he can be useful."

21.2.6 The perfectionist

Another common problem is the team member who won't agree with the rest of the team and wants a more perfect standard of faults before releasing code. The manager should handle this individual in precisely the same way Wendel was handled: Let the team figure it out.

In one particularly nice instance, a team gave their perfectionist, Carl, the role of Guardian of Quality. They gave him a toy shield and rubber sword that he was to brandish whenever he wanted to engage in Battle for the Right. In effect, they used the technique of tickling the superreasonable—a form of incongruence that has a hard time persisting in the face of humor. The same is true for blaming, another common stance for the perfectionist. In this case, Carl lightened up and began using his considerable analytical powers to the team's advantage. If he had not, I'm sure he wouldn't have lasted long on the team, thus solving the problem in another way.

21.3 Dissolve Nonfunctioning Groupings

There are times when a team member is unable to work with others and has to leave the team. Many managers consider this too radical a solution, and they struggle to prevent the departure. Usually, such departures would not be such a big deal if these placating managers didn't make such a fuss about them. With very few exceptions, the teams and the departing member have done just the right thing by mutual consent, without wasting the manager's time.

Although I believe it's possible to make almost any group into a productive team, the value produced doesn't always justify the investment needed to make the team function. If the team doesn't solve its problems by itself after a reasonable effort, you as the manager may have to intervene and change the composition of the team.

21.3.1 Nonfunctional ownership

Perhaps the main impediment to successful teamwork is an individual's attitude of "Because it's *mine*, I won't let others touch it, or even see it" or "If it's not *my* idea, it can't be the best idea." This incongruent egoistic attitude, of course, stems from low self-esteem, which translates into the fallacy "If my code is defective, then I am defective."

Such a closed attitude invariably leads to disaster in software engineering. People who feel this way have no more business handling software than people who drink on the job have driving a school bus. They may be personable, good-looking, intelligent, kind to animals, and even smell good, but keep them away from any software I'm going to use.

The problem is not the ego-involvement but the incongruence, as beautifully reframed by my software colleague, not the fictional, Andy Hardy: "I always like problems because I like the solutions. To me, solutions are things of beauty, clarity, and an art form.

"When I have defective code, I am troubled. My art is in some way defiled. To have someone discover the blight within my art gives me the chance to make it more beautiful. I am at peace."[4]

People who are unable to think this way are unable to work well on any software team. If the same person has already been quietly extruded from several teams because of insistence on private ownership of the product, this is the time for you to intervene. Rather than frustrating yourself by placing this person on yet another team, reduce your costs, increase your productivity, and encourage this person to find a more suitable profession.

21.3.2 Breaking up the long-term team

Sometimes, however, the trouble in a team cannot be blamed on one individual. At times, a pair of team members develop a loving or hating relationship that cannot be solved fairly by removing only one. At other times, the team has rejected one member after another and still has not become productive. Or even after waiting a long time, you may not be able to identify any specific cause of the team's dysfunction.

In such cases, you, the manager, will have to step in and break up the team. If possible, treat them like you would any employee who was not performing. Call the team together and warn them that if you do not see specific changes by a specific date, you will dissolve the team. Offer them some outside facilitation. Don't offer yourself. Make it clear that you are not going to pick out one or two scapegoats, but will break up the team entirely. Otherwise, team members will simply spend the probation period jockeying for position in the new arrangement.

It helps if you take responsibility, as by saying, "I thought this team would work out, but it hasn't. I lack the skills necessary to get this team functioning well in the time we have." Then learn from the experience. Team formation is not a science, but neither is it random. If you pay attention and take responsibility, you'll get better at it.

21.3.3 Dissolving temporary teams

Temporary groupings of people are attractive in a crisis because they can be formed quickly. Once properly set up, the team will organize itself and learn to function well without much attention. The other side of this self-organizing ability, however, can prove troublesome. Once a manager has appointed a group of people, it takes on a life of its own, and may be hard to dissolve when needs change.

A software quality crisis is usually marked by the existence of many nonfunctional, or even counter-functional, groupings (which are not real "teams," even though they may have that name). Although these teams cannot work well together on their task, they seem to work very well at the task of keeping together, in spite of your attempts to discontinue them.

The first principle of breaking up temporary teams is prevention: Avoid creating teams you cannot terminate if they become nonfunctional. Make every grouping short term, with a definite life span after which its existence must be evaluated. This applies to existing groups as well. Give them a few weeks to justify their existence, and if they don't do so, dissolve them. This will free up resources for more pertinent tasks.

Of course, you cannot dissolve informal groupings simply by management declaration, so don't waste your time and credibility trying to do so. But there are many groups whose existence will go on mindlessly if you don't actively intervene. During a real crisis, you can probably dispense with anything that doesn't have a payoff within a month, such as developing standards, long-range planning, writing job descriptions, or reorganizing.

If you meet great opposition in dissolving a group, try putting it on hold. If that doesn't work and the group meets anyway, try to stretch out its meeting schedule. Pay attention to what people are telling you. Some of the groups that aren't really accomplishing what they were originally chartered to do may in fact be serving a useful, if unrecognized, function. If that's what the members are suggesting, direct them to write a new charter, which you can evaluate in terms of the current situation.

21.4 Helpful Hints and Suggestions

1. Teams that are geographically dispersed present serious management problems because they miss the contact with one another. A reliable, easy-to-use electronic mail system helps, as does a generous telephone budget, but there is simply no substitute for face-to-face contact. I have found it useful to budget for getting such a team together for team building early in their life, and then to find every possible excuse to get the team members together at least once every two months from then on.

2. Endless books and articles have been written about how to select the right employee for the job or the team, with principles, guidelines, and checklists galore.[5] Many of these are quite helpful, but they do tend to give the fairy-tale impression that if you choose the right princess and the right frog, they will live happily ever after. Whatever else it does, this model makes managers over-anxious about selecting people for teams, and under-anxious about exer-

cising their control function throughout the life of those teams.

Here's a different way of looking at it. With work teams, as with marriage teams, the most important principle about selection is to choose in such a way that you believe you have picked the right person, so you will support that decision in good times or bad.

3.   Some managers try to break up teams because they become too powerful, which makes the managers uncomfortable. If you try to reduce the power of a team by breaking it up, you'll often find that the whole team quits and goes, intact, to another organization. Rather than lose the power of such a team, it would be better to look inside yourself and increase your own sense of power, rather than reducing theirs.

4.   Other managers want to break up teams because they haven't become power-ful enough. Wayne Strider, a team consultant with Strider and Cline, has developed two graphs that help lessen the anxiety that teams and their man-agers feel about whether they are a team or not, or when they will be a team, or if they will ever be a team. The underlying assumption seems to be that people think they are not a team until certain things happen or a certain time has elapsed or some other vague criterion has been met. A graph of this assumption is shown in Figure 21-2.

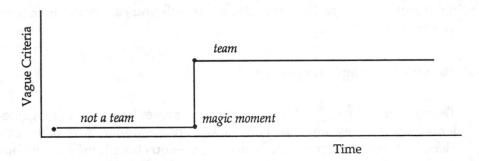

Figure 21-2.   This view that a team has a magic moment of forming seems fraught with uncer-tainty and stress for the team members and their manager.

Wayne Strider then suggests another possibility, one that is more human and possibly less stressful. "Team" could be a process, not an end state. If the focus is shifted from "team or not team" to "effectiveness," the graph might look more like Figure 21-3. In this view, a team is always a team from the date of its formation. As he explains, "Some days the team may be more effective than others. Over time, however, team members can learn how to work with each other and use each other as resources and trust each other. As a result the team can become more effective. The team itself can decide how to measure effec-tiveness and periodically take checkpoints to see how effective they're being."

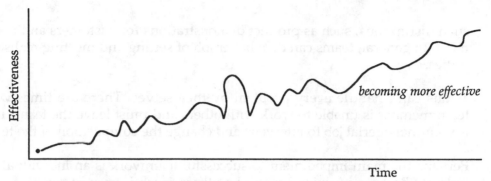

Figure 21-3. The process of "teaming" is taking place every day, with many ups and downs sometimes obscuring the attainment of higher effectiveness.

21.5 Summary

✓ As a manager, your job with respect to team building is to develop it when a team is needed, leave it alone when it's working effectively, and stop it when it's not.

✓ Forming a team during a crisis is not a trivial management task. If the organization is severely depressed, you may need a skilled facilitator in the first meetings of a new team. The composition of the team must ensure that everyone has *some* unique contribution.

✓ A better starting point than a crisis for long-lived teams is using teams that have formed naturally in maintenance or development. The trick is not to dissolve them just because their project was completed successfully.

✓ Existing teams in the organization can also be an impediment to change. They may see attempts to create special problem-solving teams as a way of breaking up their ring of solidarity, or of blaming the team for not doing a better job.

✓ A well-functioning team is the busy manager's biggest potential asset if you let the team do its work. A real team is much stronger than the typical manager, and not as likely to be intimidated by high-level management. The team's opinion is likely to carry a lot more weight.

✓ Teams are less likely to panic when the project is late. Incongruent managers don't like to see other people remaining calm when they themselves are panicking, and they often try to spread their panic to others. An experienced team, however, simply absorbs the manager's incongruence and usually has a calming effect.

✓ One piece of unmanaged work injected from the outside can disrupt any amount of planned work. Teams can establish a specialized role to handle such disruptions, such as product demonstrations for customers and management. In general, teams can do a better job of setting and meeting realistic priorities.

✓   Teams can't handle every problem by themselves. There are times when a team member is unable to work with others and must leave the team. Then it is your managerial job to intervene and change the composition of the team.

✓   Perhaps the main impediment to successful teamwork is an individual's attitude of "Because it's *mine*, I won't let others touch it or even see it" or "If it's not *my* idea, it can't be the best idea." This closed attitude invariably leads to disaster in software, and must not be allowed to persist. If you decide to change this attitude, typically you have to exchange the person for someone else. Not everybody is cut out for the software business.

✓   Sometimes teams become dysfunctional for no identifiable reason, or because of the involvement of several people. In those cases, you have to step in and break up the team, usually after putting the members on warning.

✓   Once a manager has appointed a group of people, even in a crisis, it takes on a life of its own and may be hard to dissolve when needs change. Thus, avoid creating teams you cannot terminate if they become nonfunctional. When you do create temporary groups, give them a definite life span, after which they will have to justify their existence again.

✓   Groups that seem to be dysfunctional may simply be providing a different function than you intended. Before you break up a group, try to determine what functions it serves.

21.6 Practice

1.   Imagine that you are a new manager and, after a few weeks, you realize that one of the projects assigned to you will surely fail. It is due in one month, and the project manager (who is from the customer organization) says there is no problem. So do his staff members who are on the project, but every indication is for a failure. What should you do? How can congruence help you resolve this situation?

2.   There are a number of interesting relationships between teams and turnover. If a company has, say, a ten-percent turnover in staff, that could very well create a much higher rate of team destruction. Assuming that one person leaving could break up the team, and that team size was five members, ten-percent

turnover could destroy fifty percent of the teams.

On the other hand, solid teams may well survive the departure of one or even more members, so ten-percent turnover may lead to zero-percent team destruction. Or all the losses may come from a few teams; it's well known that people working on effective teams do not readily leave an organization, unless they all leave together because of being poorly managed.

Diagram and discuss the variables involved in teamwork and turnover, and develop a diagram of effects relating the important ones.

Part V
Epilogue

These three volumes have been a long journey for me, and perhaps for you. When I started, I imagined that the final volume would consist of a recipe for precisely what to do to create a quality software engineering organization—a recipe with ingredients such as CASE tools, project organization, training practices, testing techniques, and configuration management approaches. Along the way, I've discussed such ingredients, but I've never given the recipe. This was no mistake, but a conscious omission, because without a capable chef, a recipe is merely a mess of ingredients.

I'm now in the process of writing *Volume 4*, tentatively titled *Anticipating Change*, with the full recipe. I certainly have all the notes in my files, and many of the chapters are already written. But I'm going to wait awhile before finishing it, to see if these first three volumes influence the number of capable chefs out there. I already know that there are plenty of chefs who would make a mess of it, then blame me for giving them the wrong recipe.

I've certainly messed up some perfectly sound recipes for software engineering success myself. When I haven't felt good about myself, I've bullied people, ignored them, blamed them, blamed myself, run away from difficult situations, or shrouded my head in clouds of abstraction. Through all this, I've learned that there's simply no sense trying to solve software engineering problems, or create software engineering organizations, when I'm not able to be congruent. So I work on that first, and that's what I hope you do, too.

Decades ago, I went into computing because I believed that computers could be a major factor in making a far better world. I've wavered at times, but I've never lost that vision. Perhaps I'm a naive dreamer, but I've always felt that this better world would be created by people who were driven by similar vision. Unhappily, I've encountered many people who were driven by something else: personal gain, power over others, or perhaps simple meanness. I don't understand such people, I don't deal well with them, and I think they hurt our profession. No sense preaching, though, because they can surely sense that I have not been writing for them, and they have left these pages long ago.

For the rest of you, there's an ancient story that sums up what I think you can accomplish through congruence or, if you like, character. I think of this story whenever I'm a little down from a bout with one of those others—the greedy, the power-hungry, or the mean-spirited. I'm sure I can't live up to the righteousness of its hero, Hsün Chü-po, yet it makes me feel that my attempts to improve my behavior will ultimately make a difference.

Hsün Chü-po Visits His Friend

Hsün Chü-po[1] traveled a great distance to see his friend, who was stricken ill. It happened that at this time the prefecture came under attack by the Tartars.

"Death will soon claim me," his friend said to Chü-po. "Please leave while you may!"

"I've come a long way to see you," Chü-po replied, "and you ask me to leave? Is this proper conduct for Hsün Chü-po, to cast aside the principle of righteousness and run away, leaving his friend behind?"

Then the Tartars came, and they said to Chü-po, "Our great armies are here and the people have fled the land. What manner of man are you that dare to linger?"

"My friend lies ill, and I cannot endure the thought of leaving him," Chü-po answered. "Spare his life and take mine in its stead!"

At this, the Tartars marveled. "Indeed, we are iniquitous men who have come to the land of the righteous." So they gathered their troops and departed, and the prefecture was saved from destruction.[2]

Appendix A
Diagram of Effects

An important skill of Steering (Pattern 3) managers is the ability to reason about nonlinear systems, and one of the favorite tools for this purpose is the *diagram of effects*.[1] In Figure A-1, the diagram of effects shows the effects of management pressure to resolve software failures (system trouble incidents or STIs). We can use this diagram as an example of the major notational conventions.

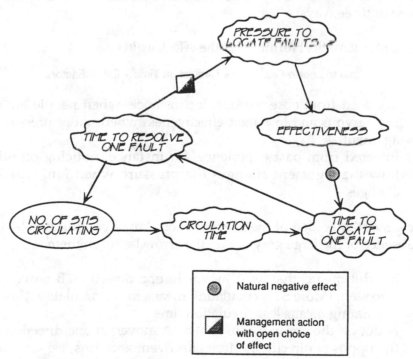

PRESSURE TO
LOCATE FAULTS

EFFECTIVENESS

TIME TO RESOLVE
ONE FAULT

NO. OF STIS
CIRCULATING

CIRCULATION
TIME

TIME TO
LOCATE
ONE FAULT

○ Natural negative effect

◪ Management action
with open choice
of effect

Figure A-1.   Sample diagram of effects.

A diagram of effects consists primarily of nodes connected by arrows:

1. Each node stands for a measurable quantity, like Circulation Time, Effectiveness, Time to Locate One Fault, or Pressure to Locate Faults. I prefer using the "cloud" symbol over a circle or a rectangle as a reminder that nodes indicate measurements, not things or processes as in flowcharts, data flow diagrams, and the like.

2. These cloud nodes may represent either actual measurements or conceptual measurements—things that could be measured, but are not measured at present because they may be too expensive to measure, or not worth the trouble, or just not measured yet. The important thing is that they can be measured, perhaps only approximately, if we are willing to pay the price.

3. To indicate an actual measurement currently being made, use a regular, elliptical cloud, as for No. of STIs Circulating in Figure A-1. Most of the time, however, effects diagrams are used for conceptual—rather than mathematical— analysis, so most of the clouds will be appropriately rough.

4. An arrow from node A to node B indicates that quantity A has an effect on quantity B. We may know or deduce the effect that leads us to draw the arrow in one of three ways:

    a. a mathematical formula for the effect, as in

        Time to Locate One Fault = Circulation Time + Other Factors

    b. deduced from observations, for instance, when people are observed to get nervous and lose their effectiveness when under pressure from management
    c. inferred from past experience, for instance, noticing on other projects how management changes the pressure when fault resolution time changes

5. The general direction of the effect of A on B may be indicated by the presence or absence of the large gray dot on the arrow between them.

    a. No dot means that as A moves in one direction, B moves in the same direction. (More STIs circulating means more circulation time; fewer STIs circulating means less circulation time.)
    b. A dot on the arrow means that as A moves in one direction, B moves in the opposite direction. (More effectiveness means less time to locate one fault; less effectiveness means more time to locate one fault.)

6. A square on an effects line indicates that human intervention is determining the direction of the effect:

a. A white square means that human intervention is making the affected measurement move in the same direction as the movement of the cause (just as a plain arrow indicates a natural same direction).

b. A gray square means that human intervention is making the affected measurement move in the opposite direction as the movement of the cause (just as a gray dot indicates a natural opposite direction).

c. A half-white/half-gray square means that human intervention can make the affected measurement move in the same or the opposite direction as the movement of the cause, depending on the intervention. In the case of Figure A-1, management can react to an increase in the amount of fault resolution time by either increasing or decreasing pressure to locate faults. The square shows that this dynamic depends on the manager's choice of response.

Appendix B
Satir Interaction Model

The Satir Interaction Model[1] says that everyone's internal observation process has four major parts: Intake, Meaning, Significance, and Response, as shown in Figure B-1. For the purpose of this explanation, I act as the observer.

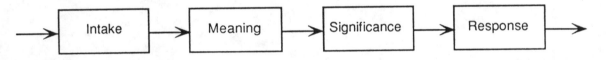

Figure B-1.   The four basic parts of the Satir Interaction Model.

Intake
In the first part of the process, I take in information from the world. Although some people may believe that intake just happens to me as a passive participant, I am actually exercising a great many choices.

Meaning
Next, I consider the sensory intake and give it meaning. The meaning doesn't lie in the data; data have no meaning until I provide meaning.

Significance
Data may suggest certain meanings, but never the significance. Without this step, the world I perceive would be an overwhelming flood of data patterns. With it, I can give priority to a few patterns and largely ignore the rest.

Response
Observation is rarely passive, but elicits response. I may not, and should not, respond to every observation immediately. I am always sifting observations according to their assigned importance and storing them away to guide future actions.

Appendix C
Software Engineering Cultural Patterns

This volume makes extensive use of the idea of software cultural patterns. For ease of reference, I summarize here the various aspects of those patterns.

To my knowledge, Crosby was the first to apply the idea of cultural patterns to the study of industrial processes.[1] He discovered that the various processes making up a technology don't merely occur in random combinations, but in coherent patterns.

In their article "A Programming Process Study," Radice et al. adapted Crosby's "stratification by quality" scheme to software development.[2] Later, Watts Humphrey of the Software Engineering Institute (SEI) extended their work and identified five levels of "process maturity" through which a software development organization might grow.[3] Other software engineering observers quickly noted the usefulness of Humphrey's maturity levels. Bill Curtis proposed a "software human resource maturity model" with five levels.[4]

Each of these models represents points of view of the same phenomenon. Crosby named his five patterns based largely on the *management attitudes* to be found in each. The names used by the SEI are more related to the *types of processes* found in each pattern, rather than to the attitudes of management. Curtis made his classification on the basis of the *treatment of people* within the organization.

In my own work with software engineering organizations, I most often use the cultural view[5] combined with Crosby's original focus on management and on attitudes, but I find each view useful at various times. The following summary incorporates material from each point of view.

Pattern 0 Oblivious Culture

Other names: This pattern doesn't exist in Crosby's, Humphrey's, or Curtis's models.

View of themselves: "We don't even know that we're performing a process."

Metaphor: Walking: When we want to go somewhere, we just stand up and go.

Management understanding and attitude: There is no comprehension that quality is a management issue.

Problem handling: Problems are suffered in silence.

Summation of quality position: "We don't have quality problems."

When this pattern is successful: To succeed, individuals need three conditions or beliefs:

✓   "I'm solving my own problems."

✓   "Those problems aren't too big for what I know is technically possible."

✓   "I know what I want better than anyone else."

Process results: Results depend totally on the individual. No records are kept, so there are no measurements. Because the customer is the developer, delivery is always acceptable.

Pattern 1 Variable Culture

Other names:

Crosby:	Uncertainty Stage
Humphrey:	Initial Process
Curtis:	Herded

View of themselves: "We do whatever we feel like at the moment."

Metaphor: Riding a horse: When we want to go somewhere, we saddle up and ride … if the horse cooperates.

Management understanding and attitude: There is no comprehension of quality as a management issue.

Problem handling: Problems are fought with inadequate definition and no resolution (but with lots of yelling and accusations).

Summation of quality position: "We don't know why we have quality problems."

When this pattern is successful: To succeed, individuals (or teams) need three conditions or beliefs:

✓   "I have great rapport with my customer."

✓   "I'm a competent professional."

✓   "My customer's problem isn't too big for me."

Process results: The work is generally one-on-one between customer and developer. Quality is measured internally by its function ("It works!"), externally by the working relationship. Emotion, personal relations, and mysticism drive everything. There is no consistent design, randomly structured code, and errors removed by haphazard testing. Some of the work is excellent, some is bizarre, and it all depends on the individual.

Pattern 2 Routine Culture

Other names:

Crosby:	Awakening Stage
Humphrey:	Repeatable Process
Curtis:	Managed

View of themselves: "We follow our routines (except when we lose our nerve)."

Metaphor: A train: When we want to go somewhere, we find a train, which has large capacity and is very efficient ... if we go where the tracks are. We're helpless when off the tracks.

Management understanding and attitude: There is a recognition that quality management may be of value, but there is no willingness to provide money or time to make it all happen.

Problem handling: Teams are set up to handle major problems. Long-range solutions are not solicited.

Summation of quality position: "Is it absolutely necessary to have problems with quality? Maybe if we just don't deal with them, the problems will go away."

When this pattern is successful: To succeed, people in these organizations need four conditions or beliefs:

✓   "We realize the problem is bigger than one small team can handle."

✓   "The problem is not too big for us to handle."

✓   "The developers must conform to our Routine process."

✓   "We hope we don't run into anything too exceptional."

Process results: The Routine organization has procedures to coordinate efforts, though its members only go through the motions of following them. Statistics on past performance are used not to change, but to prove that they are doing everything in the only reasonable way. Quality is measured internally by the numbers of errors ("bugs"). Generally, the organization uses bottom-up design and semi-structured code, with errors removed by testing and fixing. Routine organizations have many successes, but a few very large failures.

Pattern 3 Steering Culture

Other names:

Crosby:	Enlightenment Stage
Humphrey:	Defined Process
Curtis:	Tailored

View of themselves: "We choose among our routines based on the results they produce."

Metaphor: A van: We have a large choice of destinations, but we must generally stay on mapped roads, and must be steered to stay on the road.

Management understanding and attitude: There is comprehension of quality as a management tool: "Through our quality program, we learn more about quality management, and become more supportive and helpful."

Problem handling: Problems are faced openly and resolved in an orderly way.

Summation of quality position: "Through commitment and quality improvement, we are identifying and resolving our problems."

When this pattern is successful: To succeed, people in these organizations need four conditions or beliefs:

✓ "The problem is big enough that we know a simple routine won't work."

✓ "Our managers can negotiate with the external environment."

✓ "We don't accept arbitrary schedules and constraints."

✓ "We are challenged, but not excessively."

Process results: They have procedures that are always well understood, but not always well defined in writing, and that are followed even in crisis. Quality is measured by user (customer) response, but not systematically. Some measuring is done, but everybody debates which measurements are meaningful. Typically, they use top-down design, structured code, design and code inspections, and incremental releases. The organization has consistent success when it commits to undertake something.

Pattern 4 Anticipating Culture

Other names:

Crosby:	Wisdom Stage
Humphrey:	Managed Process
Curtis:	Institutionalized

View of themselves: "We establish routines based on our past experience with them."

Metaphor: An airplane: When going somewhere, we can travel fast, reliably, and anywhere there's a field, but going this way requires a large initial investment.

Management understanding and attitude: There is understanding of the absolutes of quality management, and recognition of their personal role in this continuing emphasis.

Problem handling: Problems are identified early in their development. All functions are open to suggestion and improvement.

Summation of quality position: "Defect prevention is a routine part of our operation."

When this pattern is successful: To succeed, individuals need three conditions or beliefs:

✓   "I'm solving my own problems.

✓   "We measure quality and cost (internally) by meaningful statistics."

✓   "We have an explicit process group to aid in the process."

Process results: They use sophisticated tools and techniques, including function-theoretical design, mathematical verification, and reliability measurement. They have consistent success even on ambitious projects.

Pattern 5 Congruent Culture

Other names:

Crosby:	Certainty Stage
Humphrey:	Optimizing Process
Curtis:	Optimized

View of themselves: "Everyone is involved in improving everything all the time."

Metaphor: The Starship Enterprise: When going somewhere, we can go where no one has gone before, we can carry anything, and we can beam ourselves anywhere, but this is all science fiction.

Management understanding and attitude: Quality management is considered an essential part of the company system.

Problem handling: Except in the most unusual cases, problems are prevented.

Summation of quality position: "We know why we do not have quality problems."

When this pattern is successful: To succeed, these organizations need three conditions or beliefs:

✓   "We have procedures, which we improve continuously."

✓   "We identify and measure all key process variables automatically."

✓   "Our goal is customer satisfaction, which drives everything."

Process results: Here are all of the good things achievable by the other patterns, plus the willingness to spend to reach the next level of quality. Quality is measured by customer satisfaction and by the mean time to customer failure (ten to one-hundred years). Customers love the quality, and can bet their life on it. In some sense, Pattern 5 is like Pattern 0 in being totally responsive to the customer, but it is much better at what it does.

Appendix D
Control Models

Each software cultural pattern has its own characteristic pattern of control. The study of patterns of software control starts with the question, What is needed to control anything? Here, I discuss two possible answers to this need.

The *Aggregate Control Model* says that if we're willing to spend enough on redundant solutions, we'll eventually get the system we want. Sometimes, this is the most practical way, or the only way we can think of.

The *Feedback Control Model* (or cybernetic model) tries for a more efficient way of getting what we want. A controller controls a system based on information about what the system is currently doing. Comparing this information with what is planned for the system, the controller takes actions designed to bring the system's behavior closer to plan.

The job of engineering management is to act as the controller in engineering projects. Failures of engineering management can be understood in terms of the Feedback Control Model. Routine (Pattern 2) managers, for example, often lack this understanding, which can explain why they experience so many low-quality, or failed, projects.

D.1 Aggregate Control Model

One general approach to shooting at moving targets is the technique of *aggregation*. Aggregate control is like shooting with a shotgun or, more precisely, with shrapnel. If we simply send more bullets flying through the sky in sufficiently random directions, we will increase our chances of hitting a target, no matter how it is moving.

In software engineering, the aggregate approach says, roughly, to be sure of getting a good product, start a large number of projects and choose the one that produces the best product. From the viewpoint of an individual software company, aggregation may be a useful way to ensure success in special circumstances.

Aggregation is most commonly used when we are considering a software purchase. Of several products considered, we choose the best for our purposes. If our selection procedure is at all sensible, we should wind up with a better product than if we only considered one.

Sometimes, the use of aggregation is not fully intentional. Routine organizations frequently employ unintentional *serial* aggregation. When the first attempt to build a system doesn't turn out well, a second project is started. If the second does not turn out well either, the organization may actually return to the first, now accepting its poor quality as the better of a bad lot. Aggregation is a universal strategy, and no pattern is without its examples. In Pattern 3, however, there is a more conscious use of explicit manipulation of aggregation to aid in quality improvement.

D.2 Feedback Control (Cybernetic) Model

Whereas aggregation is like shooting with a shotgun, feedback control is like shooting with a rifle. Cybernetics, the "science of aiming," is a topic that every software engineer needs to understand.[1]

D.2.1 The system to be controlled (the focus of Patterns 0 and 1)

The cybernetic model starts with the idea of a system to be controlled (Figure D-1). A system has inputs and outputs. For a system that produces software, the outputs are Software, plus Other Outputs, which may include all sorts of things that are not the direct goal of the system, such as

- greater competence with a programming language
- software tools developed while doing the intended software
- stronger, or weaker, development teams
- stress, pregnancies, influenza, happiness
- anger toward management
- respect for management
- thousands of failure reports
- personnel appraisals

The inputs are of three principal types (the 3 R's):

- Requirements
- Resources
- Randomness

A system's behavior is governed by the formula:

Behavior depends on both state and input.

Thus, control depends not only on what we put in (requirements and resources) and what gets in by some other way (randomness), but also on what's going on internally (the state).

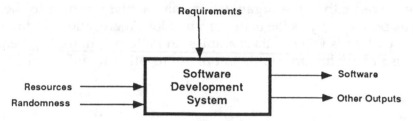

Figure D-1.   Cybernetic model of a software development system to be controlled.

Figure D-1 represents the entire model of software development as understood by Pattern 1 organizations. In effect, it says,

a.   "Tell us what you want (and don't change your mind)."
b.   "Give us some resources (and keep giving whenever we ask)."
c.   "Don't bother us (that is, eliminate all randomness)."

These are the ABC's of Pattern 1 software development, and by listening for these statements, you can reliably identify a Pattern 1 organization.

If you drop the "A" (the external requirements), you get the identifying phrases for Pattern 0 organizations, which already know what they want, without help, thank you. Figure D-1 can thus be transformed to the Pattern 0 diagram by dropping off the requirements arrow, thus isolating the system from direct external control.

D.2.2 *The controller (the focus of Pattern 2)*

To get more quality (value) from our software development with this Pattern 1 model, we would have to use the aggregate approach—in effect pumping more resources into the development system. One way to do this would be to initiate several such development systems and let each do whatever it does best. If we want more control of each system, however, we must connect it to some sort of *controller* (Figure D-2). The controller represents all our efforts to keep the software development on track, and is Pattern 2's addition to the problem of getting quality software.

At this level of cybernetic theory, the controller cannot access the internal state of the development system directly. So, in order to be able to control, the controller must be able to change the internal state indirectly through the inputs (the lines coming out of the controller and into the system). Examples of such attempts to change the programming staff may include

- offering training courses to make them smarter
- buying them tools to make them smarter
- hiring Harvard graduates to make them smarter (on average)
- offering cash incentives to make them more motivated
- offering more interesting assignments to make them more motivated
- firing Berkeley graduates to make them more motivated (on average)

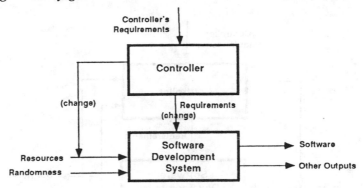

Figure D-2.   Model of a software development system controller.

The control actions are added to the system's *uncontrolled* inputs (the randomness), either by changing requirements or changing resources. Notice that no matter what the controller does to these inputs, there is still randomness coming in, which simply represents all those external things that the controller cannot totally control. The thought of these inputs is most frustrating to some Pattern 2 managers.

D.2.3 Feedback control (the focus of Pattern 3)

An effective method of limiting losses due to flu (an uncontrolled input) would be to send people home at the first sign of symptoms. The Pattern 2 controller pictured in Figure D-2 cannot do this because it has no knowledge of what the system is actually doing. A more versatile and effective model of control is the feedback model shown in Figure D-3. In this model—which represents the Pattern 3 concept of control—the controller can make measurements of performance (the line coming out of the system and into the controller) and use them as an aid in determining its next control actions.

But feedback measurements and control actions are not enough for effective control. We know that behavior depends on both state and input. In order for the control actions to be effective, the Pattern 3 controller must possess models to connect the state and input with the behavior—models of what "depends" means for this system.

Overall, for feedback control to operate, the system of control must have

- an image of a *desired* state (D)
- the ability to observe the *actual* state (A)
- the ability to compare state A and state D for differences
- the ability to act on the system to bring A closer to D

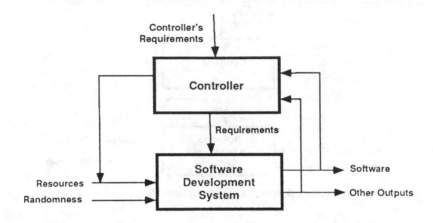

Figure D-3.   Feedback model of a software development system requires feedback of information about the system's performance, plus requirements for the controller to compare with that information. This is the model that distinguishes Pattern 3 from Patterns 0, 1, and 2. It is also used by Patterns 4 and 5.

A characteristic Pattern 2 mistake is to equate "controller" with "manager." In the Pattern 3 model, managing is essentially a controller job. To manage an engineering project by feedback control, the manager needs to

- plan what should happen
- observe what significant things are really happening
- compare the observed with the planned
- take actions needed to bring actual closer to planned

Managers who are able to do these things consistently are what we call Steering managers. Patterns 3, 4, and 5 all require Steering management, which seems to be the limiting factor for most organizations that wish to make the transition out of Pattern 0, 1, or 2 to one of these patterns. *Quality Software Management's* volumes are devoted to encouraging the transition to Steering management.

Appendix E
Three Observer Positions

Even when you are congruent, you may not be in the best position to observe what you need to work on in a crisis. One of the most effective interventions in a crisis is to provide information taken from a different point of view. Whenever you act as an observer, you have a choice of where to "stand" to make your observations: the self, other, or context.

Self (Insider) Position
Inside yourself, looking outward or inward. This position gives you the ability to realize what your own interests are, why you are behaving the way you are, and what you may be contributing to the situation. An inability to observe from this position often results in placating or superreasonable behavior. Many burnouts result from forgetting to spend time in the self position.

Other (Empathic) Position
As if you were inside another person, observing from his or her point of view. This position gives you the ability to understand why people react the way they do. An inability to observe from this position often results in blaming or superreasonable behavior.

Context (Outsider) Position
Outside, looking at yourself and at other people. This position gives you the ability to understand and place things in context. An inability to observe from this position often results in irrelevant behavior.

Nothing says you have to take any particular observer position, or any position at all. Sometimes, you become so panicked in a crisis that you are unable to take any observer position. You ignore your own feelings, don't notice what's happening to others, and have no connection with the overall situation.

In managing, you need to be flexible, observing at times from Position 1, or Position 2, or Position 3. If you cannot reach one or more of these observer positions, you may be stuck and behave incongruently (either blaming, placating, or acting superreasonable or irrelevant). In this way, you have given away some of your observational power, just when you need it most.

Notes

Preface

1   Vaughn Beals, Chief Executive Officer of the Harley-Davidson Company, explaining to television interviewers in 1992 how the Harley-Davidson people saved their company and beat the Japanese competition.

Part I

1   F.P. Brooks, Jr., "No Silver Bullet: Essence and Accidents of Software Engineering," *Computer*, Vol. 20, No. 4 (April 1987), pp. 10-19. Reprinted in T. DeMarco and T. Lister, eds., *Software State-of-the-Art: Selected Papers* (New York: Dorset House Publishing, 1990), pp. 14-29.

Chapter 1

1   For those who have not read *Volume 1* or 2, Appendix D explains the cybernetic or feedback model of control.
2   W.R. Ashby, *An Introduction to Cybernetics* (London: Chapman and Hall, 1964).
3   B. Curtis, "Managing the Real Leverage in Software Productivity and Quality," *American Programmer*, Vol. 3, No. 7-8 (1990), pp. 4-14.
4   W. Humphrey and B. Curtis, "Comments on 'A Critical Look,'" *IEEE Software*, Vol. 8, No. 4 (July 1991), pp. 42-46. This article was commenting on another article: T.B. Bollinger and C. McGowan, "A Critical Look at Software Capability Evaluations," *IEEE Software*, Vol. 8, No. 4 (July 1991), pp. 25-41. Both articles are worth reading.

Chapter 2

1   B.W. Boehm, *Software Engineering Economics* (Englewood Cliffs, N.J.: Prentice-Hall, 1981).
2   *SEI Reports: Annotated Listing, 1 January 1986-87* (Pittsburgh: Software Engineering Institute, November 1991).
3   See Appendix C for more information on software cultural patterns.

4   G.M. Weinberg, *Becoming a Technical Leader* (New York: Dorset House Publishing, 1986).
5   Ibid., pp. 97-100.
6   L.A. Hill, *Becoming a Manager: Mastery of a New Identity* (Boston: Harvard Business School Press, 1992), p. 26.
7   P. de Jager, personal communication, 1993.
8   J.A. Autry, *Love and Profits: The Art of Caring Leadership* (New York: Avon Books, 1991), p. 19.

Chapter 3

1   N. Branden, *The Psychology of Self-Esteem* (New York: Bantam Books, 1971), p. 109.
2   For a short overview of coping styles, see V. Satir, *Making Contact* (Berkeley, Calif.: Celestial Arts, 1976). For a more comprehensive treatment, see V. Satir, *The New Peoplemaking* (Palo Alto, Calif.: Science and Behavior Books, 1988).
3   D.A. Norman, *The Design of Everyday Things* (New York: Basic Books, 1988), pp. 41-42.

Chapter 4

1   V. Satir, *The New Peoplemaking* (Palo Alto, Calif.: Science and Behavior Books, 1988), pp. 382-83.
2   Ibid., p. 108.
3   See S.E. Hardin, *Success with the Gentle Art of Verbal Self-Defense* (Englewood Cliffs, N.J.: Prentice-Hall, 1989) for a discussion of the linguistics of incongruence.
4   R. Kipling, "If."

Chapter 5

1   L.A. Hill, *Becoming a Manager: Mastery of a New Identity* (Boston: Harvard Business School Press, 1992), p. 142.
2   For lots more on self-talk and how to change it, see P.E. Butler, *Talking to Yourself: Learning the Language of Self-Affirmation* (San Francisco: Harper, 1991).
3   There are a number of ways you can begin to sharpen your awareness of your body being off center. I found Thomas Crum's Magic of Conflict workshops extremely helpful, along with his book, *The Magic of Conflict* (New York: Simon & Schuster, 1987). Both the book and workshops are based on the art of aikido.
4   D. Starr, personal communication, 1992.
5   C. Argyris, "Teaching Smart People How to Learn," *Harvard Business Review*, 1991, pp. 99-109.

Chapter 6

1   T.F. Crum, *The Magic of Conflict* (New York: Simon & Schuster, 1987), p. 174.
2   Those who would like to improve this skill of following up on a worker's task can refer to *Volume 2, First-Order Measurement* of this series.
3   R. Cohen, communicated on the CompuServe Software Engineering Management Forum, 1993.
4   L.A. Hill, *Becoming a Manager: Mastery of a New Identity* (Boston: Harvard Business School Press, 1992), pp. 19-20.

5   J.R. Schmid, *Management by Guts* (Marceline, Mo.: Walsworth Publishing Co., 1985), p. 56.
6   F.P. Brooks, Jr., *The Mythical Man-Month* (Reading, Mass.: Addison-Wesley, 1975).
7   M. DePree, *Leadership Is an Art* (New York: Bantam Doubleday Dell Publishing Group, 1989), p. 104.
8   S. Heller, communicated on the CompuServe Software Engineering Management Forum, 1993.

Chapter 7

1   I couldn't possibly give a full exposition of the MBTI, for the subject is much too broad and deep. There are now several excellent books on the subject, at least one of which should be read carefully by a manager who wants to improve effectiveness. Here are some references, starting with the original: I.B. Myers, *Gifts Differing* (Palo Alto, Calif.: Consulting Psychologists Press, 1980). The full address for this publisher is 577 College Ave., Palo Alto, CA 94306. See also D. Keirsey and M. Bates, *Please Understand Me: Character and Temperament Types*, 4th ed. (Del Mar, Calif.: Prometheus Nemesis Book Co., 1984). Finally, O. Kroeger and J.M. Thuesen, *Type Talk at Work*, (New York: Delacorte Press, 1992).
2   Kiersey and Bates, op. cit., p. 25.
3   Kiersey and Bates, loc. cit.
4   M. DePree, *Leadership Is an Art* (New York: Bantam Doubleday Dell Publishing Group, 1989), p. 131.
5   Personal communication, 1991, with L. Nix. See Appendix C for a summary of software cultural patterns. For a more complete discussion, see *Volumes 1* and *2*.
6   N. Karten's most recent book is *Managing Expectations: Working with People Who Want More, Better, Faster, Sooner, NOW!* (New York: Dorset House Publishing, 1994).
7   Keirsey and Bates, op. cit.

Chapter 8

1   G. James, *The Zen of Programming* (Santa Monica, Calif.: Infobooks, 1988), p. 37. For a complete address, refer to P.O. Box 1018, Santa Monica, CA 90406.
2   Kiersey and Bates, op. cit., p. 70.
3   If you want to understand why these four combinations are singled out, consult Kiersey and Bates, loc. cit.
4   Kiersey and Bates, op. cit., p. 47
5   See Appendix B for an explanation of the Satir Interaction Model.
6   For more on the Data Question, see *Volume 2*, starting with Section 6.2.
7   G.M. Weinberg, *Becoming a Technical Leader* (New York: Dorset House Publishing, 1986).

Chapter 9

1   The address for the Association for Psychological Type is 9140 Ward Parkway, Kansas City, MO 64114-3313.
2   Much of what I know about Chinese culture I learned from F.L.K. Hsu, *Americans and Chinese* (Garden City, N.Y.: Natural History Press, 1970).
3   Most of what I know about Hong Kong Chinese culture was learned from my friends and roommates Au Chak Wang and Christopher Ng Yin Ke.

4   D. Tannen, *You Just Don't Understand: Women and Men in Conversation* (New York: Ballantine Books, 1990), p. 119.

5   D. Tannen, loc. cit.

6   See, for example, C. Andreas and S. Andreas, *Heart of the Mind: Engaging Your Inner Power to Change with Neuro-Linguistic Programming* (Moab, Utah: Real People Press, 1989); S. Andreas and C. Andreas, *Change Your Mind and Keep the Change* (Moab, Utah: Real People Press, 1987); or G. Laborde, *Influencing with Integrity: Management Skills for Communication and Negotiation* (Palo Alto, Calif.: Syntony Publishing, 1984).

7   G.M. Weinberg, *Quality Software Management: Volume 1, Systems Thinking* (Dorset House Publishing, 1992), pp. 24-25.

8   U.K. LeGuin, *The Word for World Is Forest.*

9   R.E. Axtell, ed., *Do's and Taboos Around the World* (Cambridge, Mass.: MIT Press, 1992).

10 R. Ornstein, *Multimind* (Boston: Houghton Mifflin Company, 1986).

Chapter 10

1   L.A. Hill, *Becoming a Manager: Mastery of a New Identity* (Boston: Harvard Business School Press, 1992), pp. 54-55.

2   Simply put, the Controller Fallacy appears in two forms (substitute *manager* for the term *controller)*: If the controller isn't busy, it's not doing a good job; and if the controller is very busy, it must be a good controller. See *Volume 1*, pp. 196ff.

3   E. Yarbrough, personal communication.

4   T.R. Riedl, J.S. Weitzenfeld, J.T. Freeman, G.A. Klein, and J. Musa, "What We Have Learned About Software Engineering Expertise," *Proceedings of the SEI Software Engineering Conference* (Pittsburgh: Software Engineering Institute, 1991).

5   If you have a hard time believing that abuse has this effect on employees, take a good, hard look at M. Sprouse, ed., *Sabotage in the American Workplace: Anecdotes of Dissatisfaction, Mischief, and Revenge* (San Francisco: Pressure Drop Press, 1992).

Chapter 11

1   V. Satir, *The New Peoplemaking* (Palo Alto, Calif.: Science and Behavior Books, 1988), p. 1.

2   We must especially be aware of the tendency to mechanize human beings, as in the use of the term *peopleware*, about which Tom DeMarco and I have agreed to disagree. (He and Tim Lister are co-authors of the book *Peopleware: Productive Projects and Teams*, published by Dorset House Publishing.) On the subject of mechanization, see, for example, G.M. Weinberg, "Overstructured Management of Software Engineering," reprinted in *Software State-of-the-Art: Selected Papers*, T. DeMarco and T. Lister, eds. (New York: Dorset House Publishing, 1990), pp. 4-13.

3   See Appendix B for a summary of the Satir Interaction Model.

4   See R. Ornstein, *Multimind* (Boston: Houghton Mifflin Company, 1986).

5   For more on the Parts Party, see V. Satir, J. Banmen, J. Gerber, and M. Gomori, *The Satir Model: Family Therapy and Beyond* (Palo Alto, Calif.: Science and Behavior Books, 1991).

6   For more on rules, see G.M. Weinberg, *Quality Software Management: Volume 2, First-Order Measurement* (New York: Dorset House Publishing, 1993).

7   Rules can be transformed with surprising ease into less rigid guides, if you use the correct techniques. See, for example,V. Satir, J. Banmen, J. Gerber, and M. Gomori, op. cit.; and G.M. Weinberg, *Becoming a Technical Leader* (New York: Dorset House Publishing, 1986).

Chapter 13

1   Vaughn T. Rokosz, 1993, from a personal communication arising from a discussion of requirements. He concluded that placating can destroy the meaning of any requirements, no matter how carefully obtained.

2   W.E. Deming, *Quality, Productivity, and Competitive Position* (Cambridge, Mass.: MIT Center for Advanced Engineering Studies, 1982), p. 33.

3   J. Horn, *Supervison's Factomatic* (Englewood Cliffs, N.J.: Prentice-Hall, 1986), p. 390.

4   J.R. Schmid, *Management by Guts* (Marceline, Mo.: Walsworth Publishing Co., 1985), p. 37.

5   For help with this practice, consult either or both of these sources: N. Branden, *The Psychology of Self-Esteem* (New York: Bantam Books, 1971); D. Frey and C.J. Carlock, *Practical Techniques for Enhancing Self-Esteem* (Muncie, Ind.: Accelerated Development, 1991).

Chapter 14

1   This phrase forms the basis for the title of Alice Miller's chilling book, *For Your Own Good: Hidden Cruelty in Child-Rearing and the Roots of Violence* (New York: Farrar, Straus, Giroux, 1983). *For Your Own Good* relates how Hitler's generation was reared in Germany using the pedagogy of blame. Reading this book can provide strong motivation to change an addiction to blaming.

2   K. Tohei, *Ki in Daily Life* (Tokyo: Ki No Kenkyukai H.Q., 1978), p. 103.

3   T.F. Crum, *The Magic of Conflict* (New York: Simon & Schuster, 1987), p. 168.

4   See G.M. Weinberg, *Becoming a Technical Leader* (New York: Dorset House Publishing, 1986).

Chapter 15

1   D. Defoe, *Robinson Crusoe*.

2   J. Hyams, *Zen and the Martial Arts* (New York: Bantam Books, 1979), p. 66.

3   T.F. Crum, *The Magic of Conflict* (New York: Simon & Schuster, 1987).

4   R.A. Zawacki and P.A. Zawacki, as quoted in *Managing End-User Computing*, Vol. 6, Auerbach (1992).

5   See L.A. Hill, *Becoming a Manager: Mastery of a New Identity* (Boston: Harvard Business School Press, 1992), p. 218.

6   W.E. Deming, *Out of the Crisis* (Cambridge, Mass.: MIT Center for Advanced Engineering Study, 1986), p. 102.

Chapter 16

1   To learn more about the use of presuppositions, see S. Andreas and C. Andreas, *Change Your Mind and Keep the Change* (Moab, Utah: Real People Press, 1987). For a look at how Virginia Satir used presuppositions, see S. Andreas, *Virginia Satir: The Patterns of Her Magic* (Palo Alto, Calif.: Science and Behavior Books, 1991). In this book, Andreas analyzes a 73-minute videotape of a 1986 therapy session of Satir working with one woman. Using the tape and the book together, you can gain a real appreciation and perhaps a little skill in the effective use of presuppositions.

2   G.M. Weinberg, *Quality Software Management: Volume 1, Systems Thinking* (New York: Dorset House Publishing, 1992), p. 154.

3   P.M. Senge, *The Fifth Discipline: The Art & Practice of the Learning Organization* (New York: Doubleday, 1990).

4   C. Andreas and S. Andreas, *Heart of the Mind: Engaging Your Inner Power to Change with Neuro-Linguistic Programming* (Moab, Utah: Real People Press, 1989), p. 47.

5   S.E. Hardin, *Success with the Gentle Art of Verbal Self-Defense* (Englewood Cliffs, N.J.: Prentice-Hall, 1989), p. 92.

6   B. Bluestone and I. Bluestone, *Technology Review*, Vol. 95, No. 8 (1992), pp. 31-40.

Chapter 17

1   For more on my views on feedback, see C.N. Seashore, E.W. Seashore, and G.M. Weinberg, *What Did You Say? The Art of Giving and Receiving Feedback* (North Attleborough, Mass.: Douglas Charles Press, 1991).

2   G.M. Weinberg, *Quality Software Management: Volume 2, First-Order Measurement* (New York: Dorset House Publishing, 1993), Chapter 11.

3   I.D. Yalom, *Love's Executioner* (New York: Basic Books, 1989), p. 172.

4   G.M. Weinberg, *Quality Software Management: Volume 2, First-Order Measurement*, op. cit., Chapter 14.

5   J. Peers, *1,001 Logical Laws, Accurate Axioms, Profound Principles, Trusty Truisms, Homey Homilies, Colorful Corollaries, Quotable Quotes, and Rambunctious Ruminations for All Walks of Life* (Garden City, N.Y.: Doubleday, 1979).

6   T.F. Crum, *The Magic of Conflict* (New York: Simon & Schuster, 1987), p. 120. Here, Crum quotes from a taped lecture on self-esteem by Jack Canfield.

7   J. Volhard and W. Volhard, *Open and Utility Training: The Motivational Method* (New York: Howell Book House, Macmillan), p. 21.

Chapter 18

1   D. Pye, *The Nature and Art of Workmanship* (New York: Van Nostrand Reinhold, 1971), pp. 23-24.

2   For more information on the dynamics of this circulation problem, see *Volume 1* of this series.

3   G.W. Russell, *IEEE Software*, Vol. 8, No. 1 (January 1991).

4   See, for example, W.S. Humphrey, *Managing the Software Process* (Reading, Mass.: Addison-Wesley, 1989).

5   B.W. Boehm, *Software Engineering Economics* (Englewood Cliffs, N.J.: Prentice-Hall, 1981).

6   M. Mantei, "The Effect of Programming Team Structures on Programming Tasks," *Communications of the ACM,* Vol. 24 (1981), pp. 106-13.

7   G.M. Weinberg, *The Psychology of Computer Programming* (New York: Van Nostrand Reinhold, 1971).

8   F.T. Baker, "Chief Programmer Team Management of Production Programming," *IBM Systems Journal,* Vol. 11, No. 1 (1972), pp. 57-73.

9   P.W. Metzger, *Managing a Programming Project* (Englewood Cliffs, N.J.: Prentice-Hall, 1973).

10   For two contrasting modern views, see, for example, R. Thomsett, "Effective Project Teams: A Dilemma, a Model, a Solution," *American Programmer,* Vol. 3 (1990), pp. 25-35; and R.A. Zahniser, "Building Software in Groups," *American Programmer,* Vol. 3 (1990), pp. 50-56.

11   M. Manduke, communication on the CompuServe Software Engineering Management Forum, 1993.

12   For a conflicting view on the use of special teams for quality assurance, see, for example, S.T. Stamm, "Assuring Quality Assurance," *Datamation* (1981), pp. 195-200.

13   W.S. Humphrey, *Managing the Software Process* (Reading, Mass.: Addison-Wesley, 1989), especially Chapter 3.

14   Ibid., Chapter 14.

15   P. Tournier, *The Violence Within* (San Francisco: Harper & Row, 1978), p. 69.

16   See, for example, A. Kohn, *No Contest: The Case Against Competition* (Boston: Houghton Mifflin Company, 1986).

17   For more on this subject, see the discussion of the Pressure-Performance curves in *Volume 1, Systems Thinking* of this series, pp. 248-53.

Chapter 19

1   M. DePree, *Leadership Is an Art* (New York: Bantam Doubleday Dell Publishing Group, 1989), p. 104.

2   T.N. Whitehead, *Leadership in a Free Society* (Cambridge, Mass.: Harvard University Press, 1936), pp. 98-99.

3   G.M. Weinberg, *Quality Software Management: Volume 2, First-Order Measurement* (New York: Dorset House Publishing, 1993), Chapter 10.

4   Personal communication from Randall W. Jensen, long-time critic and correspondent, 1993.

5   See B. Curtis, "Managing the Real Leverage in Software Productivity and Quality," *American Programmer,* Vol. 3, No. 7-8 (1990), pp. 4-14.

6   See, for example, B.W. Boehm, *Tutorial: Software Risk Management* (Washington, D.C.: IEEE Computer Society Press, 1989); T. DeMarco and T. Lister, *Peopleware: Productive Projects and Teams* (New York: Dorset House Publishing, 1987); R. Thomsett, *People & Project Management* (Englewood Cliffs, N.J.: Prentice-Hall, 1980); or H.D. Mills, *Software Productivity* (New York: Dorset House Publishing, 1988).

7   For information on this type of planning, see *Volume 2* in this series, Chapter 17.

Chapter 20

1   For a full development of the technical leader concept, see G.M. Weinberg, *Becoming a Technical Leader* (New York: Dorset House Publishing, 1986).

2   The concept of a standard task unit is developed in Part V, Zeroth-Order Measurement of G.M. Weinberg, *Quality Software Management: Volume 2, First-Order Measurement* (New York: Dorset House Publishing, 1993).

3   J.R. Katzenbach and D.K. Smith, *The Wisdom of Teams: Creating High Performance Teams* (Boston: Harvard Business School Press, 1993), p. 4.

4   N.R. Augustine, *Augustine's Laws* (New York: Viking Penguin, 1986), p. 235.

5   C. Alexander, S. Ishikawa, and M. Silverstein, *A Pattern Language* (New York: Oxford University Press, 1977), p. 618.

6   Personal communication in a note to M. Green on the CompuServe Software Engineering Management Forum discussing the *Quality Software Management* series, 1993.

7   J.R. Schmid, *Management by Guts* (Marceline, Mo.: Walsworth Publishing Co., 1985), p. 56.

8   For more on the MOI model, see G.M. Weinberg, *Becoming a Technical Leader*, op. cit.

9   See L.A. Hill, *Becoming a Manager: Mastery of a New Identity* (Boston: Harvard Business School Press, 1992).

10 Personal communication in a note on the CompuServe Software Engineering Management Forum discussing the *Quality Software Management* series, 1993.

11 Katzenbach and Smith, op. cit.

Chapter 21

1   B. Richter, communication on the CompuServe Software Engineering Management Forum, 1993.

2   A. George, communication on the CompuServe Software Engineering Management Forum, 1993.

3   E. Hand, communication on the CompuServe Software Engineering Management Forum, 1993.

4   A. Hardy, communication on the CompuServe Software Engineering Management Forum, 1993.

5   See, for example, A.K. Korman, *Industrial and Organizational Psychology* (Englewood Cliffs, N.J.: Prentice-Hall, 1971); or W.F. Cascio, *Applied Psychology in Personnel Management* (Reston, Va.: Reston Publishing Co., 1982).

Part V

1   He was a native of Ying-ch'uan (central and southern portion of the present Honan Province) and lived in the period of Emperor Huan (r. 147-167) of the Eastern Han Dynasty.

2   Erh-k'o P'o-an ching-chi, t. John Kwan-Terry, in *Traditional Chinese Stories*, Y.W. Ma and J.S.M. Lau, eds. (New York: Columbia University Press, 1978). For six inspiring stories from the United States in the twentieth century, see P. Gluckman and D.R. Roome, *Everyday Heroes of the Quality Movement* (New York: Dorset House Publishing, 1993).

Appendix A

1   For a more detailed description, see G.M. Weinberg, *Quality Software Management: Volume 1, Systems Thinking* (New York: Dorset House Publishing, 1992).

Appendix B

1   V. Satir et al., *The Satir Model, Family Therapy and Beyond* (Palo Alto, Calif.: Science and Behavior Books, 1991).

Appendix C

1   P.B. Crosby, *Quality Is Free* (New York: McGraw-Hill, 1979), p. 43.
2   R.A. Radice, P.E. Harding, and R.W. Phillips, "A Programming Process Study," *IBM Systems Journal*, Vol. 24, No. 2 (1985), pp. 91-101.
3   W.S. Humphrey, *Managing the Software Process* (Reading, Mass.: Addison-Wesley, 1989).
4   B. Curtis, "The Human Element in Software Quality," *Proceedings of the Monterey Conference on Software Quality* (Cambridge, Mass.: Software Productivity Research, 1990).
5   G.M. Weinberg, *Quality Software Management: Volume 1, Systems Thinking* (New York: Dorset House Publishing, 1992).

Appendix D

1   N. Wiener, *Cybernetics, or Control and Communication in the Animal and the Machine*, 2nd ed. (Cambridge, Mass.: MIT Press, 1961).

Listing of Laws, Rules, and Principles

Ashby's Law of Requisite Variety: The action taken by the controller must be congruent with the situation, in that there is at least one controller action to deal with each possible system action. (p. 6)

The Basic Principle of American Capitalism: To prohibit placating, give customers alternative sources of services. (p. 172)

The Big Secret: All people like to have their work appreciated. (p. 224)

The Blaming Style of Coping: "I am everything; you are nothing." (p. 28)

Brooks's Aphorism Modified: There is no silver bullet, but sometimes there is a Lone Ranger. (p. 1)

Brooks's Law: Adding manpower to a late software project makes it later. (p. 78)

Brooks's Law Refined: Assigning new people late in a software project to the tasks other people are already trying to do makes the project later. (p. 78)

The Congruent Commenting Standard: If there is one standard, there must be at least two standards. (p. 195)

The Congruent Manager Model: Leadership is the ability to create an environment in which everyone is empowered to contribute creatively to solving the problems. (p. 80)

The Controller Fallacy: If the controller isn't busy, it's not doing a good job; and if the controller is very busy, it must be a good controller. (p. 128)

Deming's Point Eight, "Drive Out Fear": "Most people on a job, especially people in management positions, do not understand what the job is, nor what is right or wrong. Moreover, it is not clear to them how to find out." (pp. 167-68)

The Giver's Fact: No matter what it appears to be, feedback information is almost totally about the giver, not the receiver. (p. 220)

The Helpful Model: No matter how it looks, everyone is trying to be helpful. (p. 208)

The High-Quality Software Delivery Principle: Management is the number one random process element. (p. 8) The number one random process element stands in the way of improving all the other random process elements. (p. 9)

The Houdini Approach to Management: You mystify them with complicated formulas and transformations, so they don't see what you're really doing. (p. 53)

The Irrelevant Style of Coping: "Nothing counts for anything." (p. 36)

The Loving/Hating Style of Coping: "It is nothing; you and I are everything." (p. 35)

The Mana Model: Certain people have big magic (mana) and certain people don't. (p. 16)

The One-Dimensional Selection Model of Management: A common management model that is based on three faulty assumptions: Managers are born, not made; people can be ranked on a one-dimensional scale; and the scale for programming is the same as the scale for management. (p. 15)

The Paranoid Model: Things are going wrong because somebody is trying to hurt me. (p. 209)

The Personal Effectiveness Principle: If you cannot manage yourself, you have no business managing others. (p. 9)

The Placating Style of Coping: "I am nothing; you are everything." (p. 29)

The Principle of Addition: To prevent an addiction (X), prohibit X; provide an alternative solution (Z) that really works; and soften the short-term pain if necessary, but not with X. (p. 161)

The Principle of Choosing to Be a Manager: If you don't really want the job of manager in the first place, everything you do as manager will be incongruent. (p. 20)

The Rip van Winkle Approach to Management: You wake up after two years and demand to know, "Why is this project two years late?" (p. 53)

The Stupid Model: Never attribute to maliciousness that which can otherwise be attributed to stupidity. (p. 211)

The Superreasonable Style of Coping: "It is everything; you and I are nothing." (p. 33)

The Team Formation Principle: Everyone on the team has some unique contribution. (p. 265)

Wain's Fifth Conclusion: "Nothing motivates a man more than to see his boss put in an honest day's work." (p. 224)

Author Index

Subject Index

ABOUT THE *QUALITY SOFTWARE MANAGEMENT* SERIES

Volume 1, Systems Thinking discusses the patterns that are necessary to develop high-quality software. *Volume 2, First-Order Measurement* explores the basic measurement activities every organization must do to consistently produce high-quality software.

PRAISE FOR *VOLUME 1, SYSTEMS THINKING:*

"one of those landmark books that comes along at the right time and addresses the right set of issues."

— Shel M. Siegel, *CASE Trends*

"With the current frenzy for Total Quality Management, ISO 9000, and Baldridge Awards dominating the industry, it's refreshing to have someone as down-to-earth as Weinberg focusing on the need for high-quality management as a necessary prerequisite for high-quality software."

— Warren Keuffel, *Computer Language*

"As always, Weinberg writes clearly, illustrates his main points with recognizably real-world examples, and lays out the series of traps awaiting unwary managers."

— Phil Dorn, *Computerworld International*

RECENT REVIEWS OF *VOLUME 2, FIRST-ORDER MEASUREMENT:*

"brimming with simple techniques and examples of their application."

— Roger D.H. Warburton, *Computing Reviews*

"What struck me as amazing as I read *First-Order Measurement* was not that so many software projects fail, but that so many manage to succeed. This book should be required reading for anyone who cares about project success."

— Naomi Karten, President, Karten Associates

"enlightening, practical, humorous, and enormously inspiring."

— Ed Yourdon, *The American Programmer*

"This book, and indeed, this series, are becoming indispensable volumes in my attempts to improve the quality of my work. ... It is rare that a technical book of this magnitude can be said to be a pleasure to read. However, I can certainly make that statement about this book, and indeed about the series as a whole. I highly recommend that you get this book and use the insights contained within it."

— Naor Wallach, *Newsbytes News Network*